DR JOHN TATE retired from the post of University Teaching Fellow in the Birmingham School of Planning, University of Central England, in 2002. His specialist teaching area was Environmental Economics. He has been a Regional Organiser for the Pike Anglers' Club of Great Britain since the club's inception, and was Regional Organiser of the Year in 1995. He was made a Senior Fellow of the PAC in 2000 and is a member of the PAC's advisory panel. He is currently also Honorary Secretary of what he describes as a 'rather prestigious local fishing club'. John lives in his native Black Country with wife June and a miniature Dutch lop-eared rabbit called Harry. June and daughter Natalie both fish, providing the weather isn't too cold.

Tales from a Worcestershire Whirlpool

The Ramblings of a Compulsive Angler

Tales from a Worcestershire Whirlpool

The Ramblings of a Compulsive Angler

John Tate

With a foreword by Professor Barrie Rickards

ATHENA PRESS
LONDON

Tales from a Worcestershire Whirlpool
The Ramblings of a Compulsive Angler
Copyright © John Tate 2007

All Rights Reserved

No part of this book may be reproduced in any form
by photocopying or by any electronic or mechanical means,
including information storage or retrieval systems,
without permission in writing from both the copyright
owner and the publisher of this book.

ISBN 10-digit: 1 84748 110 8
ISBN 13-digit: 978 1 84748 110 8

First Published 2007 by
ATHENA PRESS
Queen's House, 2 Holly Road
Twickenham TW1 4EG
United Kingdom

Extracts from *The Field* by Lynne McTaggart reproduced with permission
of Curtis Brown Group Ltd, London, on behalf of Lynne McTaggart,
Copyright © Lynne McTaggart 2001 and also by permission of Harper-
Collins Publishers Ltd © Lynne McTaggart 2001.

Every effort has been made to trace the copyright holders
of works quoted within this book and obtain permission. The publisher
apologises for any omission and is happy to make necessary changes in
subsequent print runs.

Printed for Athena Press

*For Richard Smith of Leominster in the County of Hereford,
the Compleat Angler*

*In Memoriam
Victor Bellars
1921–2006
Stuart Thompson
1973–2001*

Contents

Foreword	11
Preface	13
Cider with Rosie	19
Under Bredon Sun	34
God's River	45
Gromit and the Great Sea Monster	60
Duck Guzzler	77
Middle Earth	88
Red River Rock	109
Quantum Field	126
Band of Brothers	140
Phoenix Rising: The Legacy of Dr Kuznets	153
Pestered by Riff-Raff	166
The Black Beast and Other Frighteners	179
I Shall Be Glad When I Have Had Enough of This!	196
Civilisation Lost (or Gained?)	209
One for the Mortuary	226
The Rocks Remain	240
Acknowledgements	252
Useful Websites	256

Foreword

Every so often one picks up a book which cannot be put down, and I am sure that you will find, as I did, that *Tales from a Worcestershire Whirlpool* is one such. It is beautifully written, capturing the very atmosphere of angling, of places and of people, with much the same skill as a Chris Yates or an H T Sheringham. It is a book of great breadth, not only of angling, but of concepts. Thus there is a very good section where John confesses to being an anti-angler! And then he goes on to deal with the problems within angling, and the pressures to which the sport of angling is subjected. 'Civilisation Lost (or Gained?)', then, should become a classic reference for sound philosophy if this book gets its due deserts. But if you really want to bend your mind, try 'One for the Mortuary', where a lot of things, including John's black humour (as in the chapter title) help to pull him back from the black hole. No: start at the beginning, because this is a book which builds, which grows on you from the very start. Bit by bit you become captivated, not least because he is a very fine storyteller. Look, I haven't said anything about the angling! The book is full of it! However, it is angling as it should be, with all its trials and tribulations, its failures and successes, its thinking, and, most important of all, put in the full context of the lives we lead. It would be fair to say that John puts his family and friends before angling; angling is important, vital even, but only as a part of the fabric of life. Viewed in this way, you maintain a sense of proportion and perspective, and I think you see things with a kindly and humorous eye, as he does in this book. This is a great book and I feel sure that in time it will be recognised as one of the major contributions to our sport.

R Barrie Rickards,
Professor Emeritus, Emmanuel College, Cambridge,
September 2007

Preface

Pike Anglers' Club of Great Britain Dudley Regional Association insignia. (Barrie Rickards / Pike Anglers' Club of Great Britain)

What is your earliest memory when you found yourself an admittedly temporary resident on this hallowed planet? Perhaps I should use the plural here – memories? I have many, somewhat jumbled up, one of which is gazing out of our front window at a vast snowfield during the dread winter of 1947. I was not even two years old. It made quite an impression, still vivid after sixty years, but nothing like that of my Dad taking me to a nearby farm pond with a piece of cane, to which was attached cotton with a matchstick for a float. Dad would have none of the 'bent pin' business – he simply tied the red worm on and waited for the fish to get a firm grip! We filled a bucket with jack bannocks (sticklebacks to you) and the bright red bellies of the male fish still stand out in my mind.

Like it or not, I was fated to be an angler. Genetics and

conditioning certainly must have played a part but, in my blackest moments (usually after a fishing club committee meeting), I wonder whether I had, prior to this incarnation, been forced into some sort of a deal by my guardian spirits. Yes, I could return to the physical plane and have another go at getting it right, but the price this time would be that I would be chained to a fishing rod. This would be both a burden and an opportunity. It was the vehicle through which I would be tested, and it would inflict significant pain; on the other hand, properly managed, the angling career that was laid out for me would be a source of great joy, achievement and, most importantly, a way of interacting with, and at times serving, my fellow men (a 'politically incorrect' – and inaccurate – term; there have been women as well, bless their hearts; we are all *Homo sapiens* after all, aren't we?). In short, among other facets of my life to be, angling would be a vehicle for my spiritual evolution.

'Give me the boy and I will give you the man' is an old Jesuit saying. The first five or so years of life undoubtedly lay powerful foundations for what is to come. The jack bannocks (eaten overnight by next door's cat, which had managed to knock over the bucket) were just a start. On a visit to The Vine Inn at Clent, another bucket appeared, carried by a man with a real rod and wicker creel. In it was a carp, caught in the pond opposite, a mysterious and wondrous creature, which, having been shown off, was duly returned to its watery home. I was not to be a carp angler, however; my spiritual mentors had dealt me a somewhat different hand of cards. Grandfather would sometimes sit me on his knee and relate stories of great pike, fabulous beasts that had resided in Lord Dartmouth's lake on the latter's Patshull estate. Between the wars, Grandfather had the run of the place; he told me of keepers and punts with their wells filled with roach live baits. He showed me his gaff, which I still possess, a fearful piece of equipment, which was attached to a long, cane pole with a brass head. He had a huge red and green *Fishing Gazette* pike float – what leviathan was large enough to pull that under, I wondered? I was allowed to hold the pike rod, made, I think, of greenheart, so heavy I could hardly lift it. He spoke of great battles, with hooked fish going right under the punt and tangling with the anchors, of taking three fish of over sixteen pounds in three casts. He brought one of these home, live and wrapped in a wet sack, driving the Model T Ford as fast as he could, with my dad hanging on to the fish. He then gave his sister Hannah the task of releasing the pike in the local canal. Halfway across the field behind their houses, the fish got lively. Hannah panicked and abandoned it high and dry in the grass. It had to be retrieved and introduced to its new home by Dad. Grandfather even had a pet pike in his water butt! He was a pike conservationist well before his time – all fish caught had to be removed, so he took them alive, where possible, and introduced them to the Black Country canals. Whether they arrived safely or not depended on how many punctures or breakdowns they experienced on the way home! Dad was a dab hand at improvised car repairs and a great defender of the gaff as a means of landing pike, later scoffing at what he regarded as our puny (knotted) nets, which he felt did more harm than good. Faced with all this, I had no chance – the supernatural 'powers that be' had stitched me up well and truly from the very start.

It got worse. When taking his car in for repairs, at Tite's, our local garage, I was presented with an entire gallery of monsters staring fearfully down from a shelf above the workshop. There were probably a dozen or more pike, the first that I had seen, all in bow-front cases. Mr Tite said that he had taken them from the Wye (even today, the very name sends a tingle of thrill down my spine). Where was this place, would I ever be able to catch one of these leviathans? On the way home from the Battle of Britain Air Day at RAF Cosford, around 1950, I was taken to see Patshull. There was an ancient keeper's cottage, a gate and a bridge. The lake seemed enormous – at that age I did not realise that there could be so much water in one place. Lily pads encircled the bay adjacent to the bridge. I seemed to be in another dimension and was reluctant to return to the car. Then there was the Lapal Canal, or to give it its formal title, the Dudley Number 2 Canal. This ran from Darby's End, deep in the Black Country, to the leafy Birmingham suburb of Selly Oak, where it joined the Birmingham–Worcester, proceeding via what was (I think) then the third longest canal tunnel in England. This latter had collapsed in 1917 (one version of the story says the process was 'helped' with a little explosive – the owner was losing money). This left the Lapal Arm going nowhere and it was abandoned. One day I was taken a walk along it and, in a wide basin close to the (then) Manor Lane bridge, a huge green fish was spooked from under our feet. The vision is as clear as yesterday (clearer, actually!). Such, again, was the emotional intensity of the experience that it was somehow burned permanently onto my memory. Grandfather said it was a tench, and a good one at that. As with the pike, how I longed to catch one!

Even at that tender age, I knew, deep down, that angling was going to play a big part in my life. My base would be my native county and its environs, though, sadly, my home town is no longer in that county. The thirty-foot coal seam, which defines the extent of the Black Country, resisted the bureaucrats' attempts to move it and the Black Country has stayed firmly attached to its roots, which still stretch well to the south into Worcestershire, despite the latter having been robbed of its northern towns. I was taught to fish on the canals and pools of what is still a great place to live. My rivers have been the Avon, Severn, Teme and Wye; my fish, not surprisingly, pike and tench, but barbel, chub and roach as well (barbel had not even been stocked in my early years). Latterly, grayling have been added to the list. Given Grandfather's influence, however, it was inevitable that pike would dominate and, in the following pages, you will meet my pike-fishing companions within the Dudley region of the Pike Anglers' Club. We are a quirky lot and this is a quirky book. It is as much their story as it is mine, and is a tribute to their companionship over some three decades. Black Country folk are not just a tough lot; they have incredible humour, born of hardship and of the great struggle to free mankind from the shackles of poverty by harnessing the resources of the earth to an advancing technology. There is a fair amount of a 'don't take things too seriously' attitude in the book, though I have included some serious material as well, especially on the state of angling in Britain today. I have also seen fit, for better or worse, to build a framework drawing on conceptual material ranging from quantum mechanics to economics. This is not your ordinary 'how to do it' or 'look what I have caught' tome. That said, a number of my companions have angling records second to none, though, as modest people, they shirk publicity and get on with quietly enjoying their sport, sharing their successes (and failures) only with close associates. Indeed, many of the 'names' promoted by the popular angling press would fade into insignificance when faced with some of their achievements. I sometimes feel that we are more of a 'specimen group' than a Regional Association of the Pike Anglers' Club.

One such person is Richard Smith, to whom the book is dedicated. Dick is a Warwickshire lad by birth (dear me), but has spent much of his life living and fishing on the Wales/England border – he quite happily makes a round trip of some eighty miles to attend our meetings. Dick's angling successes are legion, ranging from thirty-pound pike (two in ten days from different waters, neither of which had previously produced a thirty), huge carp, a Welsh record dace, five-pound-plus chub, two-pound roach, eighteen-pound trout and a range of big sea fish. In his last telephone call to me, he announced a skate of one hundred and ninety-five pounds from off the west coast of Scotland. He then suggests to me that I write a fishing book! If anyone should be penning a weekly column in the press, it is Dick, yet to the best of my knowledge he has never written a word in an angling career as long as my own. I have now done my bit, mate, so you now do yours!

Though I have included some 'how to do it' material, much of what follows is anecdotal. Fishing is meant to be fun! What is more, some strange things happen and I have included some paranormal material, primarily for light entertainment. That said, at another level, this aspect is deadly serious, particularly that relating to UFOs. There are so many reliable reports, especially from the military, that no impartial analyst could ignore them, particularly those relating to apparently intelligently controlled objects observed simultaneously both visually and on radar. Explore this at your peril but do not blame me if you then have doubts about being alone in remote places!

My angling journey has been one of wonderful comradeship and immense reward, as the following chapters hopefully demonstrate. In parallel, once one gets involved in running our 'sport' (in reality it is far more than this), one embarks on a path of pain, stress, frustration and outright anger. Much of this latter, for me, has been in the defence of old *Esox*, but at times my activities have spilled over into the defence of angling itself. Angling also almost cost me my life. This book is a record of that journey.

Cider with Rosie

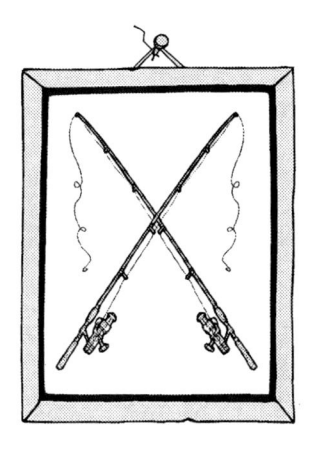

On my seventh birthday, I was presented with my first set of tackle. Compared with the ridiculous children's gear one sees today, it was remarkably functional. The rod was about nine feet long, made of bamboo (with strange burned circles on it), with a lancewood top. The reel was bakelite, a centre pin of course, with silk line. There was a goose quill float with a red top, a box of shot and packet of hooks to nylon. I was taken to the Birmingham–Worcester Canal at a place called Stoke Prior, just outside Bromsgrove. Willows lined the far bank and beds of lilies almost met in the middle of the canal, leaving a short width of open water for the occasional narrowboat (in those days these were few and far between). Grown men were fishing in spaces between the rushes. Dad said that they were using maggots, a bait I had barely heard of; I can hear the click of the checks on their centre pin reels even now. The tackle was assembled; Dad baited with a worm and cast out. I was handed the rod. The float was under-shotted and lay flat on the surface. Not for long! Suddenly, it shot along the surface and disappeared – Dad said 'Strike', I heaved, and after a titanic struggle a perch of at least four ounces was being unhooked. The disgorger was a forked matchstick! My first real fish – I know now that one always remembers best things of high emotional intensity, and this was one of those moments. I went on to catch others (with a properly shotted float), much to the chagrin of the maggot-danglers. Dad never thought much of maggots as bait, as I explain in the next chapter.

The Severn below Worcester Bridge (a 'real' water) was the next stage in my apprenticeship. Using a small grayling type float, bleak, dace, roach, gudgeon and even a chub were added to the tally. Again, the best fish came to worms. I ticked off the species against the index of an old book belonging to Grandfather. Entitled *Fishing*, it was written by G C Davies and Arthur Kent and published in 1894. Cost was one shilling (twelve proper pence – five of the new, devalued version). Today, it makes fascinating reading – if you think particles for carp are relatively modern, think again. If you think dry fly fishing for carp is new, think again as well! I continued to fish Stoke Prior with a mate, one Phil Burford and, acquiring a bicycle, was able to venture out by myself. Bread became the 'in' bait (Dad's influence) and a pool at Stakenbridge near Hagley produced its crop of roach, for the princely sum of two shillings a day. There is an old saying, 'never go back'. Take heed! The canal at Stoke Prior today lacks a single willow or lily, the water is the colour of chocolate, and there are boats everywhere. The river at Worcester has 'No Fishing' signs; it is a swan sanctuary, infested with literally hundreds of the things, all queuing up to be slowly poisoned by misguided do-gooders feeding them bread. Rats wax fat. Similar signs adorn the pool at Stakenbridge. Yes, the 1950s was a golden age; I will not even debate the point. (Why anglers get pushed around so is explained, painfully, in 'Civilisation Lost (or Gained?)'.)

When I was fifteen, I pulled a flanker on Phil Burford. Close to home was Leasowes Park, designed and built by William Shenstone, a landscape gardener, poet and local worthy, back in the mid eighteenth century. The spring fed streams, passing over a series of waterfalls, fed into a lovely pool, variously named Breeches Pool (because of its shape), Priory Pool (because

Shenstone built a mock priory adjacent to it) or the Lady Pool (after its ghost). Overhanging trees, rushes, weed beds and a notice saying 'Danger, water forty feet deep' – what a place; but – wait for it – it held pike. Yes, pike, those fabulous monsters that I had seen in Tite's garage. We faced a problem – to obtain an annual permit (costing one pound), one had to be aged sixteen. My mom had been at school with the head of the Parks' Department and a phone call later I was in, a year early! That summer, I caught more roach; Dad was right about maggots, the locals used hempseed, and ten pounds of roach in an evening was almost the norm. I acquired an Allcocks Isis rod and a Young's centre pin reel. The former was again of bamboo and had an amazing property, even by today's standards – it had two lancewood tops, one for match fishing, the other for pike! What a weapon. The fish came on single grains of hemp, fished tight in by the rushes. Evening routine was the same – home from school, swallow tea, grab tackle (stuff the exam revision) and walk/run down to the pool. One glorious night, I hooked a roach that I could not lift out and had to shout to an adult fishing along the dam for a landing net. He weighed the fish for me on his spring balance after detaching the handle – one pound, eight ounces, a personal best that was to last for over twenty years.

Physics, maths, geography and the rest of the school curriculum might have got short shrift but I complemented my activities at the time with reading. Then, as today, I was a bibliophile (television you could keep) and I positively devoured the fishing section in the local library. Bernard Venables I adored, his word pictures were better than any modern photograph. Richard Walker was the supreme technician – triangular nets, Arlesey bombs, Avon rods, learned discourses on hook shape, field craft, thermoclines; I even turned one of my dad's trilbys into a Walker-style hat. There was a delightful book by Jack Hargreaves entitled *Fishing for a Year* and C W Thurlow Craig's *Spinners Delight* was a revelation, even if Grandfather had pike-fished the Montgomery Canal years before him. Two works, however, stood out and still do today. The first was BB's *Be Quiet and Go A-Angling*. This to me still is the epitome of what a fishing book should be – evocative, inspirational, captivating, informative and beautifully illustrated. In a sense it is difficult to understand the power of the book over me – BB was no lover of pike and I have never really come to terms with carp. That said, I loved the stories of Thorney Pond, the salmon from the Border Esk and the great trout from the Blythie Brook. I have often wondered how much of it was actually true. The second tome was, and is, if anything more powerful. It was H A Gilbert's *The Tale of a Wye Fisherman*, written about a river not so far away, the one, no less, from where those pike in their glass cases had come from. This remarkable work is returned to in the chapter entitled 'God's River', but it moved me in a way difficult to describe. Even the place names Gilbert talks about have an otherworldly ring to them – Pontshione and the Turn Pool, Aberithon Pool, Goitre, Aberedw, The Nith, Glanwye, Llowes and Doldowlod. One incredible place was called Hell Hole of the Rocks – what image does that convey? Gilbert was no slouch of an angler himself – his best salmon, a monster of forty-nine pounds, came from the Quarry Hole at Aramstone, above Ross. He knew Robert Pashley – the doyen of Wye salmon anglers – a man whose name is revered even today by the good people of Walford, Goodrich and Kerne Bridge. Gilbert had some pertinent observations as to what makes a good angler, something I return to in the chapter called 'I Shall Be Glad When I Have Had Enough of This!'.

Strangely, some forty years later, I was to meet Gilbert's granddaughter. The near pristine copy of his book in her shop window at Hay was something of a giveaway. Despite being obviously busy, she kindly drew me a family tree to place the book into context. Back in the early 1970s, my life plan had been to eventually ditch academia and open a shop selling old fishing books in that delightful, quaint little border town, and of course fish for pike in my beloved river. This was one possibility within the quantum field; however, that was not to be. What did materialise was a shotgun-toting, bareback-riding, tree-climbing tomboy called June who was also an angler. She took me rudd fishing on one of our first dates and had to stop after an hour in order to give me a chance to catch up!

Books were not the only reading. I splashed out six (old) pence a week on the *Angling Times*, edited by Jack Thorndike.

There was a weekly piece by Walker, now a demi-god: I hung on his every word. Fred J Taylor (and the Taylor 'brothers' – Joe and Ken – I believe one was actually a cousin) made contributions that almost had the same status. It was a serious paper in those days, lacking the sensationalism of its modern counterpart. This was a time of rapid evolution in coarse angling thought and practice and the *AT* drove it along. Monthly, and nearer to home in its emphasis, was the *Midland Angler* – 'The Official Organ of the Birmingham Anglers' Association'. This was full of local news and even ran a specimen fish competition. The great Walker himself made the occasional contribution – one of my first copies (1957) contained the story of Pat Russell's introduction to the carp of Redmire Pool. He took a twenty-seven-pounder on this first trip. Walker, like my dad, was damning over the use of maggots, insisting that baits like bread and worms produced better fish. He then brought hell and damnation on himself by writing a piece about catching loads of big roach from a southern chalk stream using, you've guessed it, maggots! The anti-Walker brigade, led by a Mr Bristow, had a field day in the letters column. RW did not help his case by admitting that, to get the fish feeding, he chucked in at least a gallon of the things! This was the pre-barbel era locally – the middle Severn was renowned for its chub; one prized peg, highlighted in the *Midland Angler*, was the Eric Shrimpton run at Alveley – bait was bread flake in matches; wasp grub, a rather better bait, was banned. Chub to over five pounds often turned up in matches, particularly in the winter, and the Quatford area produced good bream of between five and six pounds (I would guess that the latter are still around; no one today ever bothers to fish for them). The lower river, now renowned for its big barbel, was primarily a bream venue; the method was called 'bobbing' – basically a form of float legering with a free-running, pilot-type float. It was an age of innocence, decent values and proper priorities, now sadly long gone.

In the late 1950s, my horizons broadened somewhat to include the Warwickshire Avon ('Under Bredon Sun') and eventually Patshull Pool ('Duck Guzzler') and the Teme ('Red River Rock'), but close to home I missed out on some whopping roach and, event of events, took my first pike, appropriately from the Breeches Pool. The latter was not the only local water to hold good roach. When constructed by Shenstone it had been much larger, but in 1792 an impressive aqueduct was constructed across its centre to hold the Dudley Number 2 Canal, the scene of my encounter with that tench all those years before. The ecology of the canal arm was little short of incredible. The water was gin-clear, green fronds of elodea and myriophillum were everywhere. It swarmed with sticklebacks and newts – in the spring there was frogspawn by the ton. I saw my first kingfisher there. On the downside there was a pair of aggressive swans, and leeches – these latter still give me the horrors. In the late 1950s, there was a limited pollution – it was the sight of those fish corpses that spurred me to be a lifetime supporter of the Anglers' Conservation Association (ACA). The last half a mile or so, beyond the Black Horse pub and up to the collapsing portal of the Lapal Tunnel, was an eerie place; the canal entered a tree-lined cutting, there were two ruined cottages and a narrow area, full of weed. This latter was where boards were slotted in to enable the level over a middle section to be raised – when released, an artificial current was generated which helped carry convoys of boats through the tunnel. We hunted rats here (they may have been water voles!) with our catapults – today this sort of activity, entirely natural for young boys, would no doubt result in an Antisocial Behaviour Order. This section of the canal reminded me of the Tydden Arm, as described by Thurlow Craig in *Spinner's Delight*.

Unlike the Tydden Arm, the glory of my canal was its roach. It was not unique in this respect. Around that time, a chap called Albert Oldfield was making the headlines with big roach from the Macclesfield Canal. I have one of his articles in the *Midland Angler* before me as I write, entitled 'When Nature Makes a Comeback' and published in 1961. All this was, of course, prior to the boom in pleasure boating – much of the canal system had been abandoned after 1918. The roach in the Lapal Canal were canny creatures, the shoals always keeping tight in to the far bank – we could see them well enough, catching them was another matter. Weed, overhanging trees, drag and the difficulty of getting distance with our centre pins resulted in total defeat, though Phil

Burford did manage a small carp. The only person to have any success, as far as we could ascertain, was Maurice Eley, who took two fish of over two pounds on bread one balmy summer evening. One memory stands out. As I was lying face down, looking into the aquarium that was the narrows, a shoal of five roach appeared from my right. They swam, some four feet down, right underneath my nose. They must have been the elders of the population and the leader was enormous. I may not have caught a three-pound roach but at least I have seen one.

The canal died a slow and horrible death. A hot summer (1962 or '63) plus a leak in the aqueduct resulted in massive deoxygenisation. Roach died by the hundred. We weighed one stinking corpse – around two and a quarter pounds – and there were dozens like that. The arm past the pub was drained – what were left of the fish, including some good bream, perished in a muddy ditch, the entire cutting being backfilled with spoil from the construction of junction 3 of the M5 motorway. If the place existed in its 1950s form today, it would no doubt have all sorts of fancy designations, plus the obligatory 'No Fishing' signs. By the time of the canal's demise, however, my thoughts were elsewhere. A cataclysmic event had occurred which was literally to change my life for ever – I caught my first pike. The first encounter had happened on a wet Saturday afternoon when Phil Burford and I were fishing the pool at Stakenbridge. It was autumn and, I have to admit, we were fishing with maggots and cloud bait. I think we must have attracted every fish in the pool – it was a roach, perch or bream every chuck. Suddenly, the swim exploded, a massive (to us) swirl and a tail literally waving in the air. We had not even realised that there were pike in the place! We piled in the cloud and maggots; kept catching, but the pike (several of them) had a field day. We had induced the sort of feeding frenzy one only encounters infrequently. Needless to say, we had no pike tackle and eventually packed, leaving things to calm down, soaked to the skin. Pike fever took hold. I bought some brass spoons and traces from Dennis Whale's tackle shop and fitted the pike top to the Isis. With a newfangled fixed spool reel (an Intrepid something or other), I found myself, complete with Grandfather's gaff, casting into the depths of Breeches Pool. All that happened was that the spoons quickly snagged (so much for the forty foot depth). One day I lost the last spoon, walked the half mile or so up Mucklow Hill (complete with gaff) to the tackle shop, purchased a single spoon and trace, returned to the pool, and lost the lot first chuck! Why I did not repeat the Stakenbridge technique, and use a live bait, I really do not know.

It was Phil Burford who changed things. At the end of a roach session on the pool in early March, he chucked in part of a sandwich when we were leaving – there was a swirl and a pike, the first I had seen in the pool, violently appropriated it. (Has anyone else witnessed pike taking floating bread? Have we pike anglers missed out on something?) The next weekend we returned, and I made sure that I had a green and orange *Fishing Gazette* float, trace and number four treble. We started roach fishing, Phil in the peg where we had seen the pike (it must have been without a permit), me to his right. Soon, Phil shouted 'Pike'. I dismantled the roach rig, fitted the pike top and reel with twelve-pound ICI Luron 2 (dreadful stuff, all springy), plus float and trace/treble. Lip-hooking a small roach, I muffed the first cast, but the second one was spot on. Almost on impact, the big float shot under, reappeared for a second and disappeared completely. What emotions were felt during those few, short seconds! I cranked the reel to tighten the line and struck (a little soon, in reality), the rod arched over and I was forced to give line for the first time in my angling career. After what seemed ages, but was probably less than a couple of minutes, the fish shot toward the rushes under my feet and Phil didn't muck about with the net. (Where was the gaff? I honestly can't remember!) My first pike was on the bank and my future sealed. Before we could even take in what had happened, an adult angler, well-known on the local match circuit, picked up the fish and smashed its head against a nearby oak. I do not even remember unhooking it. It weighed a little less than five pounds, no monster, but was carried home in triumph via a piece of line through the gills. I was stopped in the street by curious passers-by; we took the fish into the Royal Oak, Phil's dad's pub, and it did the rounds of the bar. Mom said that I was 'as white as a sheet' when she opened the front door – I was still fifteen and had just lost my (angling) virginity. The fish was photographed with the old Brownie box camera (dating from 1925) and buried in the back garden, to be eventually dug up to enable me to retrieve its jaw bone.

That summer it was O levels; we had time off school to revise. I did mine by the pool. S—d exams, all I wanted was pike, and I succeeded (and so did Phil, now fishing legally). The fish were small but it hardly mattered (the water has recently produced a twenty-pounder). Our problem was the rig – free-roving live baits always swam towards the bank-side rushes and we tended to fish close in. There was nothing in Walker's writing or Mr Crabtree about paternosters, though they were there in Grandfather's old book – using such an ancient method never even crossed our minds. Phil did, however, make one breakthrough. The Taylor 'brothers' were at the time publicizing the use of dead herrings, fished static on the bottom. One day, Phil ran out of live baits and put on a dead gudgeon. 'You will never catch anything on that', says I. Away goes Phil's float and in comes a pike. 'Fluke', says I, so Phil repeats the trick. We put it down to 'one of those things' and of course never followed it up. What fools we were – Phil had stumbled on to suspended, drifted, dead baiting! The suspended dead bait would have probably been more effective when paternostered, as I now know. In the early 1960s, I do not recall these methods ever being mentioned; perhaps we should have sent a piece to *Angling Times*.

Much to Dad's disgust, we discarded the gaff and resorted to the net or to simply pulling the fish in through the rushes by hand. I always carried the gaff, however – I wanted to look the part! It did come in useful once. This was the era of the Teddy Boys and one day, fishing by myself, three of these characters, complete with drainpipe trousers, vividly coloured socks (fluorescent green/yellow) and winklepicker shoes, decided to make life difficult for me. I didn't see the obligatory flick knives but it was best not to take chances. Picking up the gaff, I gave them a graphic description of what it could do to their intestines. Like German troops in both World Wars, they would not face a determined Englishman armed with cold steel, and withdrew into the bushes uttering unpleasant threats as they went. I turned victory into a rout by taking out my catapult and putting a fusillade of stones into the bushes. There was an audible yelp as at least one found its mark. My erstwhile assailants were last seen running across the bridge with rounds from my 'catty' bouncing off the woodwork. The catapult was my constant companion except, of course, at school. I did, however, once take it on an A level geography field visit. We were standing in a ploughed field on Frankley Beeches, south of Birmingham, and Mr Duke, the geography master, was showing us some peculiar stones, which he called Clent breccias. I started collecting them. 'You're enthusiastic, Tate,' says Mr Duke. 'At this rate, you might even pass.' The good gentleman was somewhat deflated when I informed him that I was merely replenishing my stocks of ammunition.

Soon, I was able to spread my wings, fishing-wise. One location was the Warwickshire Avon, the subject of the second chapter, 'Under Bredon Sun'. Prior to this, I had discovered a book by Clive Gammon, entitled *Hook, Line and Spinner*, which focused on to the lily ponds at Bosherston, in Pembrokeshire. We took our holidays at Tenby and I found Bosherston to be a wild and remote place. It had not yet been 'discovered' (i.e. despoiled). I span for pike from the bridges over the lake's arms and took fish on plugs and Ondex spoons (Gammon used toothbrush handles – how he managed to cast them is anyone's guess). June and I still walk around the place, but the fishing is a shadow of its former self, as I explain later. Another, more spectacular example of despoliation occurred with the tidal stretch of the Afon Dwyfawr in North Wales. During my undergraduate days, I took up fly fishing for sewin on Lloyd George's little river. Every pool had its complement of silver flashing sides, fishing was at night and it was some of the best sport I have ever experienced (and I am a pike man), even if many fish shed the hook. One night I hooked twenty-one and landed six. Once, three of us hooked the same fish (my fly in its mouth, plus a wormer's hook, with another chap's fly tangled around mine). I used a torch to help sort things out and, as a result, had a run-in with a bailiff – I was not amused, I felt that my real crime was having an English accent. The fishing was not without its danger, either. It came to an abrupt end when, in August 1969, I arrived to find the river unrecognizable. The pools had all gone and all that was left was a very shallow fast stream with massive shingle banks on either side. It was unfishable and there were no fish anyway. The river, being tidal, could be fished with just a rod licence. What had happened was that the proprietors upstream had complained that the proletariat was taking too many fish! The (then) Gwynedd River Board had responded by bulldozing the place out of existence. It was (and is) the single worst incident of official vandalism I have ever encountered.

Let me conclude this chapter with a small event that was a harbinger of things to come. I should perhaps have given up fishing as a result; it was the first of countless doses of disillusion to come and involved none other than the late, great Richard Walker. In one of his weekly pieces in the *Angling Times* he described removing (i.e. killing) a number of middle-sized pike from his stretch of the Upper Ouse at Beachampton. Indeed, one of my copies of the *Midland Angler* has a photograph of him with a decent 'double', impaled on a gaff and looking none too healthy. His reasoning was that such fish had no place there and that they could easily consume decent-sized roach, chub and perch. Now Walker was his grandfather's grandson and so was I. The problem was that our grandfathers had diametrically opposing views on pike. I wrote to the *AT* (talk about David and Goliath!) and my letter was duly published. My (entirely reasonable?) argument was that while RW may well have been right, by highlighting the killing of decent fish he was legitimising such activity elsewhere, in locations where pike were doing no harm – in other words, it was not so much the act of removal that was wrong, but RW publicising it. In any case, I objected, pike are fine sporting fish in their own right and their presence is surely worth the loss of a few middle-sized chub – why didn't he fish for them and return them just as he would with any other predator? Bearing in mind that I was in my middle teens at the time (and said so in my letter), the hellfire that descended was somewhat unfair. How dare a young whippersnapper challenge the great man! It was his fishery and he would judge the damage being done – the pike were 'raiders' from downstream and he had no great wish to preserve the d—m species anyway. How often since have I heard similar arguments (one surfaced last Saturday!). I wanted to be a pike fisherman and here was the country's greatest angler advocating the destruction of my favourite fish. Should I go back to building model aeroplanes? Programming and karmic forces were, however, in the event, to prove too strong.

My obsession with pike remains to this day, over forty-five years on. What is more, I still fish with Phil Burford occasionally. We even have plans to return to the Breeches Pool. Phil walked around it recently and asked an angler if he had caught any gudgeon. The reply was that the pool was full of them. The chap was somewhat taken aback when Phil informed him that he and a friend had introduced the gudgeon back in 1960! At times, on reflection, maybe pike fishing got the better of me – certainly, responding to some of the threats we face did rather take over, but someone had to stand our corner. I have, however, done a lot of other fishing as well, as the remaining chapters hopefully demonstrate (at the moment, big roach and grayling dominate). It is worth mentioning at this juncture that Barrie Rickards once wrote that he thought that I was 'faintly mad' – I leave you, the reader, to be the final judge of that.

Where it all began – the Birmingham–Worcester Canal at Stoke Prior, Worcestershire, c.1952, with Mum in the background. Today, there is not a lily or rush to be seen. (Author)

Dad with that first ever pike. (Author)

June doing what comes naturally. (Author)

Under Bredon Sun

The Woman's Pike Rod – the one and only T72(J).
Butt reads 'Pike', 'Custom Built by Terry Eustace',
together with the name 'June Anne Tate'. (Author)

In *Be Quiet and Go A-Angling*, BB (calling himself Michael Traherne) has a delightful chapter on the Warwickshire Avon. His subject is a discourse on roach and the wider waterside environment with a fly angler. It is a summer's day under Bredon Hill. This is the part of the river that I know best; it is where I served my river apprenticeship, and a place to which I return on occasions, though, unlike BB, the season is winter and the species pike. I often think of the Avon as the forgotten river. Unlike her brash big sister, the Severn, she is quiet and gentle, rising unobtrusively on the Warwickshire/Leicestershire border, and flowing through countryside that is the very epitome of middle England. She lacks the wild aggression of her sister, even in flood; her valley is a truly green and pleasant land.

Once Coventry, with its great cathedrals, is passed, the river is joined by the Leam, a stream noted particularly for its chub. There is soon the towering edifice of Warwick Castle, where it is fringed with lilies in summer and where foreign tourists gawp at artefacts that in reality are more than a little out of context. It flows through Stratford, the Bard's river, with its weirs and swans, broadening and deepening down to Evesham where Huxley's water used to (and may still do) play host to the match anglers. Then there is Pershore, with its packhorse bridge and Abbey (and its pike), followed by Eckington with its thatched cottages. During this part of its course, it is joined by the Warwickshire Stour and the Arrow, both lovely streams and significant fisheries in their own right. Finally, below Strensham, the two sisters meet, joining hands as they move through Tewkesbury and into the Bristol Channel. The valley contains some of England's great houses – Coughton (of Gunpowder Plot fame), Ragley and Charlecote (with its deer park) – and is steeped in the very history of the land through which the Avon flows.

Bredon Hill sits quietly, unobtrusively almost, brooding as background to the latter part of the valley. For the angler, most of the river has been altered to some extent in the interests of navigation, but it is not all bad – the result is a plethora of weirs, back streams and channels. Certainly, the river is less canal-like than the lower Severn; willows and other bank-side trees abound and the natural meanders remain, no more so than at the Swan's Neck above Eckington. Lily pads provide cover for the fish in summer, forming in the winter the 'cabbage patches' so beloved of the Taylor brothers all those years ago. These can be the home of monster chub and barbel, and are always good for a roach or two. Over the years that I have known the river, we have, I feel, a significant reduction in pollution levels to thank for this bounty.

I have neglected this lovely river of late; others have reaped rewards that could have been mine (the river has, for example, recently produced at least two sixteen-pound-plus barbel). Like most river systems, one could spend a lifetime exploring, but time is finite and angling priorities have dictated otherwise. In my early years as an angler, into my twenties even, the Avon valley was my playground, access limited only by the availability of transport.

My first encounter was with my parents and it took place at Huxley's. It also provided my father with one of his opportunities to force home his message about baits – thanks Dad! The evening prior to our visit, we had been walking past a cornfield, looking for one of my model aircraft. Dad filled his pockets with ears of wheat, subsequently rubbing them between his hands and blowing away the chaff. Prior to our leaving for Evesham, he emptied the grains into a large vacuum flask and topped this up with boiling water. I found a peg between the lilies and fished a porcupine quill float with a couple of maggots. Gudgeon, bleak small roach and the occasional perch kept me happy. Dad was less content; he emptied the water from the flask and tipped some by now swollen grains of wheat into the cup. A dozen grains went into the swim. Unconvinced, I reluctantly put one on the hook. First trot down the outside of the lilies, the float dipped decisively. Up came a roach, and Dad had to use the landing net. The exercise repeated itself, again and again; I was even weeded by a fish (chub?) and lost the hook. It was not long before the limited supply of wheat ran out, but Dad had made his point. A return to maggots was a return to small fish – Dick Walker would no doubt have said, 'I told you so'.

I put this lesson to good use afterwards when Phil Burford's father took us to one of the Avon's less well-known tributaries, the little River Alne (a part of the Arrow system) at a place called Wootton Wawen. I drive through this attractive little village even today, on the way to Wellesbourne airfield, and the lovely miniature weir with its inviting, fishy pool always brings back memories of that day over forty-five years ago. We started with maggots – I think Phil and his father stuck with them throughout. They are a great minnow bait – it was one a chuck, but hardly sport. The river seemed to meander all over the place, alternating from shallow riffles to deeper stretches of three to four feet or so. Disillusioned, I switched to wheat. It was a re-run of Hampton Ferry – roach, fat ones, not as many but very welcome. Again, I was smashed, hauling too hard on a fish that had other ideas. We planned a return visit; there were stories of barbel, stocked by the (then) Severn River Board. It was not to be – a pollution (I forget the source) wiped out the whole stretch. Nature screamed, anglers lost sport and farmers rents, but few cared. Today, despite the rise of the green movement, has anything changed? Would it benefit angling if it did?

We turned back to the Avon. The Alne stretch had been rented by the Mitchells and Butler's Angling Club, which also rented the right bank of the river between the Swan's Neck and Eckington Bridge. We went with Phil's father in the week and with one of the pub regulars, one Freddy Brazier, on a Sunday. Just below the Swan's Neck (effectively at its base), the river turned through nearly ninety degrees and the current sped up across the front of a lily bed. This was roach country and, using both wheat and hemp, I learned to roach fish on a river. By now I was the proud owner of a decent rod and reel, thanks to Phil's and my budgerigar breeding business. The rod was a built cane Sealey Octofloat and the reel a lovely free-running centre pin made by Young's. The float I still have, seven inches of crow quill with a cork body – one day it may ride the waters of the Avon again! Hooks were always Allcocks Model Perfects, size fourteen and attached to fine, supple, 8X nylon. These were not cheap, but with end tackle it always pays to have the best. This swim (and others) continued to produce its red-finned bounty until Phil broke the mould by attempting to catch some bream, a species for which this stretch of the river was then noted. He succeeded, first go. By modern standards, it was crude stuff – 'fill in' the middle of the river with heavy bread and bran mix and straight leger (with a drilled bullet), a lump of flake on a size six hook to six-pound line. The rod was placed between two rests, and a 'dough bobbin' used for bite detection – high-tech this, a piece of flake squeezed between butt ring and reel, forming a V. On the strike, the bread flew off – simple and effective. What price the paraphernalia of modern anglers? The only downside was that one had to stay awake – dozing off meant missed bites. We did not fish two rods because we didn't own two rods! That first day I remember Phil, cane rod bent over, landing his first river bream – a veritable monster of well over a pound. Bream are shoal fish and they either arrived over the ground bait or they didn't – catch one and others would follow. One day I got a three-pounder – quite a decent fish for those days, but the day was equally significant because I took my first tench – and it came from a river. The 'bream' I had hooked seemed rather powerful and, unlike that species, it did not want to give in. When Phil netted it, I could not believe it – the first tench that I had seen since that day ten years before on the old canal. It took in the middle of a warm August day out in the main boat channel, nowhere near any weeds – out-of-character behaviour, perhaps? I stroked its soft flanks and admired those little red eyes – tench are truly lovely fish and it was a great prize. At that time it was actually possible to set out one's stall for tench on the Avon. According to the *Midland Angler*, the place to be was upstream of Pershore Weir and the method laid-on lobworm. Fish to over four pounds (a good size for a tench in the early 1960s) were reported. We tried it once and failed – that said, recently I heard of a good catch of tench on feeder and maggots from below Pershore (at Pensham); the fish are still there after all those years.

The summer fishing under Bredon Hill – wheat and hemp for the roach and bread for the bream – was complemented when we discovered a chub run just above Eckington Bridge. This was winter fishing and bunches of maggots the bait – it was great fun trotting my cork on crow down between the very arches of that ancient bridge. Maggots are far better winter bait than they are in summer, even Dad acknowledged that. A couple of further developments are worth a mention. The first was another of Phil's 'innovations'. One day while bream fishing, he fixed his lead to the line (with shot both sides), claiming it helped him cast. I retorted that he would catch nothing on such a rig, being firmly under Walker's resistance-minimising philosophy. I was, of course, wrong – Phil continued to catch and the bites were quite decisive. He had discovered the bolt rig, but, like the previous success with dead baits, we ignored the 'obvious' implications. The second development was the discovery that the Avon held pike. One winter day, with the river high and coloured, three of us float-fished a backwater formed just upstream of a bend. The water was warm, we humped in the maggots and ground bait and it became a fish every chuck, including some good dace. Then, as at Stakenbridge those years before, the water erupted – the local pike population had arrived. Our activities had induced a feeding spell. These were the first river pike that we had seen, and they were a good deal bigger that those nearer home. We had no tackle, but a seed was sown, soon to germinate when I acquired my own transport.

It is easy to be lyrical about the events in one's youth. Most modern anglers would not even give the time of day for such fishing, yet it was very special to me. I learned a lot and came of age as an angler. It was not just the fish – there are fond memories of the café at Pinvin where we stopped for a very greasy egg and bacon sandwich prior to fishing. This amazing emporium opened at the crack of dawn each Sunday to cater for the migration of match anglers coming off the M5 to fish the river. There were laughs, the inevitable fooling around and that great sense of well-being and expectation that only the young and innocent can experience. It was not to last; Phil went off to agricultural college and his parents moved from the Royal Oak. The Avon was closed to me, but not for long. I became friends with another angler in my sixth form group; his name was Robin Dunn and some of our exploits are detailed in the chapters 'God's River' and 'Red River Rock'. We both passed our driving tests and acquired wheels – Robin's Austin A35 van was an ideal fishing wagon. By a stroke of good fortune, it was soon put to good use in pike fishing trips to the Avon, Robin's father having stumbled on to something of a hot spot.

Through a police sergeant friend based at Pershore, Mr Dunn was put in touch with the owner of a flour mill at the far end of the town. A cutting from the river ran to the mill and was either channelled through the mill itself or over a high weir. Below both exits was a wide pool, complete with island. The far bank closest to the weir current was reinforced with rocks, presumably as a means of preventing erosion. A walkway over the weir gave access to this bank. Robin and his father tried the place first. I had an enthusiastic telephone call; they had taken a number of pike, both on live bait and on Mepps spoons. It was early September and, since the owner would only allow us there in the week, half term could not come quickly enough. The A35 van was loaded and down the M5 we went, checking in at Pershore police station before proceeding to the mill. We were shown the eel trap which contained several good eels, the largest I had seen. Robin, eager as ever, had his (metal) spinning rod set up and, while I was sorting things out, he cast and promptly hooked a pike. It was not the last time that he would pull this trick – it became almost a ritual (maybe I should have followed suit?). With a booming budgerigar business, I now sported a built cane salmon rod and Intrepid Elite reel (the latter a piece of kit somewhat ahead of its time). We caught pike well into the morning, after which sport slowed until late afternoon when there was an upturn, a pattern that became familiar. We became regular visitors to the mill and had the place to ourselves. A number 4 Mepps was the killing bait, though at times I did well on an Ondex (with a red tag). We did have some fish on plugs; live baits worked free-roving if you could catch them. One day I had a take under the weir and, after a slugging fight, the fish came adrift. Robin cast across and immediately hooked a fish which turned out to be a chub of well over three pounds. It had scales like newly minted shillings and was a decent fish for the Avon at that time. I took perch to nearly two pounds and some reasonable chub as well, though Robin's fish remained our record. We found that coloured water was, if anything, a bonus – the pike seemed more, rather than less, inclined to take the spoon, unless the weather was very cold. The mill was our private piece of paradise and I learned a lot about pike behaviour there. It was the early to mid 1960s and, compared with today, pike fishing was still somewhat in the dark ages. Those dreadful gags had to be used if the fish had ingested the spoon too deeply; the use of a gloved hand under the gill cover had yet to be thought of. I did possess a decent landing net though, a large circular one that folded up to be carried and attached to Grandfather's gaff handle. The mill probably produced my first double, a fish that thumped the eight-pound scales down very firmly indeed, suspended of course by the chin.

Inevitably, it had to end as our days as undergraduates began. I stayed at home, Robin was off to Cardiff. We managed a few sessions during Christmas vacations, but soon Robin left for France with his lady love and I moved to Lancaster to do post-graduate work. My association with the Avon came to a temporary halt (soon afterwards, the mill burned down anyway –

it is now a housing estate!). It was a decade before I fished the river again, and when I did the species was again pike and my companion was June, my new wife. We had chosen the weir at Nafford, right under Bredon Hill – weirs were associated with pike (correctly) in my mind and it looked good on the map, even better when we arrived. It was early September 1976 and the long, terrible drought had come to a crashing halt with heavy thunderstorms and torrential rain. We were to try a newfangled technique, static dead baiting, though I put the spinning rod in just in case. The water was roaring though the hatches of the weir and I did not recall ever fishing the river with so much water on. Baits (sprat) mounted on Pennell-style tandem singles (I was under the influence of one Jim Gibbinson at the time) were positioned tight under the near bank. I fished opposite the island; June was below the confluence of a feeder stream. Another husband and wife pike team set up downstream and we waited. The river continued its rise, things began to look hopeless. The current was so strong that June resorted to watching the rod top. It worked – suddenly there was a yell and she was in – wifey's first pike, no monster but a beautiful Avon fish, the colour of a crucian carp, burnished gold. June was ecstatic and I was pretty pleased myself – it was the first pike I had seen on a static dead. I called her 'The Champ'; the river rose further and we packed before it broke out into the field.

It is appropriate at this juncture to mention the 'woman's pike rod'. The angling world has June to thank for this novel concept. I have to add that there is a certain incongruity here – when shooting, wifey forsakes light 'women's' guns in favour of a twelve bore; when piking, she could not get on with male-designed rods at all. Her response – design her own! The problem was the handle (I should say problems). According to my beloved, pike rod handles are too long and too thin. Given that women are shorter (generally), she could not see the point of wasting cork on a great long handle. The woman's pike rod thus saved on cork (it was the 1970s) but had a handle still long enough to be pushed into the abdomen/groin when playing a big fish. Her main gripe, however, was the diameter – women tend to have long manicured nails and, with the narrow butt, the rod was difficult to hold since her nails stuck into the palm of the hand. We went to see rod-builder extraordinaire Terry Eustace. Now Terry and June are both Brummies and have the same sense of humour. Terry listened patiently and, believe it or not, thought June had a point (or points). His only stipulation was that, at the end of the day, the rod should do its job – his main concern was its balance. He offered to build the thing, and even acceded to June's request for pink whipping to match her nail varnish! Thirty years on and the rod is still going strong and does the (female version of) the job perfectly. Things may have moved on with rod materials and design, but there is only one T72(J) and maybe one day it will claim a spot in some national angling museum, unless daughter Natalie claims it first.

We continued to fish the Avon for pike for the next couple of years. As with the Wye ('God's River'), dead baits seemed to work best early in the morning, though this may simply reflect the pike's feeding pattern anyway. Nothing spectacular turned up, and we were both soon seduced by the mighty Severn (see 'Gromit and the Great Sea Monster'), Patshull Pool (see 'Duck Guzzler'), and by an offer from the late Dick Orton allowing access to at least part of Middle Earth (see 'Middle Earth'). In addition, I was soon also to encounter the 'Quantum Field', from which I have never fully returned. I was entering that stage in my pike fishing career where I wanted quality and, prolific as it was, the Avon did not hold out much prospect for a big fish. Later, when a certain Roy Stevens ('Gromit' – guess who is 'Wallace'?) joined our region of the PAC, he brought tales of good pike from the Avon. Over fifteen years had passed and it seemed that the river may have changed – had the fish been there in the 1960s and 1970s, I am sure that we would have encountered them. Gromit spoke of big doubles and a twenty-two-pounder that he had seen weighed. Back in the 1960s, the Avon had always suffered from effluent discharge, particularly from Coventry –the Bidford area, especially, was always regarded as being 'on the edge'. Our mill pool at Pershore generated a lot of surface foam, and the smell at times reminded me of the Worcestershire Stour. In 'Phoenix Rising: The Legacy of Dr Kuznets', I explain the forces that have been instrumental in bringing about positive changes in water quality on a wide front; these seem to have accrued in the Avon valley as well.

Not so long ago, at one of our Dudley PAC meetings, a young chap turned up with photographs of two twenty-pound-plus pike he had taken, on live bait, from almost literally under one of Pershore's bridges. Gromit has recently returned to the river and doubles have followed; I have been less lucky but have enjoyed revisiting old haunts with 'our Grom'. There is no doubt that the Avon is still quite prolific pike-wise and it a good place to serve, as I did, one's river pike fishing apprenticeship. Gromit and I have taken numbers of fish, but when I am around, the big ones just do not show – if Gromit goes without me, of course it is another matter. Recently, our PAC region acquired a new member, one Ray Shakespeare. Ray had been a game angler for most of his life and took up pike fishing at the tender age of seventy! He had already had some success on the Avon, and Gromit put him on to a decent area. Ray now reports doubles (usually on dead baits) and seems to have as much success as the great Grom himself. It is good to see someone new to pike fishing 'crack it'; Ray is both keen and incredibly fit – long may he catch!

Yes, the Avon is, I feel, a rather changed river. I suspect that the quantities of small fish of all species has reduced (the same is true of the Teme); what has happened is that the river is less of a match water and more a venue for the specialist. I keep meaning to try for the roach again – BB speaks of two-pounders, maybe they have returned? (Fish of over even a pound were rare in the 1960s.) The river certainly appears cleaner, though maybe it is the nature of the discharges that have altered, but the apparent lack of small fish relative to forty years ago is certainly a concern – can they feed but not breed, or are the dreaded zander to blame? (Bob Nudd, sharing my concern, includes pike as a negative factor and, of course, got himself into trouble in the process). Nonetheless, these days the Avon produces some impressive results, and it is not just the main river. There is a well-authenticated forty-pound carp, and barbel of well into double figures (I have already mentioned sixteen-pounders) – noted barbel angler Trefor West, in a talk, has described it as one of the most underrated barbel rivers in the country. John Heath, a member of my local club, has taken an eleven-pound barbel from the Arrow (on bread), and Alan Staley, who you will meet again in 'One for the Mortuary', reports big double-figure pike from the Stour (on live baits). The confluence of this tributary (not to be confused with its sister to the north) with the main river has recently gained a reputation for big perch and zander. Both John and Alan have developed bolt rig methods for the zander. These latter are notoriously lead-shy, so rather than reduce resistance, they did a Phil Burford and increased it; results have been promising. Alan has even taken good perch on bolt-rigged bleak. His first barbel from the Avon, taken last season, went well over nine pounds – he is hopeful of his first double and has invited me along for the party! The real glory of today's Avon, however, for me is its chub. Among Dudley PAC members, Paul Humphries has taken a fish of over six pounds, and even Gromit had one over four and a half pounds not so long ago while fishing for live bait. A member of my club recently took a six pound, four ounce fish, our old chub run above Eckington Bridge has produced a fish of seven pounds (a two-pounder was an event in the 1960s), and the river above Pershore has produced a monster of over eight pounds – not far off the record. Serious chub anglers could do worse than try the Avon – both its chub and barbel are reminiscent of another, more famous, stream of the same name down in Wessex. It may be that a new era is dawning for the river that BB thought so much of. Now, if I was sixteen again…

God's River

Shad brace, 1962. (Author)

'Call a dog Wye, and I shall love him,' wrote H A Gilbert in *The Tale of a Wye Fisherman*. I have already described the impact of this book on me as a youngster, and it would be true to say that, were I forced to fish only one water from now till my dying day, it would have to be the Wye. Its valley is truly my spiritual home, and it is to my regret that I do not fish the river or its lovely tributaries more often. My only (poor) excuses are that much of the river is not available for my sort of fishing during the salmon season and, when this is closed, the river is often out of sorts due to rain. Given the longish journey, most of us play it safe unless conditions are obviously satisfactory. Tony Mobley, who moved from my home town to live by the Wye, retorts that as long as it is warm, plenty of fish can be caught, even with several feet of extra water running through. This is the land of record river pike, potentially record chub and roach (Dick Walker once saw a roach that he estimated at over four pounds), double figure barbel, world class grayling, huge brown trout and perch and, last but certainly not least, shad. What more could an angler ask for? Add to this spectacular scenery, red kite and other rare species of bird, and this valley amounts to an angler's paradise. There is, of course, also a chance to fish for salmon (it is not always prohibitively expensive). Dave Hendry once had a three-foot-long lamprey on a herring while pike fishing, and even sturgeon are not unknown.

It is appropriate to begin by saying something of Gilbert's remarkable book, the first edition of which appeared in 1929, published by Methuen, with a second in 1952 published by Jonathan Cape. Inside the front cover of the book is a sketch map of the Wye system which would warm the heart of any geographer, and the photographs, albeit (and inevitably) in black and white, are true gems. My favourite is one of Doreen Davey, who caught the record Wye salmon in March of 1923. In the book, she tells the story. Here was a young woman, salmon fishing by herself in a deep Wye pool (The Cowpond), with a 'vile wind' blowing, when at dusk she found herself connected to a fish of fifty-nine and a half pounds. She hung on grimly, playing it for twenty minutes until her father arrived; eventually landing it (admittedly with her father's help) after an hour and fifty-five minutes' play. A fire was lit on the bank to give some light, as by then night had set in. What a woman. They don't make 'em like that anymore! She achieved this using a centre pin reel from which she cast her minnow. The book is effectively a history of the Wye salmon fishery, and running through it is the strong theme of conservation. There is a chapter on Robert Pashley, 'The Magician of the Wye', who took an incredible twenty-nine salmon of over forty pounds. In twenty-six days of fishing in 1936, he caught two hundred and sixty salmon and took over a hundred every year between 1913 and 1951 (with the exception of 1914–1917, when he was fighting). Dick Smith knew Pashley's ghillie – apparently one of the forty-pounders did the three forties; forty pounds in weight, forty inches long and forty inches in girth. There is also a chapter on big fish, and to Gilbert's credit, there is a piece on pike. Although his general attitude to pike was as one would expect (they 'cross-lined' for them as children – two rods, either side of the river, connected in the middle to a single bung and live bait – the pike had a one-way journey, unlike the live bait), he clearly respected the big ones, and in the second edition not only gives details of Major W H Booth's thirty-seven-pound record (number 155 on Fred Buller's list) but also of a thirty-eight-pounder taken from the same pool. This is the 'diving board' swim above Hay, and Gilbert remarks on how big fish appear to like particular spots. On giving this information to Fred Buller, I suggested that maybe someone should fish the place. Fred suggested that I take my own advice! Gilbert's book is returned to later in this chapter, and the genius of Pashley in the chapter entitled 'I Shall Be Glad When I Have Had Enough of This!'. I find it strange that some enterprising publisher has not seen fit to republish it; for me, it is a true classic. (Gilbert's granddaughter, Athene English, in her shop The Great English Outdoors, in Hay – where amongst other beautiful things, she has a collection of antique fishing tackle and second-hand books – has copies of her grandfather's book for sale.) One final point – Captain Graystone, who gaffed Booth's fish, stated that it snapped at his waders! I cannot help feeling that a pike, no matter how large, with a treble hook in its mouth and after a long fight, is unlikely to be capable of snapping at anything. Do I detect shades of the 'Duck Guzzler' story here? Why do game fishermen always love to demonise poor old *Esox lucius*? Or maybe (just maybe) it was true?

My own first encounter with the Wye was in the early 1960s and involved that most elusive of fish, the shad. I believe that both allis shad (*Alosa alosa*) and twaite shad (*Alosa fallax*) run the river, though it is the twaite that is by far the most numerous, being distinguished by a line of black spots along its back; the allis usually only has one such mark. The Wye's run of shad is possibly unique. If you are looking for a fish that fights, look no further. The fish are in the river for around six weeks during May and June; they are known locally as the Mayfish. It was May 1962, and Robin Dunn and I had been taken by Robin's father, fishing a beat about half a mile below Hay. It was a beautifully warm spring day and the farmer informed us that none other than Bernard

Venables had taken a five-pound brown trout from the water that week on a small plug. We missed the great man (and possibly witnessing his catch) by a couple of days. The walk to the river crossed over the Builth to Hereford railway, the closure of which, by Dr Beeching, sparked the famous 'declaration of independence' by the people of Hay, led by a certain Richard Booth, great nephew of Major Booth of pike record fame.

The beat had a deep pool at its centre, with a long, rocky run-in above. Below, where Bernard Venables had taken his trout, the river was wide with a gravel bottom and gentle stream; the wading was easy. We began operations here, below a salmon hut, and soon Robin's father was into a decent trout on the dry fly. Robin had paid the princely sum of one pound to have a go for the salmon. I fished a Mepps for the trout, much encouraged by Bernard's big fish. Soon, I took my first grayling, albeit out of season, and followed this with a number of others. Later experience has confirmed that grayling get rather predatory around breeding time. Equally significantly, fast-moving fish were moving upstream, at times almost colliding with my waders. I thought at first they were small grilse, but the size and shape were wrong and there were lots of them. Still wanting a trout, preferably of Venables' proportions, I moved up into the rocky neck. The rod was solid glass (I still have it), the reel my trusty Intrepid Elite with a number 1 Mepps. There came a savage pull on the rod top, then nothing. I recast and the same thing happened, only this time a silver bolt came clean out of the water. Somehow it stayed attached but the fight was heart-stopping. Eventually, more by luck than judgement, it finished up in the trout net borrowed from Robin. I looked at it. What the hell was it? The truth dawned – a twaite shad! Stupidly, but hopefully understandably, I killed it – it was an exotic, and not only did I want to confirm its identity with the book back home, but more importantly I wanted to show it off to Dad, Phil Burford and anyone else who might be impressed. I began to fish again and the process repeated itself. These fish were devils! They would snatch hard at the spoon yet avoid the hooks, they would seemingly be firmly hooked yet come off for no apparent reason and, most impressive of all, they spent most of the time in the air, going all over the place and resisting the net to the very end. It was truly a day to remember. We tried to return the following year but sadly the beat had been sold. It was to be forty-three years before I took my next Wye shad.

I was not finished with the Wye, however. My parents started taking holidays not far from Symonds Yat. I needed no prompting to join them. The Birmingham Anglers' Association had a lovely stretch of water here, and I soon got addicted to the chub that lived in the Rocks Pool, midway along the length. It was in the days before pellets (or even sweetcorn) and I legered cheese paste; a much underrated bait even then, despite people like Peter Stone singing its virtues. Making it was a pain – stale bread kneaded into paste and mixed with whatever cheese took one's fancy. It did not harden in the water but, with the correct consistency, stayed on the hook well yet came off on the strike. I caught loads of decent chub, but my target was a four-pounder and somehow this eluded me. Despite the river's reputation, Dick Smith tells me that my experience was not unique. One evening, a massive thunderstorm ripped through Yat Gorge and, despite the weather, I sat it out and took chub after chub with not a four among them. I cannot help feeling that I was a little unlucky since there are undoubtedly huge chub in the Wye. Peter Stone, in *Fishing for Big Chub*, records an eight-pounder taken around the time that I was fishing (early/mid 1970s) and a massive fish of ten pounds, thirteen ounces to a P Morgan in 1981 (Dick Smith tells me that he has reservations about this latter fish). The late Vic Bellars once had a huge fish from above Hay Bridge (which made him wish he had taken his scales with him), and there is a fish of nine pounds, one ounce to a W Johnson recorded for 1945, albeit taken in the close season. Colin Booth seems to be able to turn up four-pounders at will – maybe I was fishing in the wrong place at the wrong time? I did find another productive spot – by accident, after being chased across a field by a mad bullock. To escape the brute, I jumped down the bank, feet first, through a mass of undergrowth (complete with tackle) and found myself above a most beautiful-looking run, flanked by thick bank-side bushes. Forgetting the bullock, I discovered that there was a resident shoal of chub under the bushes. I hammered these fish on and off for several years, keeping my discovery a secret, but there was no change in size.

For me, however, above all else, the Wye means pike. I have already mentioned the cased pike in our local garage when I was a child. I knew that they came from the Wye, but it was only some years ago that I found out in a conversation with Jack Stubbs, then Fisheries Officer for the Birmingham Anglers' Association, that they had come from my old chub water. Jack Tite, their captor, had been a friend of Jack Stubbs, and had even built a fishing hut on the water. A Colorado spoon was the favourite method back in the 1940s. It was therefore appropriate that my first twenty-pounder should come from the Wye, and even today this fish remains my largest river pike. I have Tony Mobley to thank for this milestone in my angling career. It was one of those days when, despite the conditions, things went right for once. It was December and when we set out there was a thick frost; it was bitterly cold. The river was low and clear, with an almost greenish tinge. The water temperature could not have been much above freezing – not an auspicious start. Despite this, I soon took a jack on wobbled dead bait and followed it with a lovely fat eight-pounder on a sardine from under a bush. Exploring up towards where Tony was fishing, I noticed an enticing gap between two similar bushes, but the bank was steep and heavily overgrown. Taking a risk, I slid down feet first and found a solid step, enough to allow the rod rests. Adjacent to the top bush were the remains of a salmon crib. I dropped a herring just downstream of this, fixed a drop-off and struggled back up the bank. Occasionally, the float would pull under with the force of the current. Tony came along for a chat. He had not been with me long before he announced, 'Your float has just disappeared.'

'It's just the current,' I responded, expecting the float to reappear at any moment. It didn't. I looked down to the rod and the drop-off had fallen. We crashed down the bank, Tony with net in hand, and I wound into the fish. It was solid but did nothing spectacular and I remember announcing that it felt about the size of the eight. Then it powered off downstream and I doubled my estimate! When it hit the net, it rolled onto its side and, like a lot of Wye pike, it was immensely thick across the back. Tony had a game lifting it and, without a word, went off to get his camera after we had both risked double hernias struggling with it up the bank through the dense undergrowth. It was lightly hooked and the scales said twenty-two pounds, ten ounces. After missing the magic figure by ounces for so long, elation is not the word. Tony had a small bottle of whisky with him, duly consumed after the lady had been returned to her home. The pitch was promptly christened Tate's Hole, though it soon became unrecognisable thanks to changes to the bank caused by flooding, together with growth of the tree cover. Nonetheless, the great river had delivered her bounty and I was a very happy angler.

It is worth saying something about methods. In the chapter 'Band of Brothers', I describe Eddie Butler's live bait rig; I owe Eddie the title of the current chapter. Despite Eddie's earlier successes, to start with we did not rate live baits very highly; all they seemed to produce was jack. Then Dick Smith turned up a near twenty-seven-pounder on a small live dace and we had a rapid rethink! It is a question of finding the fish; live baits will obviously produce big fish if the latter are present and the jacks do not get there first. As with most rivers, it is the most consistent method if one wants some action. The edge of the current is the place to be (but see 'Band of Brothers'). That said, static bottom-fished dead baits are a sure way to catch the big ones. My first twenty was a lesson to us all. Herrings are deadly, sardines work well, though Dick Smith prefers whole 'joey' mackerel. I sometimes wonder whether the efficacy of herrings is due to the shad run. These latter are a member of the herring family, and many shad die after spawning; the pike must get used to picking up dead herring-like fish. That said, it is horses for courses and you can try whatever takes your fancy. One area where Dick Smith's experiences differ from mine (and others) is the question of time of day. For me, the crack of dawn is the time and by 11 a.m. you can forget static dead baits. Dick reckons he can catch on them all day, but then he is Dick Smith, isn't he? My experience is that a take often occurs minutes (seconds even) after that first cast in the early morning murk. I well remember this happening and I had not set up the landing net; luckily, Dave Hendry did it for me and the fish was a big double. Static dead baits are best fished under trees, behind salmon cribs and close under the bank. One great swim (until it silted up) was about three feet deep, below a tree with rushes alone the bank; one virtually lowered the bait into the river. Wye pike are not shy of shallow water. Dick reckons that they patrol tight into the bank, using it as cover, and strike out into the river going for the dace shoals – a judiciously placed bait under the bank is just the thing. Paternostered dead baits (sea or coarse) should not be forgotten either; big baits can be used if required. My Teme rig (see 'Red River Rock'), using trotted dead bait, is also very effective, in my experience better than plain sink and draw since one can control the position and movement of the bait better. Again, this can be fished close in; Dave had a twenty-five-pounder from the Wye on this simple rig. All in all, Wye pike are pretty catholic in taste and experimentation seems the order of the day. We do not use artificials since their use is usually prohibited, though Jack Tite's success with the Colorado spoon should not be forgotten. Someone whom I will not name once cheated and tried a plug – he promptly hooked a salmon, which he had to deliberately lose because the bailiff was rapidly approaching in a boat! It should also be remembered that the two largest-ever Wye fish apparently both took salmon lures; Major Booth's thirty-seven-pounder was caught on a small Phantom minnow.

There are also good pike to be had from the tributaries. Gilbert mentions a forty-pounder killed with a pitchfork on the Monnow (a cracking little river – I learned to swim in it at the ripe old age of thirty), and Robert Gibbins, in his delightful *Coming Down the Wye*, a thirty-one-pounder from the same tributary. I would guess that these fish could be visitors, raiders from the main river, though one never knows. Eddie Butler was once approached by a riparian owner on the Monnow to get rid of a huge fish that had taken up residence in a pool below Skenfrith. I do not think he ever got around to the task. Then there is the Lugg, which used to be well-known for its pike. Over twenty years ago, my brother-in-law and I had a few days' chub fishing on the river. Peter float-fished and took plenty of dace as well. His problem was that a silly pike, which weighed just over nine pounds, persisted in grabbing pretty well every dace he hooked. I was kept hard at work with the pike rod. We christened the pike

Wally and he (she?) came out more times than you would believe. Being caught didn't dampen his ardour whatsoever. One evening, I walked the damn creature several hundred yards downstream before releasing him. Next morning, he was back in Pete's swim, up to his usual mayhem, having swum over shallows less than six inches deep and through thick weed. I put him back yet again, this time upstream, but within the hour Pete announced that he had returned. I cast out a dace and it flashed beneath the surface as the pike took it. Sick of playing the same fish, I forced the rod on to Pete, who protested that he was equally sick of the whole process as well. With a cheesed-off look on his face, Pete wound down to the fish. The rod slammed over and he was instantly back winding on something that was clearly a good deal bigger than Wally. I had literally given away a good fish. It went seventeen pounds, ten ounces and did a tolerably good job of wrecking my landing net. The pike was forty inches long and very hollow; it was July and the fish had clearly not recovered from spawning. At the back end, it would easily have gone twenty. At least Pete was happy, which is more than could be said for yours truly. Wally disappeared.

One cannot talk about the Wye without mentioning the barbel. How they arrived in the river is anyone's guess, and a potential record is always on the cards. That said, unless they arrived by some (difficult to specify) natural process, their introduction was an act of gross irresponsibility. To permanently change the ecology of such a major river, something that had evolved since the last ice age, is to shoulder an awful responsibility and has to be condemned. That said, I love fishing for them! Any barbel is a very special fish. Our best was taken by Colin Booth, on meat, from his beat below Hay and went over eleven pounds. There are reliable reports of much bigger fish. Since the waters we fish tend to be salmon beats, our barbel fishing does not usually begin until October and it clashes with pike fishing; the answer is to do both. Pike tend to take static dead baits in the morning, as already noted, and barbel feed well in the afternoon, particularly if the swim is baited while pike fishing. This is almost our standard approach and pays dividends, as I found out the first time I tried it one October over ten years ago. I desperately wanted a Wye barbel and took the pike rod almost as an afterthought, shoving three herrings in a boilie bag in order to minimise carriage. The moral of this story is to always be prepared, and take enough bait; a big low-pressure system was on the way and my three herrings were to prove woefully inadequate. The river was very low and the only place to put the pike bait in the barbel swim was upstream and mid river. I was whacking in the maggots when the top of the pike rod nodded and the herring was away. Within ten minutes of arrival, a fourteen-pounder was in the net. Stupidly, I cast off the second herring and was duly reduced to one. Out it went and soon the barbel swim was ready. The next thing I knew, the alarm was howling and the line was belting down the pool. I hit the fish at least forty yards downstream and, boy, could it pull! Eventually I worked it up towards me and was treated to a series of spectacular tail walks. By the time I managed to net it, after several abortive attempts, both angler and pike were seriously exhausted. The fish went twenty-one pounds, six ounces. How many more I would have caught, had I had more herrings, is anyone's guess, but later I took my first Wye barbel (several actually) before the storm hit (low pressure and dead baits always seem to go together). Gromit had a good day as well, taking several doubles. We drove through torrential rain and floods returning home, and Grom's car lost all electrics in the pitch dark, waiting to turn right on a notorious bend off the A449 outside Kidderminster. It was a hairy few minutes, but at least we would have died happy.

There is, of course a lot more to the Wye system than pike, barbel, chub or even salmon. I refer to the first species I took from the river, the grayling, and here the tributaries come into play. There are big grayling in all of them, but for me the Irfon and Ithon are supreme. I really have Colin Booth to thank for his pioneering work on both these lovely streams. The Ithon is, if anything, gentler; running through lovely pastoral upland country. By contrast, the Irfon literally tumbles out of the mountains and rushes from pool to pool over a rocky, rugged bed, seemingly in a desperate hurry to reach the Wye. I love them both but, thanks to Colin, know the Irfon slightly better. Colin has taken grayling to two pounds on the dry fly from this lovely little river and his fly fishing friends have, I believe, had them to over three pounds, a quite remarkable size for such fish. The Irfon is not for the fainthearted; the wading is difficult on the slippery bedrock and the banks steep and often tree-lined. A broken limb is easily on the cards, so beware. Maggot fishing is allowed on some stretches of both rivers during the salmon close season and, unless you are a skilled fly fisher, this is the way to proceed. There are big chub as well. Colin has had some fantastic catches on the float from both tributaries and also from the main river. The Wye and Usk Foundation has access to some superb water and is well worth contacting, though the tickets are not cheap (when alone in such spectacular, rugged country with rod in hand, money does not enter into the equation). Colin and I fished one of the Foundation's beats on the Irfon last winter and I took my first two-pounder (on trotted maggots). My personal best went eight times that day! With that huge dorsal fin in the strong current, big grayling are a tough proposition and, like shad, they leap. Five-pound line and four-pound bottoms are the order of the day, with fourteen barbless, forged hooks (do not forget the big chub). While playing one of the grayling, a salmon came clean out of the water at the other side of the pool, pushing me into emotional overload. The whole event, whole day even, was almost like a dream. How can such places still exist in twenty-first century Britain?

Apart from the whole area being unspoilt by development and, indeed, being part of a national park, the Wye system has, over a century and a half, benefited from highly significant enterprise on the conservation front. Gilbert's book is important in that it charts the first efforts in this direction. In the early to mid nineteenth century, the Wye salmon fishery was being ripped apart by freshwater netting, poaching and short-sighted squabbles between riparian owners. The Wye Preservation Society was formed in 1862, and the fight went on for over forty years; eventually the value of the fishing fell to such an extent that the freshwater nets were able to be bought out and eliminated. John Hotchkis was the driving force, though the great Victorian naturalist Frank Buckland also appears to have played a role. It was Buckland who introduced young salmon from the Rhine into the Wye, and thereby perhaps laid the foundation for the runs of massive fish that were to be the river's trademark for so many years. 'Sustainability' is one of the buzzwords of today's environmental movement, yet I cannot help thinking that these giants of the nineteenth century had a far better grasp of the fundamentals than anyone around today. Rather than produce piles of paper and empires of hype, they were not afraid to get their boots dirty, take risks and fight their enemies in almost hand-to-hand combat. Unlike today's urban dwellers, they were close to nature and understood its needs. Quite what a 'Sustainability Appraisal of Draft Regional Planning Guidance for the West Midlands Region' will do for the Wye salmon run and for the fishing in the river generally I have some doubt, and I helped write the b—y document!

Today, the great tradition begun by Hotchkis has been continued, with possibly increased urgency, by the Wye and Usk Foundation. The Foundation was set up as an environmental charity in the mid 1990s. To quote its brochure, 'Over the past ten years our projects have addressed a myriad of problems facing the fish species of both rivers, including over-exploitation, habitat loss/degradation and water quality problems'. It has recently bought out the nets still operating in the estuary, something not possible in Hotchkis' day, so continuing a process started well over a century ago. Funding comes from a variety of sources, but the sale of fishing tickets plays a major role. Beats can be booked direct or one can fish through the 'roving voucher' scheme. Both approaches help support the Foundation's funding. Game, coarse and shad fishing is available on a plethora of beats on the Wye itself and most of the tributaries, including the Edw, Cammarch, Llynfi Dulas and others. Recently, Colin Booth and I (plus spouses) had the privilege of being shown some of the Foundation's work when we participated in the annual walk. I had never seen a salmon redd before, let alone fish actually on them, and it was quite an experience (Polaroid glasses help). The work of this small group of angler-scientists is quite remarkable and their activities, both in opening up the tributaries to running fish and providing a good spawning environment, will stand the river system in good stead for decades to come. Our guides seemed to possess the uncanny knack of being able to think like fish. The emphasis is not just on salmon; the Llynfi Dulas, for example, has been transformed into a cracking little trout stream. These people deserve all the financial and practical help they can get; by booking through the Foundation you can do your bit and enjoy great fishing in superb surroundings as well.

For me, things recently came full circle. Fishing Colin Booth's beat on the Wye below Hay, I got among the shad. The attempt was deliberate and method identical to that used in the early 1960s. I had intended to fly fish, but my mentor at Sportfish in Winforton reckoned that the old number 1 Mepps was still the best bet. I took ten of these fascinating fish, and boy, they fight as hard as they did over forty years ago. It is a testament to those who work tirelessly to conserve the river that the shad run continues unabated, and if anything the size of the fish is bigger. Thank you, Colin, for a great day.

I conclude this chapter with the final paragraph to the second (1952) edition of Gilbert's book, written just a few years before his death. In view of what I have said, it should hopefully have a certain resonance.

> And now I come to an end. It is twenty years since I wrote the opening chapter of this book. For me the sun is setting in the west and my day is nearly done. To those who come after me I say: Protect the river and do not quarrel. Whoever you are if you love the river, your interests are the same. Fight the polluters and the water thieves and fight them to the death. With such enemies there can be no compromise. You have a noble and a glorious river – a river famous both for its beauty and for its fishing. It is a river worth fighting for by everybody who loves the valley and not by the fishermen alone.

These are wise words indeed.

A rather young author (complete with University of London scarf) with that first twenty-pound pike – twenty-two pounds, ten ounces – from the River Wye. (Tony Mobley)

Shad, 2005. (Author)

Author with a brace of two-pound River Irfon grayling. (Author)

Colin Booth with an eleven-pound River Wye barbel. (Colin Booth)

Gromit and the Great Sea Monster

Colin's nineteen-pounder, dwarfed by the big one. (Colin Booth)

I have a love–hate relationship with the River Severn. It is a brute of a river. While its reaches above Stourport contain some wonderful scenery, below that point the boats have taken over and it is a navigation that, in my youth, supported barges carrying oil as far upstream as Worcester. These were often towing others in a tandem fashion and the wash was both impressive and dangerous – bait tins, creels, rods and even the occasional angler would find themselves floating (or being swamped) in the aftermath of the passage of one of these leviathans. Today, recreational use predominates and things have calmed down somewhat, but the Hooray Henrys still make fishing in the navigable river somewhat trying at times. The other problem is nature, its effects exacerbated by the madcap drainage and navigation programmes of the past. The Severn is the ultimate spate river – even minor rainfall in Wales can transform it into a raging, muddy torrent within hours. The draining of the upland sponge, removal of trees and, below Stourport, canalisation, have resulted in a river regime that can fluctuate rather more than nature intended – Severn floods are impressive creatures, but, once past, the river can easily quickly fall back to almost summer levels, even in February. Planning fishing trips in winter is an uncertain and frustrating business.

Both summer and winter fishing therefore have their problems. Although I do not fish the river as much as he, Gromit and I have adopted rather different approaches. He is exclusively a summer angler, fishing for barbel and pike in the impressive Ironbridge Gorge. I tend to concentrate my efforts in autumn and winter in the weir pools and the mouths of tributaries and side streams, though one day I must return to the Dead Arm at Tewkesbury, a part of the old river bed cut off when the navigation was constructed. My quarry is chub and pike, though if the river is in good nick, there is nothing better than trotting a wire-stemmed stick float in the big roach country above Bewdley. The person with the best of all worlds is Colin Booth – not only does he live next to the river at Bewdley, he is a riparian owner to boot! His back garden contains an excellent chub swim and he even has access to his neighbour's fishing as well. He keeps his tackle set up in the garage and, not surprisingly, has an endless supply of live baits that he can legally use. These days, he uses a fly rod and does not even have to bother buying bait. If members of the Dudley PAC want a river report, all they have to do is ring Colin, who just looks over his balcony! Maybe he should start charging for this service?

For most members of the Dudley PAC, the Severn is predominantly a pike and zander water. We have taken two pike of over twenty-nine pounds from the river – one to John Holt from the lower river on live bait, the other to Colin Booth on suspended dead bait. I have to say that the Severn has not been kind to me, big pike-wise – perhaps the River God senses that I prefer the Wye! I have yet to take a twenty-pounder, my best being just under nineteen pounds, though I have had many big doubles. As an example, I was recently treated to a day with Chris Roadknight, fishing from his boat. We had a couple of paternostered baits out and were taking it in turns to trot a live bait on the third rod. The first take was to me – a jack. I re-baited and gave the rod to Chris. Down went the float, the light rod hooped over and a big fish dived under the boat. A great dappled side eventually rolled deep down. Holding the net, I knew what it was! Twenty-one pounds, twelve ounces of Severn pike, superbly marked. Now, if that jack had not taken my bait!

That was a winter day when the river was in good order – when in flood, the places to make for are the mouths of tributaries and side streams. I took my first fully confirmed double figure fish from such a place, back in the early 1970s, and oddly it came when I was roach fishing. Nearly thirteen pounds of pike on a one-pound bottom is an interesting proposition, but I got it out, after nearly an hour's play – I thought that I had either the chub to end all chub or a decent winter barbel. Returning with some live baits, I had a pike before I could even set up the landing net and a pattern began to emerge – put simply, the pike were either there in numbers or were not there at all. River level and temperature were critical – a warm flood, providing that the river was not in the fields, was the optimum condition. June's brother Peter and I once took seventeen fish on two rods in a morning, the best catch being twenty-one in a day to four rods. Struggling in the clinging mud made it hard work! Paternostered live baits did the trick, often gudgeon on a single treble. One winter's dusk, we had three floats disappear simultaneously – quite an experience. On another occasion, a rather larger bait put out by Tony Storey seemed to have a charmed life. Sensibly, he left it where it was, despite us catching on the other rods. Again at dusk, down went the float and the first Severn twenty-pounder that we had seen hit the net. This spot was later to produce a fish of over twenty-seven pounds to another angler – Noel Clark was a witness to it being weighed in a local tackle shop, stiff and dead. Even today, pike killing remains an issue, particularly around the towns – Bewdley, Bridgnorth and Stourport being particular problem areas. Tony Mobley was a witness to a twenty-six-pounder being killed by a match angler just above Bewdley Bridge – he was just too late to intervene. And match anglers complain about the river being 'infested' with jacks!

A thorny issue with Severn pike is that of baits. It has to be said that the river is, like it or not, predominantly a live bait water. To be more precise, Severn pike seem to go for moving baits – even bait droppers and swim feeders are not immune when being retrieved. In my experience, bait droppers are superior – perhaps they should be fitted with hooks? Non-live baiters can thus have success with lures and suspended dead baits. The latter, mounted either on a paternoster or fished sink and draw (with or without a float), is a useful live bait substitute. Colin Booth had his massive fish on a suspended dead chub, paternostered under a weir sill, and Adrian Writtle lost a monster below Upton on a dead roach, similarly presented. Dave Hendry saw this latter fish, weakening following a long fight, and it was big, very big. Unfortunately for Adrian, the hooks were more firmly in the roach than the pike and, shaking its head, the latter gained its freedom. Sea baits such as sardines and herrings work also, provided they can be made to move.

Static, bottom-fished dead baits are something of a puzzle. Above Stourport, where the river is more in its natural state, such baits work, albeit slowly. Dudley PAC members have had pike to over the magic twenty pounds on herrings, and static bottom-fished coarse dead baits have produced many doubles for Gromit from Ironbridge. This of course does not mean that such baits will not work in the navigated area, only that they can be desperately slow. I am not qualified to explain this phenomenon, or to advise on conditions when static dead baits are most likely to succeed. Alan Staley had a decent twenty on a smelt from below the island at Tewkesbury in cold, low water, but please note that I am not saying that these were optimum conditions! That said, Chris Roadknight, who has some experience in this respect, concurs. Possibly, some pike angler, somewhere, has the answers. For members of the Dudley PAC, if no live baits are available, then suspended dead baits are the order of the day.

For zander, an additional problem seems to be resistance. Zander do not like paternosters! I well remember Adrian Writtle and I having run after run one day below Upton. The bobbin would drop, the bite alarm shriek, ten feet of line would go and the bait would be dropped. We pretty well ran out of baits without connecting to a single fish, each bait having distinctive slash damage near the tail. The experience has been repeated elsewhere. The first time I managed to get a free-running, float-fished bait into a swim, I took a zander of eight pounds, four ounces and other, smaller ones followed. Colin Booth and Steve Sault once had two twelve-pounders in the boat together, one on float-fished live bait and one on a lure. How one tackles zander from the bank where trotted live bait is made difficult by vegetation I am not sure, but, as I detail in 'Under Bredon Sun', John Heath reckons that he has a partial solution – bolt rigs. Alan Staley has come to a similar conclusion. Small baits, heavy fixed leads, with everything clipped up tight – carp principles apply. I have not tried it (yet) but I am assured that it works. Whether fishing at night would improve matters, I do not know – does anyone fish the Severn for zander after dark, I wonder? Given the state of the banks and the deep, treacherous water, I would not be prepared to take my chances, particularly in winter.

The Severn's weirs, like the tributaries and side streams in times of flood, are an almost guaranteed pike location – provided that the water levels are not too high. In the latter situation, the lock cuttings are worth exploring, particularly if it is warm or temperatures are rising. Tewkesbury weir is one (well-publicised) location but there are a number of weirs, with the top one being Lincomb, just below Stourport. Dudley PAC stalwart Frank Nock is the expert here – Colin Booth and I know more about one similar place downstream. We fished this weir intensively for three or four seasons and took a lot of pike, the only one over twenty pounds coming to Colin's rod. Here, the ratio of doubles to singles seemed higher than elsewhere – numbers of fish were above fifteen pounds, and even June got in on the action – when the weather was warm! Big fish would usually scream off with the bait, often towing a heavy lead. Sometimes the big float would reappear under the far bank, only to disappear again, leaving one wondering what great power was on the other end. Tightening up to a pike literally under the far side of the river required a powerful rod and an element of luck. The big problem was hooking, particularly with a large bait in a powerful flow. I well remember a fight with one big fish that hit the bait under the weir lip and was level with the tail of the island before I was able to catch up with it. It could have been my Severn twenty-pounder – everything was locked up solid and it seemed an eternity before I managed to get the fish even on to my side of the river. Like the fish that Adrian lost, it eventually shook its head, catapulting the bait skywards, taking the hooks with it. Coarse fish are notoriously tough-skinned, and the whole operation was always a compromise between the requirement to keep the bait on the hook and getting the hooks to pull free when the bait was in the pike's mouth. Eventually, I partly solved the problem with the following rig which attaches the rear treble to the bait via a 'flyer' on a weak link.

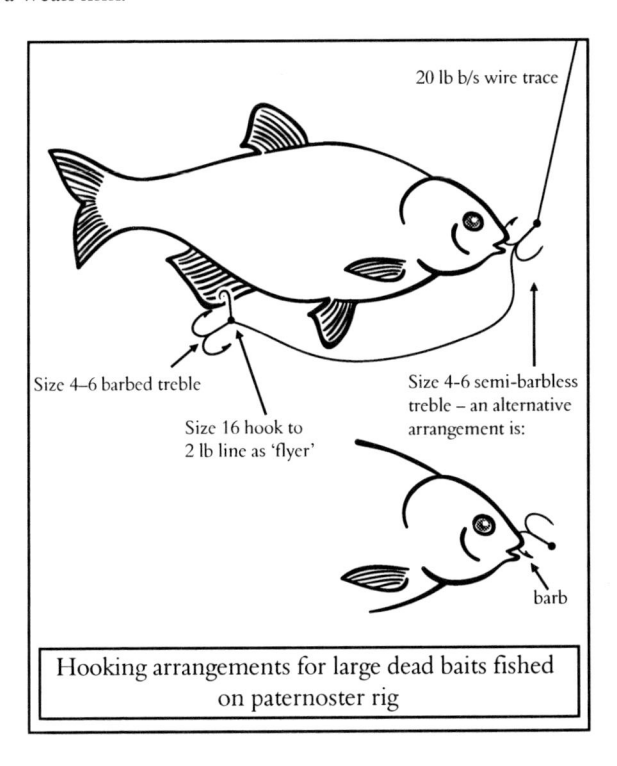

Hooking arrangements for large dead baits fished on paternoster rig

The rig allows an earlier strike – if the bait is partly swallowed, the treble in the bait's mouth, having only a bait-retaining barb, avoids unhooking problems. Most fish are hooked in the scissors with the bottom treble – being barbed, it helps prevent the loss of a fish through the well-known head-shaking manoeuvre. The first time I tried this rig, I took pike of eighteen pounds, ten ounces and seventeen pounds, six ounces in quick succession, both hooked in the scissors. For any bait, live or dead, that requires more than one treble, this is now my standard rig and it has stood the test of time. I will now let Colin Booth tell the story of his big Severn pike, not far off thirty pounds in weight, which was taken off 'our' weir in September. What it would have weighed at the 'back end' is anyone's guess – a Severn record, perhaps?

A Big Severn Pike

It was a Sunday evening in mid-September 2000. I am standing knee-deep in the river outside my house, adding yet another small chub to the keep net but at the same time shivering in a strong, cold, downstream wind. The seasons have changed with a vengeance in the space of a few days. The surface of the river is littered with leaves as a result of recent unseasonal gales. The August bank holiday heatwave now seems a distant memory. I put the rod down and go indoors to fetch a thicker fleece.

I return to the riverbank to witness a shocking and gruesome sight. My keep net is littered with dead and dying fish and is surrounded by dislodged fish scales and flesh, as if the *Texas Chainsaw Massacre* had taken place on Tesco's fish counter! Obviously, this was the work of a pike, probably a decent fish (river pike anglers who insist upon putting all their efforts into the deepest water they can find – take note!).

Immediately my thoughts turn to similar experiences in the past and eventually I make sense of what has just happened. In my dedicated river pike angling days of a decade or more previously, I had identified this precise time of year – when summer suddenly turns to autumn – as arguably the best time to fish for Severn pike. Clearly it is not the time of year to seek a spawn-laden record fish, but the pike are fighting fit and it is certainly peak season in terms of the numbers of 'runs' one can expect. Moreover, as a pike turning up in my swim is a rarity, I reason there must be a general feeding bonanza in progress along the whole river. My first thought is to get tooled up, return the following day and exact revenge on the fish that has savaged my chub. However, the chances are that fish will be long gone, and I know of far more productive pike swims a few miles downriver...

Late morning the next day sees me wipe the last of the dust off the pike tackle, load it into the car together with a bucket into which I have decanted the contents of the pike-savaged keep net, and drive like a maniac along the Worcestershire lanes until I reach the weir pool car park. There is no one, let alone an angler, in sight! 'No bloody soul has been here for weeks,' says the downbeat lock keeper who takes my money and quickly disappears back into his house.

A couple of hours later I begin to question my own reasoning for being there. Having set up two rods in my usual 'one upstream, one downstream' configuration, I find myself sitting uncomfortably between them checking each motionless drop-off bobbin in turn so frequently that I have started to develop a crick in my neck worse than must be suffered by the most dedicated of Wimbledon umpires! As used to be my standard practice, the best available bait, a scale-perfect six-ounce chub, is suspended by way of a three-ounce lead in the featureless downstream mid-river 'hot spot' that provided me with a beautiful twenty-one-pounder and a score or more other fish over ten pounds some fifteen years previously. My worst bait (a fish head with a body which resembled four tea bags stitched together) is positioned upstream, just over the sharp near-bank ledge – a textbook pike feature that, typically, used to have a reputation for producing nothing more than jacks and the very occasional low double figure fish.

It is eerily quiet. There is no traffic noise. There are no boats, no dog-walkers, no geese or gulls, not even a duck to be seen or heard. Only the voice of John Simpson on *The World at One* on the radio reassures me that Saddam Hussein hasn't launched a sudden nerve gas attack! However, needless to say (or I wouldn't be writing this!) the next half hour is to be far from uneventful. Indeed, I can honestly say that, whatever happens in the future, it is a thirty-minute period of time that I will forever remember as by far and away the most enjoyable of my angling career...

A routine glance to the left and, at last, the long-awaited adrenaline rush suddenly kicks in. The bobbin on the upstream rod is left swinging in the breeze as line pours steadily from the spool of the antique Daiwa Millionaire multiplier. As I pick up the rod in a state of panic, the reel spool stops turning and I calm down quickly when it becomes apparent that the pike has taken its meal into slack water under my feet. I recall that this is activity typical of a small jack (a good fish will almost invariably head out into midstream). Deflated, I put the reel into gear, check the star drag, tighten the fifteen-pound line and strike the fish hard twice, fully expecting to see a three-pound fish flaring its gills and thrashing about on the surface. Instead, after the second strike, the three-pound test curve rod is nearly wrenched out of my hand and all I can do is hold on as a very heavy and powerful fish ploughs into mid-river, taking almost twenty yards of line off a hard-set reel clutch in a matter of a few seconds.

I manage to stop the first run after thirty yards or so. I then apply maximum pressure in an attempt to regain the initiative and get some line back on the spool. The fish is having none of this and responds by taking another fifteen yards! How the hooks hold in the powerful far-bank current I'll never know, but after five minutes or so I gradually manage to gain line and steer the as yet unseen fish into deep, steady water twenty yards from the bank where it sulks near the bottom for a while. Having been given the chance to get my breath back, am I beginning to enjoy this! Little do I know that the fun is only just beginning.

Another five minutes pass and I am getting the upper hand, giving line where necessary but preventing each of the pike's numerous attempts to re-enter the main current. I begin to giggle uncontrollably in the manner of a certain likeable TV fishing programme presenter. It is at this point that I hear a voice behind me. 'Doing any good?' says the elderly gentleman, who is seemingly oblivious to the fact that my rod is bent to the corks!

'Do you fish?' I asked.

'Yes,' says Jim (I never did catch his name but we'll call him Jim). 'Would you like a hand with the landing net?' I am about to respond in the affirmative when I suddenly hear the bobbin on the downstream rod clatter against the rod rest and watch line pouring off the spool.

'You take that one!' I yell to Jim, who calmly picks up the rod but doesn't bother to strike, eventually winding in a dropped and badly chewed bait.

I turn to concentrate on the job in hand for a minute or two, gradually gaining line until the fish is reasonably close to being ready for the net. For his part, and without being prompted, Jim lobs the shredded bait on the second rod back into mid-river and duly resets the bobbin, stating with authority that 'They often come back for a second bite!' He then picks up the landing net as I carefully steer the big pike towards it. Hearing a clatter, I look around to see the second rod suddenly become airborne like a javelin! Something had come back for a second bite, that was for sure! Equally clearly, Jim had managed to leave the reel in gear! My response is to quickly drag the first fish over the rim of the net, throw down the first rod and wade into the river. I just manage to grab the butt of the second rod before it goes over the ledge into the main flow.

It quickly becomes clear that I am attached to a second good fish that also decides to seek the sanctuary of the far bank trees. Jim interrupts my renewed concentration. 'What shall I do with this one?' he says, staring down at the big fish in the net that is beginning to recover its energy. 'Oh, unhook it and put it in the keep net for now,' I calmly reply. Jim's response is a grey, silent stare that you would expect of a man being asked to sign his own death warrant! Fortunately, the colour returns to his cheeks when I point him in the direction of a pair of wire cutters and moments later I see him duly slip the big fish into the pegged-out keep net.

The second fish fights well, but, oozing with the confidence gained by having played and landed the first fish, I give it no quarter whatsoever and it is in the net within five minutes. Watched by Jim, I unhook the pike and proceeded to weigh it. 'Nineteen pounds exactly,' I say, 'not a bad fish, eh!' It is then that Jim points over his shoulder and slowly but deliberately issues the words that I shall never, ever forget. 'I've got news for you, young man – the fish in that keep net over there could eat this one.'

Shaking like a leaf I remove the hooks from what is by far the biggest pike I have ever seen. In my nervous hands, the scales hover between thirty-one pounds and thirty-two pounds but refuse to settle. Deducting two pounds for the sodden landing net we agree on twenty-nine and a half pounds. Both fish are released unharmed. I fish on in a daze for a while, taking two eight-pounders before driving home early in a state of euphoria that was to last for weeks.

There is an old adage among Severn pike fishers that if you want a big fish, you must use a big bait. For live baits, this poses both moral and practical problems, but a big dead bait, fished on the above rig, overcomes them both, partially if not completely. Severn pike, like all predators, can become preoccupied and, if this occurs, correct bait size is imperative. On one occasion, I witnessed a pack of pike corner a shoal of good roach in a bay at the mouth of a tributary. Mayhem ensued as the pike struck again and again. My small roach live baits were completely ignored – those pike wanted half-pound-plus food and nothing else. On the other hand, small live baits usually give great sport, and, especially when presented on a standard float rig, can produce both zander and some big perch as well. Pete Wass had a perch of three pounds, one ounce from the weir on such a rig, with good back-up fish as well, and who knows, some big Severn pike may come along not having read the rule book!

Weirs are not just about pike. For me, they have also meant chub. For many years, I always had a session or two each summer, my diary showing that the best catch was thirty-three fish, to nearly four pounds. Try as I might, as on the Wye, I just could not get a four-pounder. Rolling leger with a quivertip rod using a variety of baits was always productive. Meat and cheese paste were staple baits, though I did well on cherries – a forgotten bait these days (like wheat) but used properly, deadly on its day (slit them open, remove the stone and fish on a large hook, making sure that the point is well proud of the cherry). Then one day, my dentist, Chris Phillips, fist firmly in my mouth, announced that he had taken a number of four-pound-plus fish from the weir on casters. Gromit and I returned to the weir. Before committing myself to the feeder, I catapulted some cubes of flavoured meat across into the deepish run under far bank. Out went a piece of meat, the half-ounce lead allowing it to bump gently along the gravel. Suddenly, it speeded up, I struck, and a good fish charged up towards the weir lip. Line pulled off the clutch and I thought that I had a barbel, but there was something different about the fight. Eventually, I was able to work the fish towards the net, held by Gromit. A bronze side turned in the water – 'Carp', I announced, disappointedly. 'You have got a six-pound chub', yells Gromit. He was not far wrong – it was a chub weighing five pounds, eleven ounces and remains my personal best. I bagged up for the rest of the day but it was back to the old story – the best of the rest went three fifteen. Occasionally, a plan does come right. Oddly, fishing feedered maggots in an attempt to catch live bait, Gromit caught a rudd, followed by four or five more. There was no mistaking them – how they arrived in the Severn is anyone's guess – escapees from a still water following a flood, perhaps? Whatever their origins, they had clearly stayed together.

The weir was the scene of one of those events that comes only once in one's angling career. For me it caused a blank day, but it was a memorable blank nonetheless. I was chub fishing and Gromit decided that he would try for the pike. He quickly knocked out a couple of none-too-small baits, put them out below the weir lip and, Gromit being Gromit, started to doze off. I commenced to chub fish in the run below, from where I had taken the big one. Not long afterwards, looking up towards the weir, I was startled to observe what appeared to be a huge, black plastic sack just to the right of Gromit's live baits. It was cylindrical, around ten feet or so long and four feet across. It rose and fell, rather like a submarine doing practice dives. I attempted to raise my companion from his torpor, but the roar of the weir drowned my shouts. I struggled over the rocks to Gromit's swim. The great black mass was holding its position close to the weir lip, I presumed due to the undertow. It never entered my head that it was alive! Clouds of bubbles emanated from the upstream end, then horror of horrors, a great whiskered head appeared – in its gaping jaws was a good-sized chub. There was a horrible crunching sound as the chub met its end. The creature dived again. By this time, Gromit was beginning to sort himself out (living almost next door to a pub did not help; the man's an old soak). The intruder, a rather large sea lion, had dived close to our friend's two rather generous live baits. Any second, one (or both) of his floats was going to go under, with potentially interesting consequences, particularly for 'the fool at the other end'. 'You'd better get those live baits in quick,' I shouted. This was done and we sat, powerless to prevent the mayhem in the weir pool that ensued. Chub after chub was crunched in those fearful jaws; eventually, having no doubt cleared the place of such tasty snacks, the monster dropped back and cavorted off the tail of the island. Then, incredibly, as the lock gates opened, it followed a boat into the lock – presumably this was the technique used to get so far upstream in the first place. It exited the lock, much to the relief of the boat's crew, and disappeared upstream. By this time, the grapevine was working, and when it appeared in the next weir, television camera crews and the press were waiting to turn it into a celebrity. Eventually, having presumably dined sumptuously on the fare upstream, it tired of its coarse-fish diet (eating chub is enough to put anyone off) and withdrew back to the ocean – lockkeepers downstream being forewarned of its arrival. The next edition of the Dudley PAC's journal *Halcyon Days* contained the headline 'Wallace and Gromit Eaten by Sea Lion'; typically somewhat inaccurate, though knowing our reputation, it may have represented wishful thinking on behalf of the editor.

Now let me turn to more serious matters. The Severn is a legal navigation up to Pool Quay, above Shrewsbury, though powered craft rarely proceed much upstream of Stourport. In the early 1980s, an organisation calling itself the Severn Navigation Restoration Trust came to prominence with proposals to establish powered navigation right up the river to Shrewsbury. It was able to include the term 'restoration' in its title because Severn 'trows', as they were known, had, from medieval times until the nineteenth century, been used to transport cargo on this upper stretch, being pulled by horses or, at rapids, by the trowmen themselves (with the advent of the railways, these stalwarts and their families moved into the industrialising Black Country – hence Tromans is a common local name). The proposals were supported by some local councils, notably that of Bridgnorth, on the basis that extra employment would be generated. The scheme was opposed by a range of organisations – anglers (fronted by the Birmingham Anglers' Association), nature conservation trusts, landowners, canoeists and rowing clubs which formed themselves into an umbrella organisation calling itself the Severn Liaison Group. The proposals were ambitious to say the least, involving massive engineering works to construct weirs and locks right up to Shrewsbury. As with all such projects, costing was uncertain and environmental damage likely to be significant. The scheme would have changed the Severn for good, with the features of the existing canalised reaches being replicated for many miles above Stourport. The impact on the fishing was a matter of speculation; what mattered to the opposition was that the natural state of the river valley would have been seriously compromised. Those proposing the scheme backed up their case with a cost-benefit study, comprising two documents, an interim report and a final study. To an outsider, these would appear impressive enough, containing as they did an array of tables, options, economist-speak and a lot of data. Now it so happens that water resource economics, including project appraisal, is one of my specialisms and, through the Birmingham Anglers' Association, I was asked to make an evaluation of these seemingly significant reports. What I found appalled me. Behind a facade of objectivity what really existed was a mishmash of confusion, improperly transposed data, poor theory, lack of primary research and outright bias. I described the interim report as potentially 'a piece of pseudo-scientific propaganda designed to misinform and mislead the general public' and this was the better of the two. Perhaps I should not have been surprised – the author of both reports was an expert on the margarine industry!

The enthusiasts were not to be deterred. At Whitsun 1985, they decided to reinforce their case by staging a mass boat rally involving a convoy moving upstream from Stourport to above the usually navigated area and finishing at Bewdley. The Birmingham Anglers' Association, to which the Dudley PAC was affiliated, decided, courageously, to organise a counter-demonstration. On the morning in question, we congregated on the right bank, opposite the basin from which the convoy was due to depart. It was quite clear what the River God thought of the Severn's potential violation – the river was up and coloured, and pushing through with a force that only the Severn can achieve. Now, high water should have helped the boats over the fords, especially those just downstream of Bewdley town. But the boaters had made an error – many craft taking part were narrowboats, built primarily for use on the canals. Exiting the basin, the first of these hit the current sideways on and swung viciously downstream. Only the skill of the crew saved it from disaster. Many gave up then and there. Those that did proceed were shadowed by the protesters all the way upstream to Bewdley, the cry 'Salmon before sailors' echoing across the river. One audacious narrowboat did make it up as far as the fast water at Ribbesford. Now such craft are not exactly renowned for being over-powered and, going full out in the current, it was virtually standing still. The river, now really annoyed, won, and the boat swung sideways, crashing into the right bank, which happened to be owned by the Birmingham Anglers' Association. A crew member leapt ashore with a rope, intending to tie the narrowboat to a tree while the shaken crew sorted itself out. Waiting on the bank was an irate club bailiff who, in no uncertain terms, told the person that he was trespassing and that no mooring rights existed. The police, already in evidence, were mentioned. The altercation was short and decisive. The boat was last seen retreating downstream past Redstone Rock, seemingly only partially under the control of the crew. Only a handful of cabin cruisers made it to Bewdley – to face banners hanging from the bridge and unspeakable objects dropped from it. Impressively, the quayside pubs had notices saying 'Boaters Go Home'. If those who had braved the Severn's and the anglers' wrath had not already got the message, the good people of Bewdley left them in no doubt whatsoever. (Tony Mobley initially had a plan to hang a banner from the Bewdley Bridge saying 'Rape a River on the Rates', but thought better of it – I thought it was a brilliant idea, but Tony is more circumspect than I).

The great rally fiasco broke the opposition's back. While the Severn Navigation Restoration Trust still seems to issue the occasional press release, I suspect that proposals to turn natural rivers into navigations have had their day. Its website criticises human intervention for a 'river in crisis' and then proposes even more intervention to put the problem right! What is more, according to the Trust, the river above Bewdley is 'underutilised'. These arguments fool no one. Significantly, the earlier 'cost-benefit studies' are not referred to. I wonder why? A more recent scheme to open up the Warwickshire Arrow for power boats (to Alcester) has foundered, though better access to canoes on the Arrow is still on the agenda. We must remain on our guard, though with sustainability now firmly on the national agenda, the sort of irreversible damage to the environment inherent in canalisation is, hopefully, no longer acceptable. One thing is certain – given the Great Sea Monster's predilection to negotiate locks, placing a few minor obstacles such as weirs in its way would have had no effect on its progress whatsoever!

Author with five-pound, eleven-ounce River Severn chub. (Author)

Chris Roadknight with a magnificently marked twenty-one-pound, twelve-ounce pike from the River Severn. (Author)

Colin Booth with a twelve-pound-plus Severn zander (pikeperch).
(Colin Booth)

Duck Guzzler

The Lodge Bay, Patshull. (Author)

I have already introduced Patshull Great Pool, which was my grandfather's pike fishing playground in the years between the wars. When one is young, early impressions make a strong impact and, as a consequence, the lake (which is what it really is) has always had a special place in my affections. Early attempts at catching the pike were failures but the float fishing, especially for the roach and perch, was much more of a success. Some of the lessons learned relating to the roach are spelled out in more detail in 'Pestered by Riff-Raff'. That pike fishing was with lures and herrings; the lake was deep and, though I had perch to nearly two pounds on the plug, the pike refused to play ball. I may have been one of the first to 'dunk' herrings in those fair waters, but for some reason, they were a total failure. The place has a hard, sandstone bottom and, from later experience, there was no earthly reason why the pike should not have obliged – I have since wondered whether a pre-baiting campaign might not have conditioned the fish to switch their allegiance away from the lake's indigenous species. Anyway, as a result I became totally disillusioned with dead baits, and it was only when I followed in Grandfather's footsteps and switched to live baits that I took my first Patshull pike.

Memories of those early days are very special. I often fished with a cousin and we travelled in my old Austin A30, bought eighth-hand for ninety quid (and which ran for eight years, even if the sills were reinforced with concrete!). The drive through the lanes, past Grandfather's bungalow in Wombourne, and out through Trysull, Seisdon and Pattingham, was always full of anticipation. Having overheated struggling up the Clive Hill, it was always a relief to park the car under the trees and to walk to the keeper's cottage, where his elderly wife issued the day tickets through an open front window. Two shillings was hardly an extortionate price to pay for access to such a lovely, and faintly awe-inspiring, place. It was also remote; walking across the bridge, one turned right and crossed meadowland covered with ancient chestnuts, passing Lodge Bay on to a straight length where the sandstone was interspersed with bank-side trees, many of which had fallen into the water. Towards the end of the fishing was the old temple, adjacent to which was the Glory Hole, a deep, armchair peg which did actually live up to its reputation at times. It was along this bank that we learned to use slider floats with bread, red worm or even maggot (sorry, Dad), together with liberal amounts of cloud bait. Good roach were common, but the real eye-opener was the perch, many between one and two pounds with one fish, which took live bait and was eventually lost in the tree roots, being a good deal bigger. It was a lovely, fishy, peaceful place; kingfishers flashed between the fallen trees and the great crested grebe, which on occasions used to take Grandfather's live baits, were ever in evidence. One day, returning to the car, the keeper showed me a dead carp, well into double figures, that had turned up in Lodge Bay – these fish were in the lake long before more recent stockings. One unpleasant experience was when I found a cow, massively bloated due to eating grain, but still alive. The look in its eyes was quite haunting – I ran back to report it to the keeper, but, despite the vet's efforts, it died; its corpse was dragged away across the meadow behind a tractor.

With the formation of the Dudley region of the PAC, Patshull became an obvious location for our 'fish-ins', being local and open to all. On the first such event, we were allowed privileged access to the top of the lake and were able to fish off a causeway. We all took fish (which was what it was all about) even though they were not large. When demonstrating how to unhook a pike to young Paul Bloomer, the fish kicked and drove one of its front teeth through my glove and into the ball of my thumb. Not a good example to set to a new member; there was blood everywhere. Some big fish began to turn up; whether these were indigenous or had been stocked I do not know, but it was clearly a water that was going to get some attention from members in the coming seasons. Then came apparent disaster. The following is a piece I wrote for an early edition of the Pike Anglers' Club journal (before it had been christened *Pikelines*).

Patshull Farewell

The four orange-topped floats were barely visible through the murk of the early dawn. Some eighteen feet below the calm surface our roach live baits worked vigorously, giving high hopes of an early take, an event which was usually the prelude to a good day. Across the water, the lights of the fishing lodge reflected on the surface of the Great Pool as behind us the early morning traffic wended its way along the winding lane as less fortunate mortals made their way to work.

This, however, was no ordinary fishing day. The initial blow had in fact fallen a few weeks earlier when, at a PAC 'fish-in', we had been informed that the entire water was to be turned into a 'put and take' trout fishery, an announcement that was received with a mixture of incredulity and shock. To be told that one's bread-and-butter fishery was about to cease to exist took some swallowing, for even though the great days of Patshull were long gone, piking in this neck of the woods is a pretty scarce commodity, particularly in the depths of winter when our local rivers are unfishable. Indeed, during the last year or so things had appeared to take a turn for the better with not just more fish coming to the net, but better quality fish as well, including a sprinkling of twenty-pounders with a twenty-six-pound fish being taken the week before. This made the news a bitter pill indeed, for we had high hopes of a first-class pike fishery developing on our doorstep.

More details had become available from the lad in the fishing lodge that morning. The decision was final and all coarse fishing would cease that day. 'What about the pike?' we had enquired.

'The big ones will go into the Church Pool,' we were told. We didn't enquire as to the fate of the smaller pike but had a pretty good idea of what was going to happen to those unlucky enough to find their way into the nets. Anyway, we couldn't see the much smaller Church Pool sustaining a head of large pike, particularly since the majority of coarse fish had been removed to make way for king trout some years ago. We secretly hoped that predictions from fellow PAC members that the Great Pool was virtually impossible to net effectively would prove correct, though doubtless any pike falling to the lures of the trout fraternity would have a one-way journey. Outside, the notice on the wall of the fishing lodge which read 'All coarse fish including pike to be returned to the water' seemed a trifle hypocritical to say the least.

As the winter sun rose over what remained of the trees, hope of an early run faded and we were able to reflect on how the estate had changed over the past few years; on how the area that we were fishing had previously been totally inaccessible due to dense undergrowth, fences and stern notices; on how the trees opposite had been savagely thinned out to allow for boat moorings and a car park; on how the area across the bridge had once been rough pasture interspersed by horse chestnuts and was now a golf course around which had been cut a metalled road. Young Paul Bloomer, my fishing companion, seemed to find it difficult to believe that where a Calor Gas tanker now rumbled, cattle had recently been able to graze and badgers roam. Even the fallen trees which had lain in the water for decades had been removed so the trout anglers would not lose their precious tackle, destroying a number of pike and perch lies in the process.

Soon three other anglers arrived on our bank, a couple of young lads, neither of whom had ever caught a pike and yet whose enthusiasm for the fish was magnetic, and a solitary 'specimen hunter' type whom I had met before and whose knowledge of the water seemed unrivalled. The latter soon netted a brace of small fish, which did something to add life to our flagging hopes, though our live baits seemed to sense that perhaps the depths were not as dangerous as they at first seemed since they gradually quieted down, only moving the floats gently on the slight swell, whereas earlier they had been giving us heart attacks, holding the floats under the surface for seconds at a time – young Paul's baits in particular had seemed to possess a bionic quality.

By midday the sunshine was quite hot, with the thermometer reaching 60°F. A solitary bat appeared, no doubt feeding on the midges brought out by the unseasonal warmth. About this time, we were greeted with a gruff 'Any good?' and found ourselves face to face with a rather rugged-looking character dressed wholly in green (including 'Dick Walker' hat) and carrying an expensive-looking plug fishing outfit. 'What do you think of the news?' we were asked.

'It's sick,' I replied.

'It's more than that, it's b—y diabolical,' was the reply. 'I was born and reared next to this place, fished it as a kid. I spent twenty-five years in the army, a lot of it abroad, dreaming of fishing for the pike at Patshull again and hoping to eventually retire here. Now I have done just that and this happens. I've even spent over £200 on carp gear recently – got interested in them, good fun in the summer – that's wasted as well.' By now the others had gathered around and we were treated to a discourse ranging from the history of Patshull ('Been a pike fishery from time immemorial') to the economics of put and take trout fisheries. At the end of it, we were all near to tears! 'There is nothing that we can do about it,' said the specimen hunter. 'Coarse anglers are always bottom of the pile and we pike anglers are underneath the lot.' At this juncture, as if to emphasise the point, a gleaming Rolls Royce purred over the newly-strengthened bridge, taking the right-hand road to the plush new golf house. Realising our state of complete helplessness, the meeting broke up, but not before several rather wild suggestions had been made about possible (radical) courses of action.

'I know who would be as upset as we are, had he been alive,' I said to young Paul – 'My dear old grandfather. He fished this place for pike over seventy years ago when it was dead private, and took some fantastic bags of fish. He was one of the few lucky ones who were allowed to fish by Lord Dartmouth. It was done in grand Victorian style with punts and live baits laid on by the keepers. Even his lordship used to come down and have a go occasionally. When I was a kid, Grandfather used to sit me on his knee and tell me of the fish he had taken. The big bind apparently was the number of greater crested grebes on the water – they were adept at removing live baits from the hooks!'

By mid afternoon, we were still fishless, though the specimen hunter had scored again with a fish of around seven pounds taken on a Sidley-style sunk float paternoster. We changed baits for the final hour or so with the shadows lengthening, though somehow it didn't matter anymore whether we caught fish or not. The old soldier bade us a sad goodbye with a telling reference to 'spotted vermin', and silence descended on the bank as we crouched behind our rods almost in a state of stupor. After twenty years fishing the place, I found it difficult to believe that I would probably never return. I tried to picture in my mind how the place had been when I had known it, but somehow I found this impossible, so drastic had been the changes of the recent past. The fact dawned that the pike floats we were watching were probably the last that would ever grace the surface of that once fair water and as darkness grew there was extreme reluctance on both our parts to pack. We were witnessing the death of a pike water, and it was not a pleasant experience.

After we had packed, I left young Paul with the tackle by the roadside while I walked back to collect the car. Memories of the water flooded back as I trudged down the darkened lane alongside the lake; the bag of roach from the Glory Hole taken during what must have been a force ten gale; the huge perch hooked in the underwater jungle of a sunken tree that had thrashed on the edge of the net and smashed a six-pound line almost within touching distance; the hours spent fishing static dead baits, chasing the mystical twenty-pounder before I realised that such methods were unlikely to succeed. As I neared the car park, I found myself walking along a newly erected perimeter fence – wire mesh a good ten feet high that made the approach more like the road into Stalag Luft IV than the entrance to a sporting estate – and my thoughts turned back to Grandfather. I had a strange feeling that the spirit of the long-dead pike angler might come back to haunt the perpetrators of the rape of Patshull.

It is now well over a quarter of a century since the above was written and it is perhaps pertinent to reflect on subsequent events. Our pike floats were certainly not the last to be seen on the lake; indeed, it did not take the new owners long to recognise the economic value of retaining their pike stocks. At the end of the day, hard financial calculus acted on the pike's behalf. Revenue from pike fishing outweighed the estimated loss of trout due to predation. The new owners, unlike Lord Dartmouth, were not philanthropists – they were engaged in a commercial venture and were out to maximise profitability. The estate had to pay its way and generate an adequate rate of return. Much of the change was of course irreversible, but worse fates could have awaited the pike fishery. The lake could have been turned over to sailing or could have finished up as some dreadful semi-public, local authority-controlled 'nature reserve' emblazoned with 'No Fishing' signs. It could have been taken over by a wildlife trust with similar consequences – as I note in the chapters 'Quantum Field' and 'Civilisation Lost (or Gained?)', Greens are most certainly not angler-friendly.

The pike fishing at Patshull actually seems to have had something of a golden age in the 1980s and early 1990s. Within the Dudley PAC, Dennis Hibbs took a massive fish of thirty pounds, twelve ounces, though he had to endure a whole number of (expensive) blanks before his final success. Adrian Writtle took a fish of twenty-seven pounds, two ounces, and I believe my old buddy Paul Williams had a twenty-five. The first two of these fish came on live bait from the Lodge Bay, the area of the lake that I had viewed as a child. Others had success, including the late John Sidley and friends. John, open and honest as ever, naïvely publicised his use of (rather large) live baits in the angling press and brought hellfire and thunder upon himself from the match-fishing brigade. Coming soon after the RSPCA's infamous Medway report, which, in conjunction with certain factions in the angling establishment, wanted to offer live baiting up as a sacrificial lamb to appease the tiny minority of the population who were 'antis' (and, of course, draw fire away from match fishing), it was an unwise move. The hare had started to run and presented the Dudley region of the PAC with a big problem; but that is another story. I did actually go back – once. We held a fish-in at Patshull; it still being a place where all members could go, access not being predicated on any club membership. The ensuing informal competition was won by Gerald Angell with (I think) a single double. I shared a punt with Max Taylor and, as a result, Max and I became p—ss brothers.

I was at the time pike fishing with the late Dick Orton, recently resigned from the National (Rod Caught) Record Fish Committee (another story again) and who at the time was writing a monthly conservation column in *Angling* magazine. Dick had a thing about pheromones, which of course are present in one's urine. It explained why women were more successful anglers than men, he declared, referring to the list of huge salmon taken by the ladies. Men's urine, however, had the opposite effect – driving fish away. Woe betide any bloke who peed over the side of the boat when Dick was around! Now Dick was a persuasive character with whom you did not argue; his great booming voice and massive frame were enough to see to that. I became an ardent adherent to the pheromones theory. When the practical implications of the theory came into contact with Max Taylor's sense of humour, a side-splitting outcome was pretty well guaranteed. Max drank flasks of tea (quite the most disgusting beverage invented – give me coffee any day). Needs must and I strictly forbade him to perform over the side of the punt, but hardly wanted to paddle in the stuff either. The only answer was the live bait bucket, still containing a few roach. After all, the urine would dilute down anyway, the roach would not be too bothered, would they? And so it transpired. Now I am not exactly known for the size and strength of my bladder and soon was contributing to the roach's discomfort. The water in the bucket became a lighter shade of green, but the roach managed to survive and were eventually returned to their watery home, no doubt complaining about human attitudes to water quality. Since we had shared the bucket, Max declared that we were now p—ss brothers and we have been ever since. Despite these radical precautions, we blanked anyway!

The management of the estate, seeing money in the pike fishing, decided to talk it up somewhat. They seem to have come up with the story of the Duck Guzzler. Now, this component in their promotion campaign may have had some basis in fact, I just do not know. The story was that there was a huge pike in the lake, which, of course, guzzled ducks, apparently by the dozen! The media took up the theme, including the (game) fishing correspondent in my local *Halesowen Chronicle*. The legendary creature had, of course, been hooked on a number of occasions and had always vanquished the opposition. It had also been seen, usually when some unsuspecting duckling disappeared in a massive swirl. Game fishermen, despite their gentlemanly demeanour, are of course often a little on the naïve side when it comes to coarse fish, and pike in particular. Our correspondent always referred to pike as 'snappers' and, to him, a low double off the Severn was a savage monster. He took to the Duck Guzzler story with gusto. The intention was to pull the money in – more pike anglers meant more cash to spend on trout! It was a good story – the thing of legend – milked for all it was worth. Now I have few problems with Patshull containing a monster pike; the place was, after all, being heavily stocked with trout and I have seen the impact of this on the size of pike elsewhere (see 'Middle Earth'). What I do dispute is the bird thing.

In nearly fifty years of pike fishing, I have never seen a pike take a bird, though they take floating dead fish readily enough and, as noted in the first chapter of this book, even bread. That said, it does happen – on occasions. I can vouch for only two instances. The first was on Lifford Reservoir, deep in darkest Birmingham. Two cousins of mine observed a swan, attempting to take to the air, with a pike hanging on to its leg! The fish was dragged through the water until it managed to let go; the bird presumably finishing up with a somewhat lacerated appendage. The second finished up with its photograph in *Pikelines*. Ian Jarvis and friends found a dead pike of over twenty pounds which had choked on a grebe, the bird being half in and half out of the fish's throat. On speaking to Ben Solloway, the fishing keeper on our local estate (a man reared on the waters and a third-generation keeper), I was told that he has encountered such an event only twice in his lifetime; one bird was a Canada gosling, the other a young coot. As he pertinently observed, 'You have got to be in the right place at the right time'. Ben has seen the body of a pike with a rat in it, this latter wrapped in line – was it being used as bait? His most bizarre experience, however, was when Blitz, his fully grown Alsatian dog, was attacked by a pike close to the shore outside his cottage. The dog was splashing in the shallows when a decent-sized pike shot out of the deeper water and went straight for it, only veering off at the last minute when it realised that it was literally biting off more than it could chew. The dog, nonplussed, stood its ground and did not seem to know what to make of the situation. Alsatian versus pike would be an interesting fixture!

Anyway, according to our correspondent, the Duck Guzzler has not been seen lately, though pike fishing is still allowed on Patshull Lake during the late autumn and winter. Various pike matches and championships are held there. It still produces some reasonable fish, though, given the trout that go in, I am surprised that more big pike do not show. Colin Booth, co-ordinator of the Dudley PAC's fly fishing section, has had some great sport with trout; only last week he took the biggest from the water this season, a rainbow of seven pounds, eleven ounces. This latter has earned him a 'trout master' award – well deserved, especially for a pike angler! I wonder what Grandfather would have thought of all this, eighty-odd years on? He would no doubt have been staggered by the amount of change and disappointed that his favourite species did not have a higher profile, but I do not think that he would have been too downhearted. In his day, the pike had to be removed and preservation seems to now be the order of the day. What he would have thought of our huge landing nets, I really do not know. The punts and live baits are still there and, apart from the stages and drastic reduction in tree cover, the lake itself is probably little different from the days when he fished it. He was also a fly fisherman and would, perhaps, have approved of the trout. I used to play with his fly rod as a child – made of greenheart with a whipped handle and highly sophisticated ferrules, it must have cost a fair amount of money in its day. I used the bottom two sections, equipped with a solid glass top, as a substitute roach rod for a time. What became of the rod, I cannot recall – it would, in the condition that I originally remember it, be worth some money today and merit a place in an angling museum. The workmanship in it was remarkable – I wonder how Grandfather would have reacted to our modern rods?

The transformation of Patshull, now over a quarter of a century in the past, was, in some senses, the precursor to the commercial fisheries that we see springing up around the countryside today. This is not the place to discuss the pros and cons of such activity, though this private enterprise has undoubtedly contributed to the growing popularity of our sport. On the trout front, fly fishing is enjoying a boom, and a lake like Patshull has to earn its living. Colin Booth has offered me a day's trout fishing on the lake; despite my earlier anger and pessimism, it is an offer that I intend to accept. Casting a fly on those hallowed waters may not be full compensation for the loss of the roach and perch fishing, but a decent rainbow in estate lake surroundings has a certain attraction. Who knows, we may witness the Duck Guzzler seize a coot or moorhen – a pike fly or two in the kit might not be a bad idea.

The Great Pool at Patshull today – do 'duck-guzzling' monsters really inhabit its depths? (Author)

Middle Earth

Pike conservation, Black Country style. (Author)

First the red-topped pike float was there, bobbing in the increasingly choppy water. Then it was gone. Forty feet below the boat, a great pike had taken my half mackerel, and line was pouring off the spool. The Eustace T40 took on its battle curve, a three-and-a-half-pound test curve beast of a rod, made from hollow glass and designed to tame the monsters of the Irish loughs. Canal reservoir fish, in the warm water of mid autumn, usually pull hard, but I had never before felt anything like this. The power was fearful. 'That's a big fish,' said my companion. 'Take it easy'. I was confident of the tackle – a big ABU reel, eighteen-pound Sylcast and twenty-pound-plus wire. I could make no impression on that fish; any attempt to pump it resulted in a violent wrench the other way. At that relatively early stage in my pike fishing career, I had yet to take a twenty-pounder, though eighteens and nineteens had been fairly regular visitors to my net. This was it – my first twenty! But there was something wrong. None of my previous fish had behaved like this. No nineteen-pounder had treated me thus. The rod top was being dragged well under water every time the fish plunged, my arm was straining in its socket – the pike was literally playing me. 'I am never going to land this,' I said. 'Stick at it,' said my companion.

I did just that. Twenty minutes later, I had barely gained an inch of line. The waves were battering the side of the boat. Above us towered the dam wall and the wind, blowing straight into it, was causing the line to whistle. We had no engine, only oars. This was not a happy situation. I had just got to get that fish; it represented the end of many years of fruitless effort, searching for the elusive monster. The tackle was strong and I knew that, if I could hang on, with the virtual absence of snags the brute would give in. It had to. There was one problem – the front anchor rope, the rear mud weight having been raised when I hooked the fish. Like many big reservoir pike (in my experience at least), this fish was fighting under the boat, pretty well directly below the rod. 'Get the anchor up – please,' I begged my friend. Now, he was secretary of the club and I was a guest, fishing in his boat. Anglers had died against that dam. Neither of us was in an enviable position – I desperately wanted my fish and my friend wanted us both to stay alive. 'There isn't a problem,' he replied. 'You will get your fish, and your first twenty is going to be a thirty.' This remark was designed to spur me on – it did the opposite! I quaked in my waders. The water had a sound track history of making dreams come true – my dream was developing into a nightmare. It ended predictably – a horrible grating as line and anchor rope came into violent juxtaposition. The line held for a surprisingly long time – I know now that I should have knocked off the bail arm and gently pulled the anchor up, hang safety! But I was stressed and tired. The line, inevitably, gave. The stop-knot was a foot below the rod top – I had not lifted that monster off the bottom during the whole time I had played it. It was the worst moment in my fishing career, bar none. The anchor system we use now – not perfect, but a distinct improvement – is shown below.

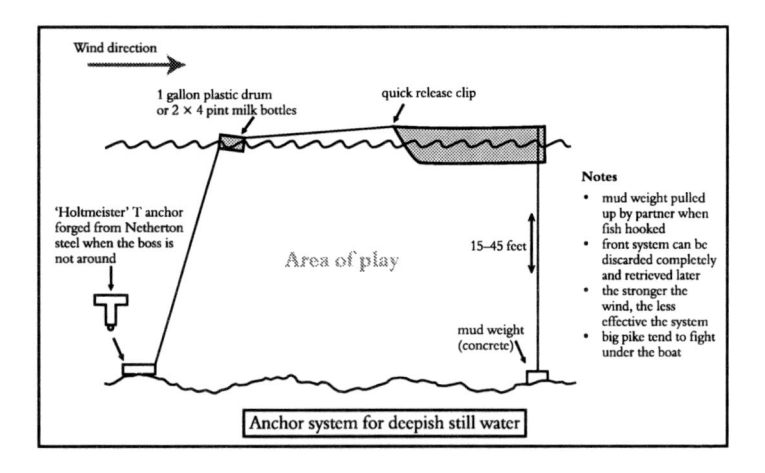

Figure: Anchor system for deepish still water

- Wind direction →
- 1 gallon plastic drum or 2 × 4 pint milk bottles
- quick release clip
- 'Holtmeister' T anchor forged from Netherton steel when the boss is not around
- Area of play
- 15–45 feet
- mud weight (concrete)

Notes
- mud weight pulled up by partner when fish hooked
- front system can be discarded completely and retrieved later
- the stronger the wind, the less effective the system
- big pike tend to fight under the boat

That was many years ago. I tell the story because it is indicative of the quality of fishing bequeathed to us by the canal engineers of the late eighteenth and nineteenth centuries. England's great industrialisation was predicated, at least initially, on the mobility brought by the canals, and canals need water. These reservoirs can be found all along the Midland canal system and nowhere more so than in and around the Black Country. They are a fantastic angling resource. The archetypal canal reservoir has key features: a dam with adjacent deep water, quite severe changes in depth, and extensive shallows fed by streams, usually coming in from surrounding farmland. Water levels fluctuate, often severely, with draw-off reaching its peak in the early autumn. The shallows become extensive again in the New Year and provide spawning grounds for pike and other fish. But they are not all thus. Some are not used by British Waterways at all and flourish, with an enhanced ecology, virtually as estate lakes. One such water, close to my home and deep in the industrial heartland, is an old clay pit – crystal clear, very deep and with rich reed growth. It reminds me of Dick Walker's descriptions of Arlesey Lake, back in the 1950s. Pike thrive in most of these waters, and some, notably Blithfield, have been turned into trout waters as well – not necessarily to the detriment of the pike fishing. Some waters respond best to moving baits, especially live baits; others are dead bait waters par excellence, these latter typically being the more traditional type, with fluctuating levels. For me, they represent bread-and-butter pike waters and have brought me good roach, tench and eels as well. Recently, following a reintroduction to fly fishing instigated by Vic Bellars, I fill in the coarse close season with some superb rainbow trout fishing on three estate lake-type reservoirs.

Some waters are highly exclusive but many, such as Edgbaston, close to Birmingham city centre, can be fished for a modest sum. Others are even free. Cheap does not mean poor! Let me tell you about Dave Hendry's Black Country Bonanza. On the edge of Pensnett Chase, close by the very crucible of Black Country industrialization, lie, abandoned, a chain of three reservoirs. They are now a Site of Special Scientific Interest and are properly wardened, but back in the 1970s and 1980s they were no man's land. On one side was the Round Oak Steel Works and on the other a large, very run-down council estate. The Fens Pools, as they are known, were pike-fished by Grandfather when the area was prosperous, the works thriving and the houses new. Big tench and bream abounded – many years ago, a Mr A Tolley took a tench of eight pounds, ten ounces from the top pool, at a time when the record stood at just over nine pounds, and, more recently, double figure tench have been reliably reported. As steel output declined, local unemployment grew and, by the time Dave decided to test the big pike potential, it was a brave man who fished there alone – even being in company would not protect one's vehicle from losing its wheels, or worse. In the early 1980s the steel works closed and, for the locals, destitution became a frightening reality. Feral youth (and feral unemployed) roamed the Chase, their ranks supplemented by itinerants who kept horses tethered on the grassed remains of the slag heaps. They were not happy people, and horror stories abounded as to the fate of unfortunate anglers who found themselves on the receiving end of their wrath. I was barraged with half house bricks while tench fishing one evening (by children who appeared to be little more than five years old), and it was not unknown for stolen cars to be rolled down the steep bank towards any unfortunate angler sitting below. Even a reinforced concrete sluice failed to survive sustained assaults on more than one occasion. Nefarious activities went on in the bushes and, for the police, it was virtually a no-go area.

Little wonder conventional wisdom among local anglers was 'Don't forget your Kalashnikov'! Plenty of ammunition and a few anti-personnel mines were also recommended, Princess Diana notwithstanding. Shotguns just encouraged the blighters, though smoke grenades were useful to cover you while you packed your tackle. Some purists insisted that the best defence of all was the British Army's Sterling sub-machine gun, a Rolls Royce among weapons if there ever was one. Bursts of 9mm parabellum were a real deterrent; members of the Territorial Army apparently conducting a thriving trade in illicit weapons hire, with training thrown in. Dave Hendry did not need all this, however; as a martial arts expert he had a fearsome reputation among the locals for inflicting appalling suffering on anyone who so much as thought of doing him harm. Moreover, he was an honorary National Rivers Authority bailiff and the first individual to attempt to establish some sort of law and order in the El Paso of the Black Country. He fished unmolested, taking one-hundred-pound bags of tench and bream in the summer and some massive pike in the winter. These waters were classic examples of pike thriving by neglect and Dave made the most of it. Dead baits were a waste of time – these old reservoirs were live bait waters pure and simple. Here is Dave's story:

Dave Hendry's Black Country Bonanza

For many years I have lived close to several canal feeder reservoirs and been told by the locals 'Yo con catch fish aut a there mate!' After translating the comment, I got to thinking, 'Why not?' I had seen anglers trying to catch pike with a variety of methods with little or no success, which was good news for the pike as those that were caught found their way up the bank, into the cooking pot, or into the cat!

These waters had an unconfirmed reputation for big pike. Many of the local youth would delight in telling me – 'My granddad caught a thirty-pounder from here'; 'Have you seen Moby Dick yet?'; 'I saw a forty-pound pike eat a swan last week!' Add that to the fact that many well-known pike anglers of the day would not fish these waters because of the fearsome reputation of the local youth (and the not so young), with parking your car being 'a bit' of a problem, and I knew that I could end up with having the pools to myself. I must add that I was to experience none of this during the time I fished there. Getting to know the locals, being an NRA bailiff and a karate black belt may have had a slight bearing on things – who knows? Now to the pike fishing!

My first visit was to the Fens Pool itself and set the ball rolling. It was 10 October 1982, the water was flat calm, and baits had been cast out before the first of the locals came for 'a chat'. The first voice said, 'Do you want me to get a fire going?' This, I was soon to find out, was the way the locals did things – set up their tackle, cast in and then burn a bush! I was soon left in peace and got my first run. The pike weighed in at eleven pounds, two ounces and was to be the smallest fish I was to catch during my campaign.

I attracted the attention of a few characters. Big Dave – yes, he was. Tea Cosy – the hat he seemingly never took off. Most memorable was Cocky, a young lad who would ask half a dozen anglers if he could get them some chips from the local chip shop and then persuade them all to buy him some as well. This resulted in him both feeding himself and making a profit! Putting all this to one side, the pike fishing was getting better. My idea of using large baits in areas where no one would fish seemed to be working. One trick was to fish next to sunken cars and other vehicles. One van I fished next to usually seemed to hold good fish willing to take the bait and then, obligingly, run away from the safety of the snag. I never once lost a fish this way, although I did have one pike of twenty-one pounds, six ounces go in through the back doors, turn around, and come out again! The first season disappointingly came to an abrupt end due to prolonged ice cover. My tally was rather better than expected. Eight pike, including two twenty-pounders, were taken, with an average weight of sixteen twelve.

The second season was to be a little different, as I intended to try fishing all three pools in the chain. First visit was to the Middle Pool where earlier I had seen a large pike lying under some overhanging trees. I decided to fish an area where the pool narrows to about thirty yards with a deep gully running through the middle. Heavy weed on the ledges meant care would be needed to land the fish. Once set up, I retired to the remains of the boat house, burnt down by someone with a grudge against sailors, no doubt. An hour or two passed during which time I was kept entertained by more stories of huge duck-eating pike, courtesy of a couple of local storytellers who eventually ran out of tales and left – just in time, as one of my indicators soon dropped off. A very fit pike of eighteen pounds, nine ounces soon graced the net. The fish was duly photographed and returned. I sat back, soon to be visited by another local 'angler', who spent half an hour telling me about his large quantity of tattoos. He had no sooner left when I had my second run. This was a much stronger fish, which spent its time swimming along the bottom of the gully. Firm pressure eventually lifted its head and eventually into the net she came. Weighing in at twenty-one pounds, four ounces, the fish remains my biggest pike from this particular water.

The season progressed with me finding more of the elusive Fens Pools pike. I still had the waters to myself and, apart from a few friends, no one was aware of the fish that I was catching. The only break to my fishing was caused by the appearance of a great northern diver (a rather large budgie) which brought a larger number of 'twitchers' out to look at it – had it taken one of my baits, even I would not have survived the resulting onslaught! Soon it was back to business with my first trip to the third of the three reservoirs, The Grove. This resulted in pike of seventeen pounds, thirteen ounces and thirteen pounds, ten ounces. Other pike of nineteen pounds, eight ounces, sixteen pounds, twelve ounces, and nineteen pounds, two ounces were to come from the Fens and Middle Pools – there was more to come.

On the 18 November 1984, I took a friend to the Fens Pool, hoping he could beat his best pike of fourteen pounds. Things did not go to plan. The pool was covered in thick fog, there was no wind, and the air temperature was low. Baits were cast out but hopes were not high – until my indicator dropped off at 7.45 a.m.! My first words were 'Sorry, Pete.' A steady run, typical of all that I had experienced, was soon hit. I told Pete that it was a small fish until I realised that it was swimming towards me – then it got heavy. After several minutes and a few anxious moments, she was in the net. The weight was twenty-six pounds, two ounces. I was delighted (an understatement!). After photographing, the pike was slipped back, only to show up again a year and a day later to the rod of my friend Paul Bradley; the weight twenty-five pounds, four ounces.

This remains my best fish from the pools, with my final tally being seventeen doubles plus four twenties with an average weight of seventeen pounds, eleven ounces (and not a jack in sight). I had proved that 'Yo con catch fish aut a them pools' if you go about it in the correct manner and are prepared to put up with the locals.

I returned to the Fens Pool in December 1990 for a 'memory' trip. Things had not changed, as the first fish tipped the scales at seventeen pounds, fourteen ounces. A visit the next day to the Grove Pool resulted in a pike of sixteen pounds, five ounces. For me that was the end of the line, as people had realised that there were good pike to be caught. After seeing a fish of over sixteen pounds foul-hooked and dragged up the bank to feed the cat, I moved off. Since then, very few pike have been caught, and over the last fifteen years few anglers have bothered to fish for them. Maybe the time is right for a return visit? Maybe!

(In the summer of 2006, 'normality' returned to the area when a group of locals sabotaged the sluice on the Middle Pool and proceeded to try to net it for food! The ensuing riot was only displaced in the local media by a national terrorist threat. It may be coincidence that Dave Hendry, accident-prone as usual, was incapacitated with a shattered ankle at the time.)

As Dave states, a problem on a lot of these waters, particularly those with little control, was (and still is) that of pike killing. Once word got out, Dave's monster eventually met its end, as did more than one of the remaining twenty-pounders. Around that time, a photograph appeared in a local newspaper of another (big) twenty held (very dead) by its captor and wife over a frying pan in their kitchen – this fish was from the clay pit. The classic, however, was a magistrates' court appearance by a lady who was charged with beating her husband over the head with a dead, frozen pike! Some of us were more concerned with the fate of the fish than that of the husband.

Some waters are of course properly run, particularly those outside of the urban area. Back in 1973, Dick Orton published, in his Conservation column in *Angling* magazine, some work that he had done on the relationship between weather and pike fishing. The venue was a canal reservoir, to which he subsequently introduced me, of the more traditional type. Although Dick did not consider the effect of barometric pressure, he was a true pioneer and his results seemed to demonstrate that there was no such thing as good pike-fishing weather any more than there was bad. Dick restricted his method to dead baiting and to one water, but his article still makes fascinating reading. My own (subjective) view confirms Dick's work, particularly when differences in waters are examined – on his water, with static dead baits, the 'three Ws' (warm, wet and windy) seemed a good bet – a strong south-wester being the driving force. On another water, sunshine and high pressure, providing the air temperature is rising, seem to produce the works. Many photographs of big dead-bait-caught fish from this water have sun and blue sky as background. I once took two decent twenty-pounders (twenty-four pounds, one ounce and twenty-one pounds, twelve ounces), one on each rod, and within fifteen minutes of each other, under such conditions. Live baits, as one would expect, produce during high pressure, but again, generalisation is difficult, even when looking at one water in isolation.

It is not my intention to chronicle thirty years of pike (or other) fishing on the waters of Middle Earth. (It is odd that J R R Tolkien, in his travels, seems to have lived close by a number of them – was he an angler, I wonder?) I am a lazy piker – grabbing a few dead baits from the freezer and chucking two out in a suitable location means that I am far from being an expert, though my companions do sometimes complain of being 'Tatered', when I get things right. One trick is to run a lure through the swim prior to casting out the dead baits – big fish often lie close in and will strike if not disturbed. Having a double on the bank before my companion has even set up usually produces some ribald comments. I love fishing the shallows after Christmas, sitting in amongst the undergrowth with the grebe doing their mating dances and the local herons holding a tea party. Often I am joined by Gromit and it is a sublime experience, especially when a double or two grace the landing net. More than once we have been visited by ospreys and it is the very essence of what angling should be. If I am no expert, I did know one – the late John Sidley. John was one of the old school; he had no secrets and was always willing to help and give advice, the very antithesis of his counterparts today. Having thoroughly thrashed me one day using live baits (I was dead baiting), he very graciously presented me with his last live bait, telling me to change tactics if I wanted a pike. I did so – down went the float and out came a fourteen-pounder. I do not know who was more pleased, John or I. John, of course, was driven by what his friends recognised was a personal demon. He worked at his fishing like no other, abusing himself pretty badly in the process. I well remember Noel Clark and I being huddled under our brollies on a day of icy, driving rain. In a semi-waterlogged punt, out in the channel, was JS, his only protection being an old Barbour coat and his famous red, woolly hat. He was standing up, fishing sink and draw. In the end he came in, near to hypothermia and exhaustion. He had taken a twenty-five-pounder from the area a few days before and was intent on getting another. His only sustenance for the day was a single humbug, which he produced from the pocket which also contained his dead baits! We poured hot coffee into him and shared our sandwiches. With the punt bailed, out he went again to continue his quest.

On one notable occasion, I remember John gesticulating violently to me from the shore of a small, shallow bay. He and Gerry Rogers were pike fishing and had been sitting concealed in the undergrowth. It was February, and Gerry was in the water with a fish that John had just landed, bulging the net. It was one of the most magnificent pike I have ever seen; at twenty-seven pounds, six ounces it was like a side of bacon lying on the unhooking mat, fin perfect. I photographed the pike and sent the film to John. My photograph subsequently appeared in the angling press and in the book *Pike Fishing Beyond 2000*, published by the Pike Anglers' Club. John, being naïve it has to be said, made a mistake here – going public with this fish was a significant factor in him losing his place in the club. Publicity bans, however necessary, are of course a reflection of the pressure that good waters come under – together with the behaviour of those who chase big fish whatever the cost (John, I feel, only partially came into this latter category).

We take it as axiomatic that fish will not tolerate disturbance. But is this true of pike? Tommy Morgan, whose forty-seven-pound, eleven-ounce fish was, in my view unfairly, removed from the record list (and was one of the factors in Dick Orton's resignation from the British (Rod Caught) Record Fish Committee), used a weed-thrashing technique on Loch Lomond.

This was the controlled use of disturbance to flush fish from bank-side weed beds to 'wake 'em up a bit' and start them feeding. On one of my first trips to Dick's reservoir, we took the boat up against the dam. The anchors were two iron grapples and Dick prevailed upon me to throw them up onto the grass top of the dam to enable us to secure the boat. Such a process is not as easy as it seems. My first attempt was a dismal failure, the anchor clanging against the dam wall before falling back into the boat. This was embarrassing – here I was, the guest of a well-known and respected angling author, the organiser of the Angling Foundation, and I had just wrecked our chances of success. My second attempt was little better. I tendered my apologies and suggested that we move. Dick, experienced man that he was, did not think that there was a problem, quite the opposite. He suggested we stay put. Despite more disturbance, I finally secured the boat and we cast our coarse dead baits into the deep water. An hour later, we had taken five doubles, the best nearly seventeen pounds, to my rod. Dick's view was that we had replicated Morgan's approach.

I have since concluded that Dick could have been correct. On a windy day on another canal reservoir, Gromit, Adrian Writtle and I were fishing from the bank on a tree-lined channel. The water was well into the trees and the wind was blowing hard into the thick, partly submerged scrub at the narrow end where a stream entered. It was February and we were hoping for some big fish, particularly given the wind direction, water level and time of year. In the wind, casting was not easy and I volunteered to row a couple of baits out in the punt. Now, punts and big blows are not comfortable bedfellows, and I succeeded in losing an oar. Cursing, I manoeuvred the punt back to our bank and wondered about how we were going to get back to the car park on one oar! Mid morning, using his binoculars, Gromit located said object in among the jungle on the opposite bank. We went over in the punt to retrieve it. Chaos ensued. Wading, I had to hold the punt with one hand and pull it into the jungle to avoid the effect of the wind. I grabbed the oar and we tried to escape from the clutches of the overhanging trees. The wind on the side of the punt had other ideas and, even when we eventually escaped into open water, we were pushed down the channel into the scrub at the far end, out of control. Eventually, I had to jump overboard and tow us away from trouble, splashing and cursing as my feet sank into the mud. The disturbance was impressive. Meanwhile, Adrian had a sardine out, only feet from where our antics had taken place. I jumped into the punt and Gromit struggled to row us out of danger. There was the sound of a bite alarm. Adrian had a run on the sardine, from almost under the punt. We landed, Adrian's rod was firmly bent and a titanic struggle was taking place in the shallow water (probably not more than two and a half feet deep). I had difficulty lifting the net. The pike went twenty-six pounds, three ounces. Had we flushed it out of the scrub? Convention says that there should have been no fish anywhere near the location, yet here was a huge fish, not only unfazed, but willing to feed. We pike anglers have a lot to learn.

(At one stage in my pike-fishing career, I had a fetish for statistics. At the end of this chapter, I present my own weight-for-length tables for two of the more significant Middle Earth waters, and compare them with the generally accepted Mona scale – I leave the reader to draw conclusions from this flight of fancy.)

Let me now turn to trout fishing. I am lucky in having good trout waters close to home and, following intensive instruction on Vic Bellars' delightful Suffolk lake, have really got back into fly fishing. Still-water trout fishing, mainly for rainbows, has really taken off within the Dudley PAC, and we are getting quite good at it (some of us arrogantly so!). The fly is the ultimate renewable bait; one can dispense with the rucksack, chair and holdall and get one's string pulled, often spectacularly, and in lovely surroundings. A spring evening, casting a fly with newly arrived martins, swallows and swifts overhead, is difficult to beat as an angling experience. Trout can range from being stupidly easy to near impossible. On more than one occasion I have packed up because it was a fish a chuck; on other occasions, especially in hot weather, the fish are frustratingly difficult. Ringing the changes is always a good tactic and I have several hundred fish under my belt. Rainbows, like sewin, are incredibly strong and have remarkable acceleration – the line can enter the water in one place and the fish come clean out many yards away. Being taken down to the backing, as will happen with the better fish, can be a disconcerting experience. That said, I am reminded of Dick Walker's comment about salmon – rainbows, in particular, fight with great strength but little intelligence. Transplant a chub's brain into a rainbow and you would never land it! Fly pattern is trial and error – on my waters, orange patterns can be deadly (Montana, Cat's Whisker, Viva and an unidentified pattern I refer to as the Orange Horror). I am of course speaking of wet fly fishing here. Another good fly is Walker's Mayfly Nymph – that man again!

One of my trout waters contains pike, including some very big ones, despite (futile) attempts to remove them. My first encounter with one of these was when a trout I had hooked refused to dive, charging round and round the boat in ever decreasing circles. When it came close in, I found out the reason for its strange behaviour – directly underneath it was a log, a rather familiar-looking log, with the head of an alligator and a dorsal fin apparently the size of my hand. It was not that trout's day – talk about being between a rock and a hard thing! I fully expected a spectacular strike as I drew the fish towards the net – and yes, I was a little frightened. The pike, however, had other ideas – there were lots of other trout around – and it gently waved its tail as if saying farewell, and sank slowly into the depths. Weight? Twenty pounds easily, thirty maybe. On another occasion, I had failed to secure the fish bag to the rowlock firmly and a dead trout of around a couple of pounds floated away. I reached for the landing net to retrieve it. Before I could do so, a pike took the trout off the surface, just as a trout would a dry fly. A huge swirl and the trout had gone. A two-pound trout is quite a mouthful – how big was the pike? Has anyone ever tried floating dead baits, I wonder? Are we pike anglers missing something? I recall the pike that took floating bread on Breeches Pool in my youth and, thinking about it, have witnessed pike taking dead fish off the surface on a number of occasions. Dave Hendry once took a twenty-five-pounder from the Wye, which had drawn attention to itself by taking a discarded dead bait which had floated away downstream.

Now, in the eyes of many club members, these pike have no business in their water. They are vermin. The situation is a familiar one. Prejudice rather than science (or even clear thinking) is the order of the day. One would think that, in the twenty-first century, such attitudes would be a thing of the past. Those pike are not a problem but a resource; they represent an opportunity for some fantastic sport and increased revenue to a cash-strapped club. Big pike keep down the jacks, which represent the real nuisance to the trout angler and, I suggest, feed on the corpses of the many rainbows that fail to over-winter or die from a variety of causes, of which cormorant damage may be the most significant. When we last netted the water, we took out many hundreds of pounds of prime roach – and pike to thirty-two pounds, six ounces. The netsman remarked that the pike were 'roach-fed'. I am no fisheries scientist, but I am a pike angler, and you can imagine my frustration at this situation. I am told that conventional wisdom in the club is that our trout do not over-winter. I find this a sweeping generalisation, but, if it is true, why then attempt to constantly wipe out every other species? Some control I can accept, providing the case is made drawing on some real evidence and has a basis in fisheries science. Other trout waters now accept big pike as a positive addition to a water's sporting assets; sadly, in my neck of the woods, the 'cult of the adipose fin' precludes coarse fishing members even having a vote at the AGM. Coarse anglers, like their favourite species, are treated as second-class citizens in an antediluvian system more reminiscent of 1950s South Africa than of a forward-looking British fishing club in the twenty-first century. We have trout anglers, many of whom do not live far from the River Severn, who have never fished for barbel, and have probably never even seen one of these magnificent fish. And as for roach, bream and chub! Yet they look down on their fellows with disdain – catching a stew-pond-reared rainbow on a 'bunch of fluff' to them, given the class connotations of fly fishing and trout, is an entirely higher level of activity that sets them above the guy who stalks a River Teme chub with a lump of crust, emulating the curse of the serpent – 'on thy belly thou shalt go'. Rainbows are not even an indigenous species! Which angler is the true disciple of Isaac? It is no contest as far as I am concerned. There is an old adage in the philosophy of science – a paradigm shift can never really be complete until the old guard is literally dead. I am too far gone to test this contention, and just wallow around in a sea of despair as far as these pike are concerned. This is not to decry (still water) trout fishing per se; quite the opposite, as I have indicated, it is a wonderful experience. I love it. But anyone who is a competent float angler will not find it difficult; the reverse is not the case. At the end of the day, it is not the trout that are the problem, but the sort of people they attract. Let me now place things into perspective.

I am concluding this chapter having just returned from an evening's trout fishing. Eight fat rainbows have graced the net and I should be feeling euphoric, for the experience has been superlative. This was not to be however: yesterday morning Lindy Bellars telephoned to say that Vic had lost his last great battle, that for life itself. But Vic was immortal, you may protest, certainly if you are a member of the pike fishing fraternity. Yes, we all thought that. The news was not wholly unexpected but is difficult to cope with nonetheless. Despite this, the evening on the reservoir has been truly sublime. Trout fishing for me lacks the raw excitement of pike or barbel fishing, but this place can have a quality that, while inevitably intangible, would move all but the most insensitive of match fishers. It was sunny, warm and still. I shared the place with one other and he, casting from the stern of his boat, in turn shared things with his Alsatian, which obediently occupied the bow position, seemingly mesmerised by the evening's atmosphere. 'Oh to be in England, now that April's there' – the poem says it all. Daffodils and other flowers adorned the banks, though the green shoots of the rushes were still conspicuous by their absence. In some senses, despite the warmth, winter still lingered. There was no great hatch of fly, but the fish were swirling on the oily surface in considerable numbers, presumably feeding on something. The first martins and swallows had arrived and been given a warm welcome by the local sparrowhawk. The coots, as usual, were playing the fool and even the swans seemed less aggressive than usual. On top of the aqueduct, canal boats moved sedately along; the holiday season is about to start. The Orange Horror, a gold head this time, was doing its deadly work. As the sun dipped over Tolkien's hills, smoke from a wood fire drifted across the distant trees and a heron glided lazily down into one of the shallow bays, a killing zone now that the water was warmer. It was difficult to believe that the city is so close; this could be another place entirely in the quantum field, a million light years away from what we disingenuously call civilisation. There was a wonderful sense of peace; I thought of Vic and realised that this is his personal legacy to me. A more wonderful one there could not be – any time, any place.

Data on which Weight-for-Length Figure is Based

Length (in)	Mona's scale (lb)	Sample mean (lb)	Upper of range (lb)	Lower of range (lb)
32	10.24	11.18	12.75	10.5
33	11.24	11.9	13.25	10.31
34	12.23	11.67	12.75	10.06
35	13.28	13.4	14.94	10.06
36	14.58	15.02	17.69	13.19
37	15.83	16.12	19	13.63
38	17.15	16.52	18.88	13.63
39	18.54	18.38	21.75	15.5
40	20	20.23	27.44	16.25
41	21.54	20.75	26.19	17.81
42	23.15	21.66	23.13	18.81

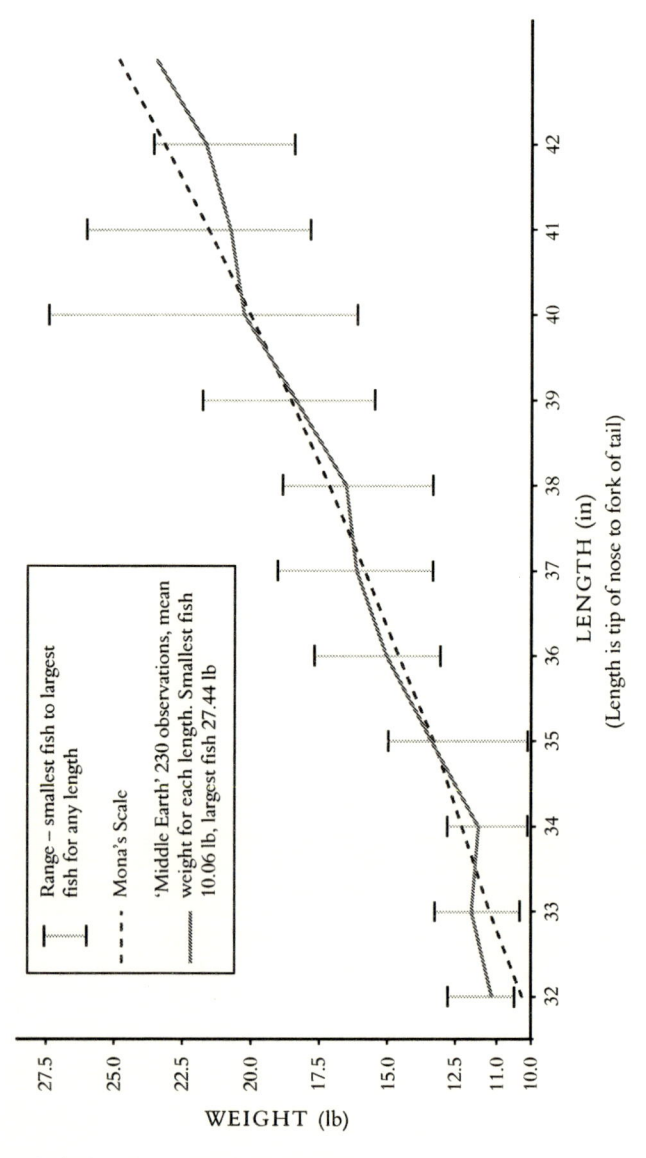

Weight for length – 'Middle Earth' compared with Mona's Scale for pike (Esox lucius) ten pounds and above.

Notes to Accompany Figure on Weight-for-Length in Pike

'Mona's Scale', as produced by a Mr Fletcher, a writer in the long-defunct *Fishing Gazette*, is still regarded as a key benchmark in transforming the length of a pike to its weight. It is based on the key statistic that a forty-inch pike should weigh (conveniently) around twenty pounds.

It can be seen that, for fish up to twenty pounds, the author's 'Middle Earth' sample does not deviate excessively from the Mona 'norm' — thereafter, however, the latter's predictions appear high for the Middle Earth pike. That said, any sample data will be subject to both sampling error and bias. In addition, the data are drawn from populations different both temporally and spatially from those sampled by Mona. Both sampling error and bias undoubtedly account for the data in the sample giving a lower mean weight for a thirty-four-inch fish compared with one of thirty-three inches.

In his books *Pike* and *The Doomsday Book of Mammoth Pike*, Fred Buller is critical of the accuracy of the Mona scale, particularly for pike of over twenty pounds. The sample data are consistent with this position. However (significantly?) both Mona and the sample data agree on the forty inches/twenty pounds equality, quite precisely, in fact.

However, as any pike angler knows, the condition of the fish is critical in any weight-for-length analysis. Condition (reflected in average girth) will itself depend on variables such as age of fish, time of year, food supply and so on. In statistical terms, there is a range of independent variables to be considered and not just one (length). This is reflected in the ranges shown, most spectacularly for forty-inch fish. Although the means are very close (20 lb for Mona, 20.23 lb for the sample), the range is vast: from a low of 16.25 lb to a high of 27.44 lb. Similar, if less spectacular, ranges exist for the other sample means.

As Buller states, Mona is 'positively inaccurate' for pike of over forty inches long (Buller, *Pike*, p.112). One might posit that any mean can similarly be misleading for pike of less than twenty pounds as well. There is a lot more that a statistician could do with better data (Buller refers to a study involving some 44,000 observations). Suffice to say that single variable models are no better in angling than they are in economics!

Author with a Middle Earth pike of twenty-one pounds, twelve ounces taken on a sardine. (Author)

David Hendry with the biggest pike during his Black Country Bonanza. Close by today is one of the largest shopping malls in the UK. (David Hendry)

A great (not so) modern pike angler – Roy 'Gromit' Stevens with a near thirty-pound fish, taken from Middle Earth in early autumn. (Amy Stevens)

John (Holtmeister) Holt with a magnificent Middle Earth common carp of twenty-eight pounds, four ounces. (John Holt)

Red River Rock

Author's twelve-pound, three-ounce Teme barbel. (Author)

If the Wye is my spiritual home, the Teme runs it a close second. Many have waxed lyrical over this beautiful valley, notably Bernard Venables. Let me quote from *The Angler's Companion* (1959):

> It is a country remote in feeling, but peaceful; wild, but warm. Wales is to the west of it, the English Midlands to the east, but it is like neither. As border country so often has, it has its own unmistakable identity – haunted a little by the Welsh proximity, English with an Englishness that has nothing in common with the plains of Warwickshire and Worcestershire beyond.

This is where I spend my summers, the river being some forty minutes' drive from home. The Abberley Hills, arguably the gateway to the middle Teme, are just visible from our bedroom window. I only have to glance in that direction to have visions of willows, Himalayan balsam, a quiet stream, great barbel and chub, double-figure pike, big roach, trout, grayling and, more recently, otters. Kingfishers are abundant; I never cease to thrill at that blue flash as the bird flies fast and low between the branches. Buzzards wheel overhead and the tap, tap, tap of the greater spotted woodpeckers is one's constant companion. The Teme rises in the Radnor Forest but I must confess that I do not know it well until much lower down, beyond Tenbury, where it is a sizable river, alternating from fast riffles to deep, almost canal-like channels. It is particularly (though not exclusively) in the latter where the big fish live, the often heavily wooded banks generating a jungle-type environment, full of snags, with the tree cover making even casting a difficult exercise. Over the millennia, the river has cut deeply into the bedrock and steep, precipitous banks make the fishing an even greater challenge. Only the foolish fish during high water; it is a dangerous place. During such times, the river runs red, the alluvium of the valley providing the distinctive colour. Venables describes it as a fascinating river, and I could not agree more. Every swim is different; a fast run can become a deep pool in mere yards; shallow water over the bedrock can transform into apparently bottomless pits, as vertical walls in the rock appear as if from nowhere. A narrow neck can quickly widen into a wide pool. Trees from each bank meet overhead, forming dark tunnels even during the sunniest of days. Fallen willows provide safe haven for the barbel and chub. Even lower down, not far from the Severn confluence, good trout and grayling can be taken in the faster water. The entire valley is steeped in history and an awareness of this adds to the whole experience. One does not (or should not) fish in a vacuum.

This environment has generated its own form of fishing, particularly for the barbel and chub. We call it 'jungle fishing' and it is not for the fainthearted. Ideally, a roving approach is needed but on occasions it is appropriate to stay put, as we shall see. Roving is also for the young and fit, and I am neither. Quality rather than quantity is the byword, and success is hard won though sweeter in the making. Gromit will have none of it; although he is probably fitter than I, it is difficult to get three or four rods into a typical Teme swim! The man always will insist on having at least one pike rod out, even when barbel fishing. I shall expand on our experiences in the jungle later, but one's first encounters with a water are always memorable.

My first recollection of the Teme is as a young child in the late 1940s when, recovering from a bad attack of whooping cough, my parents took me for a break at Ludlow. We travelled in my Dad's 1935 Ford Ten, and I well remember the weir at Dinham, with the mighty castle towering on its rock in the background. The registration of the car was ADH 100 – it would be worth some money today. My brother-in-law had some good perch from this weirpool some years ago, but I have never fished it. My acquaintance with the Teme goes back a long way.

In the early 1960s, a chap called Jim Wheat ran a series of articles in the *Midland Angler* entitled 'Around BAA Waters'. In these, he described the results of visits that he had made to a range of waters belonging to the Birmingham Anglers' Association. One of these pieces was on the Teme at Ludlow (actually, the water was somewhat downstream of the town). He caught a three-pound chub on bread and was quite enthusiastic about the place. My school friend, Robin Dunn, and I had just passed our driving tests. It was February half term. Robin managed to persuade his father to lend us his Sunbeam Rapier. Such trust was hardly justified; we hit 110 mph along the Halesowen bypass – wow! In addition to its brevity, the journey was also notable for the foul breath emanating from Robin's dog – it sure was a relief to get there for that reason alone; being in one piece was a bonus! With my newly acquired waders, I trotted maggots in a number of fastish runs; the weather was none too warm and I blanked. Robin however, as an inveterate dry fly man, managed to catch a number of small grayling on midges. Despite the time of year and the temperature, there was a hatch and he made the most of it – an impressive performance.

Student life and the acquisition of a career then intervened. August sea trout in north Wales was about all I could manage. In the early 1970s, however, I had my first encounter with the middle reaches of the river. This is a land of church spires, delightful villages, winding lanes and hop fields – Eastham,

Lindridge, Puddleford, Menith Wood, Stockton and Pensax are all names to evoke strong emotions among the exiled. Over forty years ago, an angler called Richard Holding wrote a delightful little book about this part of the valley entitled *Down Along Temeside*. The book is long out of print but is well worth chasing for the photographs alone. The work was apparently intended as a series of articles in the *Fishing Gazette* but, since it was as much concerned with social history as it was angling, it finished up as a book instead. Holding knew the middle Teme mainly between the wars, a time of great social change and not just in the towns. He was a witness to such change and paints a fascinating picture of rural life, together with details of some great local characters. Trout and grayling were his quarry; something of a contrast to today, though I am sure that the fish are still there.

My companions were Bob and Roger Allen. The former had flown Halifax bombers during the Second World War, had all sorts of hairy moments, been shot down by a German night fighter, escaped through enemy lines and survived to fly on Bomber Command's last raid of the war. A very brave man indeed, he was terrified of cows! No force on earth would get him through a field of cows – human psychology is a strange, irrational thing. With the Allens, I fished for trout with legered worms in one of the many Teme 'canyons' – even getting down the bank needed a rope and almost the skill of a mountaineer. We caught some as well, and I remember Bob playing and losing a big brown which persisted in leaping until it threw the hook. Later, Bob and Roger had a big catch of grayling, fishing float and maggot in an eddy off the car park during a flood. I was not present but many fish were around the pound mark and, switching to legered bread, Roger had a real thumper of two and a half pounds. This was a big fish, even by today's inflated standards.

It was not long after this that I was taken to a stretch of the river that was much deeper and slower. The walk was a long one; over stiles and through a small wood. Here the river had literally cut a trench into the bedrock, the banks were heavily treed and the stream was sedate, moving almost imperceptibly in places. I took some decent chub on waggler and maggot but was not overly enthusiastic about the place; the walk was a killer anyway. I did return with June a couple of years later; we caught some small grayling – leaping salmon were a real nuisance next to a fallen tree. It was only much later that I realised the significance of this spot, and the fish were barbel – big ones. The salmon, of course, were by then long gone. On the day in question, we packed early; June was far from well. (Little did we realise that this was the onset of an illness that would almost claim her life, leaving her with a condition that bugs her to this day.) I then pretty well forgot about the place, though had I thought about it, its fishy potential should have been evident.

It was to be well over a decade before my thoughts began to focus again on to the Teme. Then, in the mid 1980s, tired of catching smallish barbel and indifferent chub from the middle Severn, I rethought my summer fishing. A big barbel was a prize worth having and stories of doubles from the middle Teme were beginning to surface. Matthew Makin, a young neighbour, was keen to join me and we wondered where to start. I thought of a stretch from where I had recently taken a double figure pike and we began operations there. Matt fished hemp and casters on a feeder rig in some deep, snaggy water and took half a dozen fish (of no great size). I fished a faster run and blanked. I sought advice – look for deeper, slower water, preferably with cover and/or snags, I was told. I know now that there are exceptions to this, but it was sound advice for beginners. I thought of the trench; it fitted these criteria totally. Lugging buckets of hemp and casters, we went on a reconnaissance. Midway along, the river narrowed under a carpet of trees. Opposite was a big willow, its branches coming well across the river; above and below, trees met in shady arches across the water. Fifty yards below the downstream arch was the spot where we had seen the salmon all those years before. What was more, the depth was good – over seven feet. That day we caught barbel to over six pounds; there was better to come.

In retrospect, our tackle was too light – one-and-a-half-pound test rods, six-pound line and size fourteen forged hooks. The rods were glass Eustace T101s, lovely and soft, almost like a fly rod; these cushioned the takes and handled the line well. What they could not do was stop a big barbel getting into a snag. This peg, despite the tree, was relatively snag-free and we lost very few fish. Our personal bests began to climb. Then came a great day; it started well with me taking a fish of eight pounds, ten ounces first cast at six in the morning and just got better. At midday, with the sun blazing down, I had a savage take and line literally melted off the reel. The fish was quickly in the peg below and soon became solid. I tried the salmon angler's trick of thumping the rod with my hand and the fish broke loose. After a heck of a battle, the net went under a very big fish indeed. It was thirty and a half inches from snout to fork and seventeen in girth. My scales said twelve pounds, two ounces; Matthew Makin's said twelve pounds, four. We called it twelve, three. At the time, the record was fourteen pounds, six ounces (jointly held by T Wheeler and H D Tryon). My fish would not attract much attention today, but back in 1989 I was a very happy angler. Matt himself took a personal best later in the day; we both went home on a terrific high.

Strangely, soon afterwards, the fish moved from this swim, dropping down to the salmon hole. Maybe we had pressurised them too much. Here the fun really began, since the snags were, to say the least, severe. To get any action, we had to fish tight against the sunken tree. Even eight-pound breaking strain line was almost useless – I recall being broken on a straight pull by a big fish when using this. It is a powerful fish that can break such line without the leverage of a snag. I lost eight fish that day, landed seven, the best being nine pounds, eleven ounces. Any fish had to be stopped immediately it was hooked – we tried playing fish gently and persuading them to swim out of danger but as soon as pressure was put on, they would bolt into the snag and that was it. In the end, it was carp tackle that won the day – two-and-a-half-pound test rods, twelve-pound line (Berkeley Big Game) and size eight star point hooks. With a big feeder and a bunch of casters on the hook, it looked crude but with a bait dropper regularly putting out a carpet of bait, on occasions the fish would abandon all caution. My diary records one catch of thirteen fish. Three more doubles hit the net. Matthew Makin sadly could not make even one; he specialised in taking nines! He took to fishing more frequently than I, and I got tired of the inevitable telephone call (usually late on a Sunday – he started fishing when the match men had packed) announcing another nine; sometimes two in a session. We got rather blasé about the whole thing. A pattern emerged; use the hemp and casters during the day and switch to meat in the evening on a straight leger, with the heavy lead acting virtually as a bolt rig. This worked best when fished as close to the undercut on the far bank as possible. It meant fishing beyond the snag – a dodgy practice but it worked; all three doubles from this peg came to these tactics, together with many of Matt's nines. One fish I took is worth a mention, quite the fattest barbel I have ever caught. It went eight pounds, five ounces, was twenty-three inches long and only a fraction of an inch less in girth than the twelve-pounder. Unblemished, it was like a little fat pig and its photograph sits on my bookcase as I write. It may not be my biggest barbel, but it is certainly my best.

To digress somewhat, it was apparent to me that there was significant potential for some decent pike here as well. I regret now that I did not follow this up with any degree of determination. In winter the banks would be treacherous, I would most likely be alone and the spot was a long walk from civilisation. One dry autumn, I did give it a try. Method was mobile dead bait (a small bream; with their deep sides and silver colour, these always work well). The rig was simplicity itself; two size eight trebles on a longish trace, with a couple of swan shot eighteen inches from the bait. The top hook can be fixed or fitted Ryder-style; I prefer it fixed. A large single can be substituted for this as an alternative. John Sidley publicised a similar rig in his book on river-piking; where my rig differs is that I have the float fixed, if possible. John's rig, with a sliding float, is obviously better in deeper water, but for my purposes in shallower swims, it results in quite violent movements of the bait as the latter is pulled literally up to the surface when held back against the current. With my rig, the movement of the bait is gentler – it is possible to literally bounce the dead bait off a pike's nose. In the Teme swims I have fished, this can be deadly. The rig is shown in the diagram. Such an approach is a useful alternative to a live bait, and one can travel light, covering a lot of water. It has proved itself on both the Wye and the Severn as well. On that first day, I took two fish, one a jack, the other a fifteen-pounder. Takes as usual were sedate, the small float gently bobbing under and gradually being towed under the near bank. I have not bettered that fifteen-pound fish, but there are undoubtedly some much bigger pike in the river. Adrian Writtle caught one and the story is amusing, if apocryphal.

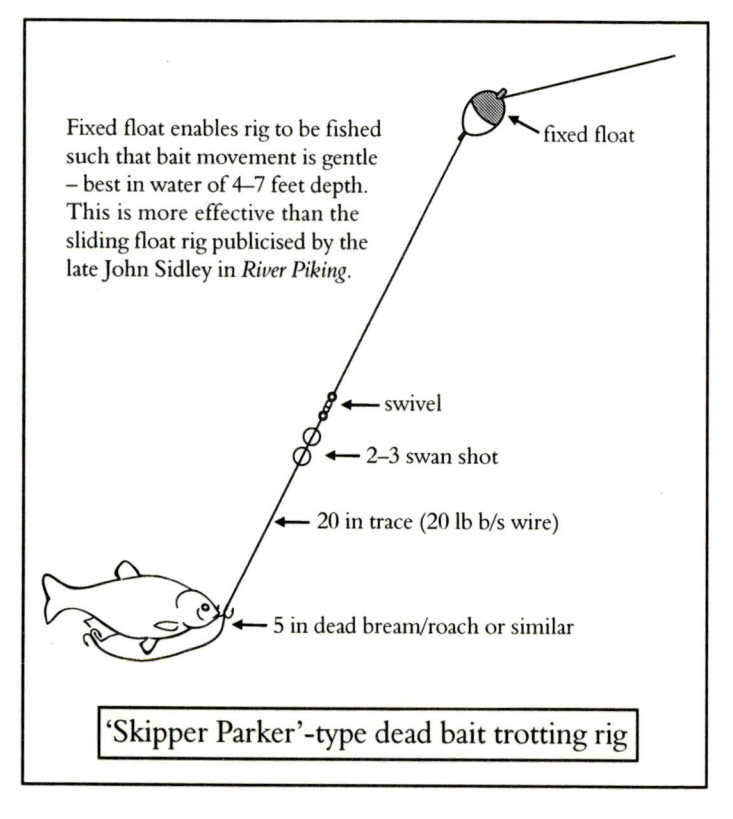

Fixed float enables rig to be fished such that bait movement is gentle – best in water of 4–7 feet depth. This is more effective than the sliding float rig publicised by the late John Sidley in *River Piking*.

fixed float

swivel

2–3 swan shot

20 in trace (20 lb b/s wire)

5 in dead bream/roach or similar

'Skipper Parker'-type dead bait trotting rig

As noted in 'Gromit and the Great Sea Monster', the use of static dead baits on our local spate rivers is an uncertain business. With regard to the Teme, Dilip Sakar and friends from Worcester wrote about the use of static dead baits in one of the early magazines of the Pike Anglers' Club. Their conclusion was similar to mine. On the day in question, however, a static dead bait produced a big fish – at the height of summer. Adrian Writtle had taken the local vicar barbel fishing. There cannot be many barbel-fishing vicars in the country; this gentleman is probably unique. Since I had inducted Adrian into the delights of the trench, I am fairly sure they fished there, but Adrian is keeping his mouth shut! Never missing an opportunity, and despite it being late June, Adrian put out a static dead bait as well (he was obviously under the influence of one Gromit). The bait was an exotic bought from the Birmingham fish market, the name of which escapes me. On the day in question, the barbel failed to show; our intrepid friends were pestered by small fish attacking the baits, always a bad omen. In desperation, so the story goes, the vicar decided to invoke divine intervention. Climbing to the top of the bank, in a bold gesture, with his arms in the air, he asked the Almighty for help. Now the latter is either a pike angler or misheard the message. I prefer to think the former (the two were barbel fishing after all). The bobbin on Adrian's pike rod promptly dropped and the bite alarm howled. After a spectacular fight, a big pike hit the net. It was a few ounces over twenty pounds. A fish of this size in June could have been nearer twenty-five at the back end and was a huge fish for the Teme. Rumours that Adrian now attends church regularly have neither been confirmed nor denied.

Let me conclude the story of the trench with an amusing and fluky incident when old Isaac well and truly pulled one out of the bag for me. It had been a poor day with only three small barbel coming to the hemp and casters. About midday, however, a big fish came right out of the water just below the snag. At least one decent fish was around. Around 5 p.m., it was time to switch to the meat. I was just bringing in the tackle when the chap fishing the peg immediately upstream climbed down the bank for a chat. He had blanked. We got talking about the fishing and he asked about big fish, stating that he had never seen a double. I told him the routine – fish hemp and casters during the day and switch to flavoured meat in the evening. Since I was about to change anyway, I showed him the meat rig; a size six hook with a hair, tied to fifteen-pound braid with a running lead of around one and a half ounces. The important thing was to get the bait as close to the undercut as possible, on the far side of the baited area. I cast and got it right first time. Within minutes, over went the rod top and I was in. All one can do in this situation is hang on like grim death, not give an inch, and pray. The fish eventually moved into open water and away upstream, a fatal move as it was fighting both the tackle and the current. Eventually, it was netted. My newly found friend was gobsmacked – at twenty-eight inches long and sixteen and a half in girth it went ten pounds, one ounce, a double! He could not believe it and secretly neither could I, but I played it cool and nonchalantly pretended that such an event was routine. After taking a couple of photographs for me, he returned to his peg with a glazed look in his eyes. Minutes later, a big piece of meat splashed into the far side of his swim.

The end of our fishing in the trench was a tragedy. Over the previous couple of years, we had become increasingly concerned at the pressure the hot pegs were receiving. When we had first begun fishing, it was rare to see another angler all day. Then a guy called Peter Kirby took a fish of well over thirteen pounds; not far off the record in those days. A photograph appeared in the national press, though to be fair the exact location was not stated. There were only two hot pegs and, although we could usually get in, it meant arriving at some ungodly hour in the morning, despite the morning fishing always being slow. Litter began to appear and it was clear that the place had been 'discovered'. The farm began to do bed and breakfast, and strange people with odd accents and claiming to come from a foreign land (other dimension?) called Kent put in an appearance. Nonetheless, they were association members and were entitled to their fishing. People staying at the farm, however, started to fish the pegs all night, despite a ban on night fishing. Nothing was done to stop this. We started to avoid the main holiday periods and continued to catch. Then in mid June 1996, at the start of the season, I had a call from Matthew Makin, in a state of total distress.

'It's gone!'

'What's gone?'

'Our barbeling!'

Matt had gone down to start the season and the place was unrecognisable. It apparently looked like Delville Wood on the Western Front after an artillery barrage. The river had had the works from the Environment Agency's drainage people. The trees had gone, all the snags removed. The trench was now a canal. Matt could not even find the pegs we had fished. Now this sort of vandalism is not uncommon on our rivers; parts of the Severn have suffered badly. The strategy (if you can call it that) is to get flood water to the sea as quickly as possible. This means ripping out any obstruction that might slow it down (and artificial channelling, though this has not happened on the Teme). Add to this what Barrie Rickards refers to as the 'draining of the upland sponge' and there is no wonder that our spate rivers are up and down like yo-yos. In the trench, the river was anyway at least fifteen feet below the top of the banks and the locals told us that it never came anywhere near to covering the fields, even in high spate. The whole thing, in addition to destroying the fishing, was a costly nonsense. It causes powerful short-term rises in level after rain, with small fish particularly being washed downstream due to lack of cover, followed by very low levels in drought resulting in deoxygenisation. This latter has become such a problem recently, particularly on the upper Teme, that the fisheries people from the Environment Agency have had to install pumps to keep the fish alive. Meddling with nature is often counterproductive; for us it was the end of some truly great fishing.

We decided to try the lower Severn. I fished this time with Adrian Writtle, Matthew Makin having lost heart (and, I think, discovered girls). My diary records eleven trips. We caught two barbel, the better to my rod and going just under eight pounds. I just could not get on with the place. It seemed little more than a large canal and, although there were features, there was no comparison with the Teme. Hoards of boaters chugged around in everything from narrowboats to large cruisers. They were friendly enough and considerate, but the atmosphere was too much like Blackpool Pier. It was not for me. I then had a small piece of luck. At a social event, I found myself sitting next to an elderly gentleman who turned out not only to be an angler, but also a member of a somewhat prestigious outfit which controlled two very exclusive stretches of the lower Teme. The club even once had a British prime minister, Stanley Baldwin, as its president. It was known to be extremely difficult to obtain membership. I poured out my troubles over my barbel deficit and he immediately offered to sponsor me. It was a generous gesture. The papers were signed and sent in. Nothing happened. Then came foot and mouth disease. The rivers were closed to angling. The club lost members. Out of the blue came an offer of membership which I seized with a juvenile enthusiasm. I was back in business.

Even today, I am still exploring my new-found piece of paradise. Despite being much lower down the Teme than the trench, a lot of this water has the characteristics of what I have seen of the upper river. It is narrower, shallower and faster. Features abound. A lot of the fish can be seen and there are some very big ones indeed. Depth seems of much less importance; groups of barbel can be observed living directly under fallen branches often in two or three feet of water. On sunny, hot days, big chub drift aimlessly just under the surface. I do not know who it was who said that 'if you can see them you cannot catch them' or what fish was being referred to, but it certainly applies to chub! I found this out on my first visits to the top stretch of river. I had persuaded Gromit to accompany me, and our Grom was clearly not happy. What's more, I had stupidly left my landing net behind, which meant that I had to fish within shouting distance of my friend. The latter had settled into an armchair swim and looked distinctly odd fishing with only one rod. I scouted upstream and, finding a track in the Himalayan balsam, found myself on a promontory with a big tree at its point. Below the tree were two big chub just under the surface. I was downstream of them and under cover, or so I thought. Out went a big piece of floating crust. It landed perfectly. The chub contemptuously faded out of sight. They did not spook; they clearly were both VIP chub and, what is more, had seen it all before. There was no time to feel deflated as, suddenly, a big barbel came up from nowhere, turned belly up and quietly absorbed the crust. I can still see its white belly and open mouth and swear that its barbules came out of the water. I struck and the hook whizzed past my ear. My action was instinctive and foolish. I had already taken exotics such as bream and tench on floating crust, but a decent barbel would have been really something.

As the sun rose, this swim was virtually an aquarium. Although the chub had gone, it was still inhabited by a group of seven good barbel. A lot can be learned from watching fish and observing reaction to baits. I catapulted some 6mm pellets into a tight area mid swim and watched the shoal, slowly, form up over the bait, the fish almost side by side. A piece of salmon-flavoured meat went upstream with just one swan shot on the line. I allowed it to trundle down towards the barbel until it was directly above them. It halted and a good fish moved up to it. The bait seemed to disappear under the fish. Take it, take it! The fish turned downstream, the rod slammed over and soon I was shouting to Gromit for the net. Watching a fish fight in clear water is fascinating; those pectoral fins sure are powerful. My first barbel from this stretch went eight pounds, six ounces, no monster but a great introduction to catching such fish in aquarium conditions. I have its photograph in front of me as I write – a beautiful golden bronze fish.

On the day that Dick Smith nearly poisoned himself (see 'One for the Mortuary'), and prior to this incident, Dick came down to my peg to tell me that he had seen a huge chub in the jungle about a hundred yards upstream. We went to look, me rod in hand. Pushing through the undergrowth, I had a fleeting glimpse of a big fish quietly doing its disappearing act. Chub never change! What we had discovered however, was a quite decent peg. The bank was steep and covered in brambles, but someone had fished there recently – in front was an aquarium beyond which the river deepened into a slow run under the opposite bank. There were sunken trees upstream and down. Next to the former was a group of barbel, and they were big. Dick thought that there were at least two into double figures. I quickly moved in before Dick got ideas of his own. All attempts to interest these fish failed, though I did manage a couple of smaller fish upstream legering adjacent to the sunken tree. Despite being high above the river, making netting problematic, I love this peg and have learned a lot from it. No matter how much you camouflage yourself, any chub that you can see is uncatchable; the same is not true for barbel. Good chub can be caught by casting into the deeper water, but trundling baits is really deadly for both species and complements the static leger (upstream or down). I fish just one swan shot on a short link (you now can buy weighted hooks for this purpose) with flavoured meat, worms, pellet or even bread crust (the latter works well in winter). The technique is to lob the bait into the current and pay off line from the bait runner, letting the bait bump under rafts and other pieces of cover. This can be done for good distances, with halts to allow the bait to settle every few seconds. It is quite something to have the rod top heave over and be connected to heavy fish way downstream. Chub will usually try to get under the near bank and even a three-pounder in such circumstances can be a difficult proposition. I once hooked what could have been the very granddad of barbel doing this. The meat was deep under a raft when the pull came and on being hooked the fish shot up towards me and across, the line scything the water under the far bank. It powered past me and on upstream against the full power of a carp rod, twelve-pound line and a size six hook. Despite fighting the current and the tackle, it just kept going, passing under the upstream sunken tree. This was not on, and I tried to take control. Clamping down on the reel and holding tight, the force was fearful. Then there was that familiar, sickening feeling as the hook pulled. I have since wondered whether it was a salmon, but the fight was very much like the twelve of all those years ago. A salmon, I feel, would have jumped at some point. Telling the story to Trefor West one night at a club meeting, he nonchalantly announced that his best barbel from this swim was a fourteen-pounder. Oops!

One little incident was significant. One day I had a number of decent chub swim under the rod top. Bringing in the bait (salmon-flavoured meat), I dropped it six feet from the bank, in two feet of water where it could be clearly seen. Five minutes later, a barbel shot out of nowhere and mouthed the meat, ejecting it before I could strike. The fish disappeared only to reappear seconds later, taking the bait in total confidence and finishing up in the landing net. Despite my not using feed, that fish had detected the bait and homed in on it from many yards downstream; such is the power of smell. Feeding with pellets or fish meal boilies of course increases one's chances even further, but it is not essential by any means. With barbel, smell is all important.

When fishing this peg, with the ancient court and church

filling the skyline opposite, it is easy to get lost in one's own thoughts. Mine tend to turn to the history of the place. It was in these meadows in 1651 that the cavalry and pike men of Cromwell's New Model Army mustered prior to the last great assault of the English Civil War. Bridges of boats had been built across both Teme and Severn; an incredible feat of military engineering done in order to ferry men across from the east bank of the Severn. The resulting charge, through Powick and into St John's, routed King Charles' remaining forces. The old bridge still shows the impact of the musket balls. That final charge marked the end of the divine right of kings and ultimately ushered in the parliamentary democracy that we enjoy today. It literally changed history – if only the meadows could speak! It is easy to imagine the clank of armour and the thunder of the horses' hooves as the charge took place, the shouts, the screams and the smell of musket smoke. I suppose the area is even more evocative for me in so far as family legend has it that the 'original Tate' was a member of the king's shattered force. Legging it back to Scotland, he got to Sedgley, met a local wench and decided that the rest of the walk was not worth it – the Tates had arrived in what was to become the Black Country. I always find it remarkable that old Powick Bridge witnessed both the first shots of the Civil War in 1642, and the last in 1651. How odd that the first and last actions of a nation-wide conflict took place in the same location!

Last summer, I explored other pegs and, despite my reservations, adopted Matthew Makin's technique of using two rods; the heavy rod against the snag (a partly sunken tree), and a lighter rod (with 'only' eight-pound line) fished tight under the nearside bank. I took a chub of two ounces under five pounds on this latter rod, on pellet, and if there is space the system works well. I also caught my first Teme trout in thirty years; what beautiful fish they are! Stopping the barbel has again proved difficult; Frank Hodgkiss was easily broken on a straight pull using ten-pound line, and we are seriously thinking of resorting to the use of heavy braid. These barbel must surely rate as one of the hardest fighting fish of all. At what point, one wonders, do such tactics become unsporting? It was in this peg that Frank and I encountered the Black Beast. At the moment, Frank and I are planning for next summer. We have heard of some pegs way downstream that sound uncannily like the trench. There are stories of fourteen-pounders and better. That braid is going to be needed.

Author with a ten-pound, one-ounce River Teme barbel taken from the trench. (Author)

An 'unlucky' young angler, Matthew Makin, with one of his many nine-pound barbel. This one missed double figures by just four ounces. (Author)

Quantum Field

A young Natalie with three of the denizens of the quantum field. (Author)

'Anyone who is not shocked by quantum theory has not understood it.' Thus spoke the great physicist Niels Bohr, who can justifiably claim to have had a better understanding than most. Being something of a New Ager as well as an angler, I have become aware that many contemporary thinkers are focusing on to the quantum world as a means of providing significant, if not earth-shattering, perspectives on the human situation. The popularity of Lynne McTaggart's book *The Field* encapsulates this trend, and the film *What the Bleep Do We Know?* has been given high acclaim. Lynne McTaggart refers to 'the coming revolution' in which we humans (and we anglers) come to centre stage in the scheme of things; a far cry from the rational materialist perspectives of the last century popularised by reductionists such as Richard Dawkins. But this is a fishing book, you may rightfully say; what specifically has all this got to do with angling? In the chapter 'I Shall Be Glad When I Have Had Enough of This!', I shall enlarge on things and for the moment will restrict myself to one set of implications.

Physicists have long recognised the existence of a background energy field that permeates the physical world of matter (including fish). It is called the zero point field and is a nuisance in that it cannot be eliminated in their calculations, even at a temperature of absolute zero. It appears to be a heaving sea of energy which underpins creation, including your local carp water. Lynne McTaggart describes it as 'a life force flowing through the universe', the psychologist Carl Jung conceptualised it as the 'collective unconscious'. It is a sea of infinite possibilities, often referred to as Dirac's Sea, after Paul Dirac, another great physicist. It means that, at a fundamental level, all life is interconnected. Incredibly, this superposition, as it is called, only 'collapses' into physical matter when a conscious observer is present. Particles only probably exist until they are brought into juxtaposition with consciousness. This turns conventional philosophy upside down – consciousness determines, and is superior to, matter – not the reverse. Thus, we (anglers) can create our own reality – focus hard enough on to something and it will happen. Such a process is effectively engineering a thought to create intentional reality. Many years ago, Dick Orton and I engineered our thoughts to envision the ultimate pike water and, lo and behold, it happened! I kid you not. For you, this is 'the water that does not exist'. You can imagine your own anyway!

Dick Orton's passion, in addition to pike fishing, was the conservation and protection of birds of prey. Alienated from formal organisations such as the Royal Society for the Protection of Birds (RSPB) – a body about which he was far from complimentary – he conducted his own lone patrols in the English hills. One day, walking over a cattle grid, he encountered a blue mist – a sure sign, according to physicists such as Julian Barbour, of the presence of Dirac's Sea. He experienced a seething maelstrom of visions and, in this altered state of consciousness, one particular vision gradually emerged. Across the cattle grid appeared a green, pastoral valley with mountains beyond. At the bottom of the valley lay a farm and beyond that, in the middle of a thick wood, there was a lake. It was no ordinary lake. Apparently formed from a *cwm*, the birthplace of an ancient glacier, it shimmered in the ethereal sunlight, like a giant eye beckoning his attention. Strange birds circled the mountain tops. Dick made his way down to the lake. He passed (appropriately) through a blue gate. Within the trees, moss-covered rocks protruded from the grass. One that he examined contained the fossil of a long-dead shellfish. Barrie Rickards would be in his element, thought Dick! High beds of reed encircled the water and lily pads formed great rafts of green beyond, their yellow flowers glowing in the sunlight. The water was crystal clear. Shoals of roach and perch were visible beneath the depths, their genetics untouched by human hand. As he watched, a great pike struck. Almost black and white in colour, it was massive in size, appearing to dwarf his personal best of twenty-seven pounds, taken some years previously from Hollowell Reservoir. He thought for a second that he had died and gone to pike-angling heaven. Then the blue mist returned and the vision faded.

Telling me about this weird experience later, he produced a map of where he had been. No water could we find. It clearly had been a dream, or had it? Had his powerful will brought about a collapse of Dirac's Sea into some physical reality? Could we replicate the experiment? Retrace his steps perhaps? In the end, such action proved unnecessary. This was where fate (destiny?) intervened; Dick clearly was still on the correct wavelength and I must have tuned into this as a kindred spirit. I was at the time in correspondence with another angler concerning a fish listed in Fred Buller's book, *The Doomsday Book of Mammoth Pike*. In a telephone conversation, out of the blue (pun intended), this guy (a sea angler!) mentioned blue mist, mountains and a remote lake. He spoke of massive pike. This was little short of incredible – it must be the same place as that in Dick's vision! What is more, and even more incredibly, he claimed to have access to the place; nay, he even stated that he controlled it! I was firmly informed, however, that only the initiated had any chance of following in Dick's footsteps. Only the pure in heart could ever encounter that mist – self-publicists, rule breakers, stroke pullers and those who measure success in terms of numbers had no hope. What is more, you had to wish the water into existence. To arrive there was like finding the Holy Grail and it could vanish at any moment if you placed a foot, or a thought, wrong.

An apprenticeship, containing appropriate hardships, was necessary to get to obtain access to the place. The lake was as much a state of mind as a physical reality. Lynne McTaggart had been right; the power of consciousness is all. In addition to purity of heart, both mental and physical stamina were required. If we wished to visit this point in space/time, bring it into existence even, we would be tested to the limit and we might only be given one chance to prove ourselves. My contact was someone akin to the Wizard of Oz; I think he inhabited a higher level of existence than I – the seventh heaven, perhaps? Dick Orton and I were given our instructions ('Listen carefully, for I shall say this only once'). Just after midnight, on a not-too-cold November morning (note this), we left Dick's home in Alvechurch and set off for the hills. I was soon totally lost but Dick was confident he could find his way. I had to have faith. He had been an officer in the Special Operations Executive during the war, so presumably he could navigate even if we were going to Oz!

I remember strange land formations passing to the left as we motored through the night – country lanes, churches, wild landscape and, eventually, a cattle grid. It certainly was misty but I could not categorically state that the mist was blue. After an interminable number of hills, there, through the hedgerow, illuminated by the dawn light, was the lake. A blue Ford Fiesta was parked by the blue gate. We pulled alongside. Two shapes appeared through the trees, our guides and the spiritual guardians of the place. Our appraisal had begun. The taller of the two sported a bright red beard and wore a huge straw hat. Given that we had arrived in the seventh heaven, I was not surprised when he said that his name was Gerald Angell! Now, Dick Walker apparently had a magic hat, but Gerald's was far more powerful. Without it, we were reliably informed, the place would vanish in a puff of blue smoke. The other guardian announced himself as one Dick Smith. Loaded up with tackle, we were led through the wood, stumbling over tree roots as we went. Wading a stream, we broke out into open country. Dick Orton asked if the lake had swans. 'No,' replied Gerald categorically. At that very moment, a white shape materialised over the mountain. It was a swan! Thunderstruck, Gerald muttered, 'That's a bad omen'. Dick Orton announced somewhat formally that it was a whooper swan which had no business being so far south; such an event was a portent of bad weather. In the quantum field, if you wish something and are on the correct wavelength, it will happen. The appearance of that swan was weird. Dick Orton looked worried. Now this was a man who had led sabotage operations behind German lines in the Italian mountains – if he was worried, where did this leave me? Just what had we got ourselves into?

We were instructed to fish off a rock promontory. A cold wind was getting up and we were exposed. I whacked out a mackerel tail on one rod and a dead roach on the other. Dick Orton, having no confidence in sea baits, put out a dead dace; casting it expertly from his Allcocks Ariel centre pin. This was it. If we ever wished to return, we had to prove ourselves worthy. Our companions set up on a more sheltered beach to our left. What was more, they were ensconced behind a rock sangar obviously built there for protection. We wondered why and soon found out. It was bitterly cold due, Dick said, to the altitude. The sky darkened and a wind got up, blowing straight into our peg. Waves lashed the rocks and spray blasted the shore. Rain began to fall, seemingly attempting to rip the very skin from our faces. The rain turned to sleet, then to snow and there was no escape. We cowered under my umbrella. I have never been so cold and Dick, twenty-odd years my senior, did not look too happy either. To cap it all, my reasonably new wavelock brolly literally shattered in one terrible gust. Eventually, looking like the abominable snowman, I climbed up the bank and dropped down into our companions' snug retreat. Amazingly, Gerald Angell was winding into a run, which he promptly pulled out of. 'Great place, eh?' said Dick Smith, informing me that we were highly honoured; the elves, hob-goblins and fairy folk who inhabited the place were putting on a show to demonstrate their approval of us. The swan had been a good omen after all. As if on key, the bobbin on Gerald's second rod dropped and, in the wind and snow, he was into what was obviously a good fish. In the net we looked at it – it was fat, and black and white, just like the fish Dick Orton had seen in his vision. What struck us most, though, was its head, the lower jaw protruding in a way that looked somewhat like the nose of the Concorde supersonic airliner. She was duly christened, but not before the elves and hobgoblins had turned nasty. One treble hook was free of the fish's mouth. In the blizzard, Gerald made a mistake, the fish kicking and pulling the barbed point deep into his thumb. We cut the trace and unhooked the fish. Unhooking Gerald was another matter! Concorde was weighed on three sets of scales and we settled on twenty pounds, two ounces. She was Gerald's first twenty. He stood there in all that weather, with the treble hook sticking out of his thumb, doing a little dance on the rocky beach and we had to forcibly prevent him from walking inadvertently into the lake. This was the raw end of pain and pleasure, to say the least. The former got worse when we took out the pliers and pushed the hook right through the flesh, snipping it away with the wire cutters. At least the numbing cold acted as an anaesthetic!

There is not much to say about the rest of that day except that we blanked yet managed to survive. At least the big fish warmed us up and eventually the snow abated. Later that week, Dick Smith rang to say that we had passed our first test. Eventually, I qualified to join the august body of spirits that guard the place, though our first encounter with its inhabitants was enough for old Dick Orton. I am now a high priest even, though the mental and physical effort of swimming in the quantum sea has resulted in fewer visits than I would have liked. It is worth relating some of my experiences in this hallowed place. Of beloved memory to us all is Concorde. She was one of the most obliging big pike I have ever encountered, though she only graced my landing net once, and that was a sad affair. I well remember watching Dick Smith play a big fish off a platform constructed (by gnomes, it was said) off the far side of an island. Chaos seemed to reign as the fish crossed over two other rods. By the time we arrived, the fish was in the net; it was Concorde, now at over twenty-two pounds. This capture set a pattern. She loved to swim just under the surface and Dick had actually seen her coming. We gained the impression she actually enjoyed being caught. Examining our diaries, a small of group of us found that we had caught her around ten times; other people may have taken her as well. Just how many times can a big pike get caught? Over several years, she peaked in weight at over twenty-three pounds and never showed any adverse effects of her regular journeys to the bank. Then came tragedy. Evil spirits, claiming to own the lake, were unhappy with the amount of luxurious weed growth. It was causing problems elsewhere, in some filter beds. They materialised one day with a boat and sprayed the place. Concorde, with her predilection to swim just under the surface, was vulnerable. Dick caught her some days later, her back covered in sores. He seriously considered ending her misery but, knowing the ability of pike to recover from seemingly insuperable damage, returned her, trusting to the power of the influence of our concern on the quantum field to do the necessary healing. Some weeks later, fishing off the island, I had a powerful take on a live bait. There in the net was Concorde, but she was a shadow of her former self. Although her wounds had healed, she weighed only sixteen pounds, seven ounces and was clearly a sick lady indeed. She was caught again soon afterwards in a similar condition and then disappeared. Appropriately, it was Gerald Angell and Dick Smith who found her body. With deep affection and great sadness, the Lady of the Lake was buried under a great oak, her spirit reintegrating with the great life force of the universe, so joining the other guardians of this hallowed spot.

Concorde was not the only big pike to inhabit the lake. In the half light of the early morning, fishing off the point where Dick Orton and I had been initiated, Dick Smith had a run on a small trout live bait. Hitting it, the rod bent little as he brought the fish in. 'It's only a jack,' he announced as I waded out with the net. Charging towards me in the clear water was a b—y great twenty-pound pike! Seeing the net, she turned and tail-walked away, soaking me in spray. Dick uttered some expletive and back-wound furiously. Eventually, I netted her and it was still sufficiently dark that we had to use torches to unhook her. She went over twenty-three pounds and had a distinctive mark on her flank, yellow in colour; it was shaped like a rose. Rose became her name, and, though not as obliging as Concorde, she became an occasional visitor to the landing net of the high priest, a role now clearly assumed by Dick Smith (my sea angler contact having teleported himself to a bass beach somewhere out in the ether). Someone expressed the view that the yellow rose-like mark on the fish was a 'kiss' from a lamprey, but if so, the scar never faded. She peaked at well over twenty-four pounds and then vanished back into the energy field from whence she had come.

Dick Smith continues to be high priest to this day. Twenty-pound pike grace his net with sickening regularity (sickening for the rest of the initiates; Dick seems quite happy with the situation!). He did two thirties in ten days recently, from different space/time locations. The better of the two involved a trip through the blue mist; the second, from a different location, appeared to him in a mystical moment. Driven by some higher force to get in his car, he motored into the night, guided only by the engagement of his higher self with the great cobweb of interconnections that drives the existence of matter. On arrival, having travelling through mist that had a slightly different tinge of blue, the water that appeared seemed both river and lake. He cast out a smelt, meditated for an appropriate time, the buzzer sounded and, after a suitably hard scrap, a fish of over thirty pounds was landed. Recognising the potency of engaging with Dirac's Sea sure does pay dividends. He just knew that this was going to happen, having actually seen the fish beforehand in his vision. Such is the power of the conscious mind when appropriately focused.

My tally of big pike does not approach that of Dick Smith's. In fact, my most memorable (as opposed to my biggest) fish from the water was just under twenty pounds. It took a half herring early one December morning and, on the strike, came clean out of the water, a spectacular sight. I managed to work it back towards the net, held by David Hendry, when it suddenly dived and, for a second, everything went solid. Then it began to take line powerfully – the problem was that the line was disappearing down into the water by my feet and the fish was tail-walking way out in the lake, having swum under an obstruction deep under the bank. I can feel that rasping sensation on the rod now – a most disconcerting experience. If ever there was a test of Berkley Big

Game, this was it. I pulled and the fish pulled back. Gradually, despite more tail-walks, it came close in. I sank the rod top deep and, incredibly, the fish swam towards me back under the obstruction and straight into the net. Dave never needed a second chance! The line was in shreds over many yards, yet it had held. Phew.

One successful initiative pioneered in the early days was encouraging our children to fish here. We instigated a children's match held each August. The lake perch were a good size and very obliging on swim-feedered maggot or legered worm. Many were over a pound in weight and some good catches were made. I well remember Dick Smith acting as Natalie's ghillie when she was around eight years old. June was float fishing a deep rocky undercut close in and began to bag up. The rules being somewhat flexible, daughter was given the float rod and perch followed perch into the keep net. One fish was one pound, seven ounces, which she played like a veteran. Sadly, when she hooked something much bigger, despite her best efforts, the cast parted – there were perch of some size around. Losing this fish spooked the shoal but she won a trophy for best fish, which she has kept to this day. Embarrassingly, on that day I too lost a big fish – in the thick weed. Dick Smith videoed the whole thing! Initiates were encouraged to take their children through the blue mist at other times; a specific category of membership was granted to them. Young Gareth Angell, fishing with his dad, took a roach of two pounds, ten ounces on a worm. It remains the lake record to this day. One of angling's great weaknesses (see 'Civilisation Lost (or Gained?)') is a general failure to promote itself with our children (though there are encouraging signs that this situation might be shifting). Our problem was that our kids grew up! Gareth, for example, is now a chief petty officer in the Royal Navy, attached to the Royal Marines. At our last initiates' meeting, it was pointed out that the children's section can soon be reinstated – most of us are now grandparents!

Other friends have entered the blue mist and faced initiation. Most notable of these was Tony Mobley. With him, the guardian spirits were really unkind. He had arrived overequipped, they deemed. With bed chair, single strap bag, bucket of live baits, rods and so on, they were probably right. Leaving the wood and climbing up onto the open ground, he suddenly complained of feeling ill and semi-collapsed onto the grass with a grey face and heaving chest. 'He's having a heart attack,' muttered the high priest. We divested Tony of all his kit and for some time he just sat, head in hands. This was before the advent of mobile telephones (which are useless elsewhere in Dirac's Sea anyway), and the farm was a long way to run in waders and heavy clothes. This is the sort of situation when you wish that you had done a first aid course. Luckily, Tony gradually recovered and was able to fish. We christened the spot where he collapsed Heart Attack Corner; it is the same spot where we had seen the swan on our first visit. Medical opinion obtained later suggested that the strap on Tony's bag had pressed on his carotid artery and reduced the blood supply to his head. Another initiate was Chris Phillips. He had a dual ordeal, first walking into mud that behaved like quicksand (we swore that the ground was hard minutes previously) and leaving his boots behind when pulled free, then getting lost in the wood with a dodgy torch on a black night when attempting to return to his car. Chris did not pursue his application any further.

In many senses, the place, inevitably, is too good to be true. Natalie and I once encountered a mass migration of baby frogs; there were thousands of them, an amazing sight. Owls abound; only last month Gromit and I were driving down the lane when we encountered a barn owl sitting on a fence post – this wonderful creature has always been a favourite for me. Water rails inhabit the high beds of reed; how they manage to walk (run) on slender floating reed stalks never ceases to amaze – they quite happily scoot under the pike rods on occasions. Buzzards and red kite wheel overhead. There are even rumours of bitterns. One day I watched a peregrine stoop from high up over the grassy hill. It fell like a brick for several hundred feet, there was a squeal from the grass, and a rabbit was no more. Otters are occasional visitors. By and large they are welcome – this environment, being beyond the blue mist, is still very much in its natural state.

All has not always been well, however. We do not own the place, though approaches to the Celestial Council on this matter have been made. Some time ago, elsewhere in the quantum field, big pike were being persecuted by selfish trout anglers. We were approached to see whether they could be found a home. A lorry arrived with a huge tank containing the fish, one of which was over forty pounds. They were released. We had high hopes but disaster ensued. The fish did not settle, some died quickly, others lingered on. They were a different colour from the native fish and easily identified. I took an eighteen-pounder that should have weighed twenty-five. What was more, our native big fish seemed to disappear, or at least they were not caught. It was a salutary lesson. Moving trout-water pike is a far from ideal solution. Worse was to come. Through the cosmic web of interconnections, evil spirits from the lower planes got wind of our piece of paradise. Envious eyes were cast. These demons were green in colour and claimed moral superiority over both ourselves and the Celestial Council. They called themselves a nature conservation trust and seemed determined to drive us out. Without any authority whatsoever, they removed the blue gate, playing dice with the very force that created the lake in the first place and which kept it in existence. The lock was stolen and a boat vandalised. Vehicles were smashed through the undergrowth and a large hut resembling a bird hide constructed. They put up notices, inviting in any entity that might encounter the place, even laying out a public car park. Harsh words were spoken and the boat damage even went to a solicitor. As a deputy high priest, I was asked to intervene. A letter was written to the Celestial Council. The reply was immediate; a semi-legal document that confirmed that the greens were interlopers and informing us of our heavenly rights. Our supremacy as guardian spirits was confirmed; we had looked after the place well over a period of several decades. The elves, gnomes and hobgoblins did not want change. The green demons were summoned to a joint meeting attended by two leaders from the Celestial Council. The quantum riot act was read. The notices were removed and replaced by ones from the Council itself. A force field was erected to keep out passing spirits. As a minor concession, designated members from the nature conservation trust were allowed access to the hut, but we anglers were to rule supreme. An uneasy peace returned to paradise. We remain on our guard.

My visits though the blue mist never pale in their emotional intensity. A group of like-minded spirits literally keeps this reality in existence through the power of their intention. Among us, none is more powerful than Dick Smith; we all bow to his authority and to his wisdom. The lake looks after him well. Last summer, I was in Washington State, staying with my cousins, deep in Bigfoot country, not far from Mount St Helens. There is a lake here (now sadly much altered by the devastating eruption in the early 1980s) which the Native Americans called Spirit Lake. It was a place in Dirac's Sea where higher beings were able to interface with us humans and was a sacred spot. The Native Americans knew all about the life force of the universe and the power of conscious intention, and they respected that life force to a degree difficult to imagine today. Until the coming of the white man they were rewarded with abundance. Our lake is a parallel place and, as long as we are around, the quantum field will continue to deliver its bounty. The love affair continues.

The quantum field delivers its bounty – the author with a pike of twenty-one pounds, two ounces. (Author)

Dick Smith with both 'Concorde' and 'Rose' on the bank at the same time – coming on separate rods, the former (foreground) weighed twenty-two pounds, six ounces, the latter (held) twenty-one pounds, eight ounces. (Richard Smith)

Band of Brothers

Author with his five-pound, six-ounce eel. (Author)

Dick Walker once remarked that the best thing in angling was not the fish that one caught, but the friends that one made. This to me is a great truth. I still occasionally fish with Phil Burford, my first ever fishing buddy of nearly half a century ago. We are members of the same fishing club and not that long ago I sat behind him in a match, giving good advice, as always. He did not win! We found it difficult to believe that our pike fishing exploits on Breeches Pool and those days on the Warwickshire Avon were so far in the past. He thought that he might still possess my grandfather's pike rod; quite why I gave it him I cannot recall. Robin Dunn, from my sixth-form days, married the French *assistante*, who was little older than himself, and pushed off long ago across the Channel, though, weirdly, I did bump into him on a train back in the early 1970s. We lads all lusted after Annie; Robin won the jackpot and turned his teacher into his wife. I wonder if he still goes fishing? He certainly landed a specimen that time around. For me, however, the true band of brothers has been fellow pikers from within my native Black Country. This chapter is their story, in so far as it is possible to recount. It is also a tribute to their comradeship over nearly three decades.

'First cause' was a young chap called Paul Williams. I had been a member of the Pike Society for a time and, when the Pike Anglers' Club was formed, Paul contacted me to see whether I was interested in forming a local branch (these are formally termed 'regions'; a term I dislike since such groups are inevitably local in scale. That said, Dick Smith, Gerald Angell, Tony Mobley and John Holmes travel to our meetings from deepest Herefordshire; Colin Booth from Bewdley, Steve Sault from Kidderminster and Richard Seal from Bromsgrove – am I arguing against myself here?). Paul and I became joint Regional Organisers for the new Dudley region of the PAC. Now, to anyone born and bred in Halesowen, as I was, the name Dudley is like a red rag to a bull. My place of birth has always regarded itself as a Black Country town in the north of Worcestershire; people from Dudley, albeit fellow Black Country folk, were culturally separate and a little downmarket. In 1974, Halesowen was taken out of Worcestershire and merged with Dudley in the new West Midlands County. No one was consulted (such is our democracy) and the merger became a takeover. The term Dudley Regional Association has therefore always grated with me; but perhaps I digress ('Black Country', I could have lived with). Anyway, Paul came from deepest Netherton (you cannot get more Black Country than that) and we became firm friends. Paul introduced me to the efficacy of the paternoster for pike; until then I was still under the influence of Dick Walker and his thing about resistance – pike, of course, quite happily drag leads; since the lead is on the bottom and often supported by a float, the resistance is often minimal anyway (though enough to deter zander). I well remember June, Paul and me, together with three lots of tackle and a bucket of live bait, squeezing into our VW Beetle for a trip down to the Dead Arm at Tewkesbury. Talk about sardines in a can! Paul took a double on a paternoster at dusk, June's and my roving baits only producing jack. It was March and the mud was fearful. Moving up to the top of the Arm, Paul and I inadvertently left June behind (we were both suffering from fish fever). She managed to get totally stuck. Out of the bushes, all hair and badges, emerged a knight in shining armour. Lifting her bodily, he carried her and her tackle to safety. He said not a word; probably thinking what the b—y hell is a woman doing pike fishing? June, thanking him and cursing me, asked his name – 'John Sidley' was the reply as he returned from whence he came.

A great character in those early days was one Eddie Butler. Eddie ran a driving school and was responsible for recruiting Tony Mobley, who remains a member to this day. Eddie was an innovator angling-wise. Among his rigs was a version of what Fred Buller calls the standing pike paternoster in his book *Pike*. Fred has a spike on the bottom of the rod (nasty), a three-way swivel (risky) and the live bait mounted horizontally. Eddie mounted the rod on a near-vertical rest with the butt in a ton-dish attached by terry clips. A two-way swivel was used and the live bait mounted head up. The diagram demonstrates things. The clutch on the fixed spool reel (Fred has a centre pin) was set loose – these were the days before baitrunners or indeed drop-offs. Eddie's river was the Wye and his best fish on this rig went thirty-two pounds. The approach was to dace fish, working the swim up with maggots (accepting gratefully the occasional decent chub), and placing a live dace just below the keep net. The latter acted, together with the dace shoal hopefully grouped up tightly, effectively as groundbait, attracting pike from a wide area. One of these days I must forsake herrings and give it a try; it certainly seemed very effective, providing the dace would oblige.

Some anglers from those early days are still with us. One such stalwart is Adrian Writtle. I first knew Adrian when he was eighteen years old and, like Paul Williams, he hailed from Netherton. He is now getting on a little (sorry Ade), and we still fish together whenever possible. He once had an interesting experience when zandering with Chris Phillips and friend in the Norfolk Fens. By the time that they had packed up and returned

Notes

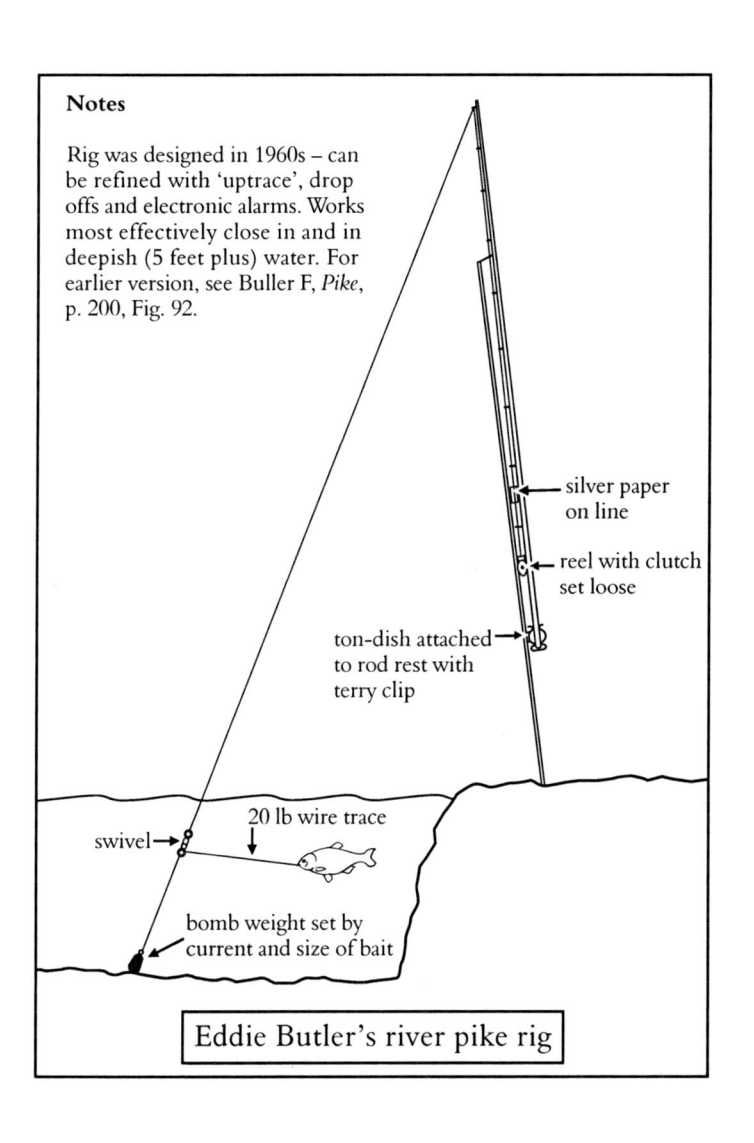

Rig was designed in 1960s – can be refined with 'uptrace', drop offs and electronic alarms. Works most effectively close in and in deepish (5 feet plus) water. For earlier version, see Buller F, *Pike*, p. 200, Fig. 92.

silver paper on line

reel with clutch set loose

ton-dish attached to rod rest with terry clip

swivel

20 lb wire trace

bomb weight set by current and size of bait

Eddie Butler's river pike rig

to the car, it was pitch dark and pouring with rain. Chris and friend got into the car and, hearing what they thought was the rear door close, assumed Adrian was in the back and drove off into the night. After a few miles, Adrian's silence was taken to indicate that he had gone to sleep (he is not known as Rip Van Writtle for nothing). After another few miles, Chris began to have his doubts and felt behind the driver's seat for Adrian's leg. The truth dawned that the latter was still standing, minus waterproofs, by a fen drain some twenty miles back. Adrian reckoned that there was not a light to be seen. He had viewed the car driving off with disbelief and assumed that the crew would be back within minutes; he actually waited for nearly an hour, getting wetter, colder and rather distressed. When the car's headlights finally appeared, he was not a happy bunny! Adrian edited our magazine *Halcyon Days* (of more anon), until the cost of producing it became prohibitive. This crazy piece of literature contained everything from politics to pornography, quotes from Isaac Walton, reviews of waterside ale houses, hilarious jokes (often at one Gromit's expense), cartoons, and a fascinating piece, 'Retrospect and Review', taken from inter-war editions of the *Fishing Gazette*. A long running saga was 'The Adventures of Balaclava Man', which featured yours truly – the day I sat down in the boat straight on to the point of my combat knife was a good story. Adrian is now very much into continental catfish; eighty-pounders are the order of the day, dwarfing somewhat his best pike taken from Patshull back in the 1980s.

Now, Black Country humour is something that one either gels with or does not. It helps to understand the language! A 'wet-eft' is a newt, 'bemoiled' is dirty, 'bostin' is excellent, 'fettle' is food, 'jack bannock' is a stickleback, 'rippit' is belly, 'swag' is a pool caused by mining subsidence, 'tacky-bonk' a pit mound and so on. The following is reproduced from *Halcyon Days*, where it was suitably illustrated. Unlike some Black Country literature, it is hopefully intelligible. It was written by Max Taylor who was once our resident comic, as well as attempting to be our chairman. It has added resonance given my recent adventure (see 'One for the Mortuary').

Last Rites

What's gonna happen to you when you 'peg it', 'pop your clogs', 'go to the great venue in the sky' or 'that more than warm syndicate of flames below ground'?

You can safely bet that on the day you are laid to rest, the river will be bang on and your favourite lake will chuck up more biggies than hitherto heard about, all from your favourite swim, which, until your demise, you had carefully baited for most of the season, but with negative results.

Yes, 'He'd have been in his oil tot', 'Filled his boots he would'. These and other well-used – though unprintable – sayings would be the hushed uttering of your piscatorial amigos on the day that long black wagon creeps past your house in second gear.

What can be done about it? Well, you could live forever; I hope you do; come to that, I hope I do! But no, even in these days of wonder drugs, hip, nose, ear and throat replacements there's still that b—y bus driver with notches to carve on his 'Please have the correct change' sign. All of a sudden you're gone – who'd have thought it, you felt good, looked well enough, even got next season mapped out. 'Gonna go there', 'Gonna fish here', 'Gonna try this', 'Gonna do that', 'Gonna do nothing now!' You've been taken from us, departed this mortal coil, dead. The final day is left to your nearest and dearest.

But we can do something about that day; sod the local crem. Anyway, between the close of the velvet curtains and the time your box hits the back burner, the tatters have had it away with the brassware – before the music stops, it's in the back of the transit and the vicar's daughter has got another goldfish!

As for burial, you could get dropped short of six feet down so that your comrades in rods (with your written consent, of course) could have the benefit of a plentiful supply of lobs. Now, that's a positive step towards making a contribution after the fact. Hmmmm. Maybe.

Alternatively, you could try this – a Viking burial by flaming raft set adrift on your favourite lake or down your local stretch of river (canal fishermen not catered for).

Indeed, a Viking burial is the only fitting way for a true lover of the waterside to depart this mortal life, plus it's much cheaper than the other options. You are picked up as normal by your fishing partner or, if he is squeamish or just fishing elsewhere that day, one of our highly trained staff. Then you are driven to the venue, obeying speed limits, though not at that funeral crawl solemnly adhered to by the black topper mob. In fact, it's just like any other fishing trip, but without your tackle; you won't need it.

At the waterside, you're laid in a one-size-fits-all box casket, pre-soaked in a non-smelling, though highly flammable, substance. The bareness of the chipboard is cleverly disguised with alder and willow branches, removed on the previous work parties and dried especially for the occasion. Fresh vegetation will be cut on the day and added to the funeral pyre. All of this is secured to our 100% burn-down, none-capsize raft. We do these in a range of burn times; no. 1 is our 'Ashfast' model, no. 2 our 'Burn to be wild' model, takes a little longer. By far the most popular model, however, is our slow burn 'Valhalla Express', with a rudder astern, shields and oars along both sides with a figurehead of your choice (from our full-colour brochure) at the prow and a mast in full sail. This is most often preferred as it gives the mourners ample time to tackle up, bait swims and bivvy up for a long session.

The 'Launch and Flame' ceremony is a very safe affair, as our own fire safety personnel are always on hand and we enjoy a 100% safety record. No one has ever been burned (who was not supposed to be) since our services have been available.

The launch itself can be performed by a loved one, a member of our staff, or even a celebrity of your choice, maybe from TV, radio or the angling world.

Ignition is by remote control and always when the raft is waterborne, due to safety regulations (complies with BS183/99(1)(a) Raft Ignition and Pyreworks Display Act, 2000).

Our basic price is about 40% of the available alternatives (except burial at sea during wartime). This can be reduced by multiple bookings. Do you have a fishing partner? Try our double-booking offer and save an extra 5%. A simultaneous ceremony can be an awe-inspiring event. Should you outlive your comrade, or vice versa, there is no time limit for a second ceremony as long as the amount is paid in full before the first raft is lit.

Save even more! Are you in a club?

Please write to Viking Burials for more details and full-colour brochure at:
Odin Taylor Viking Burial Services plc,
Valhalla House,
Waterside Trading Estate,
Somewhere in what was once Worcestershire.

Another old lag is one Frank Hodgkiss. A real trooper, Frank has been the secretary of a rather exclusive local club for thirty years or so. He has been trying to stand down for the last twenty but, typically, no one else wants the job. Frank is my roach and barbel fishing buddy, though we pike-fish together as well. He has taken an incredible tally of two-pound roach and loves to float fish for tench in the traditional way. It is no secret that he has the hots for a certain lady who just happens to be my wife. The following also appeared in a certain publication, and was written by June as a way of putting the gentleman in his place. It is worth noting that, prior to the events described, I had taken an eel of five pounds, six ounces which was forty inches long and nine in girth. Due to my yogic activities, I am also sometimes referred to as the Maharishi.

My Night with Five Men and a Whopper

It all started out innocently one Friday in July. It was a typical summer evening – wet, grey, overcast and humid. I was not at all surprised when the male chauvinists watched me struggle along the dam wall loaded up like a packhorse, having to stop halfway to disentangle my Lord and Master's tackle from his Barbour coat. Typically, it started to thunder and lightning just as eight carbon rods swished into action, inviting instant death on us all from Her up above. What a brilliant night for eels!

Soon, eight bunches of lobworms were settled in the gloomy depths of the 'ressa'. Bite indicators were adjusted, generating a cacophony that sounded like the beginning of the *1812 Overture*. One particular gentleman had great difficulty in this operation as he had already downed a number of cans of Breaker, topped up with a certain spirit made by Bells and supplied by Yours Truly. Even so, there was still an impressive row of full cans strategically positioned on top of the lifebelt support to keep them safe from a certain Ade, who had been eyeing them up enviously since his arrival. Bivvies in place and food and booze laid out, I then had to fight off several invitations of company at my or their place, providing I supplied the Bells.

Just when things were settling down, a lone figure was seen staggering along the path looking as if he was about to have a coronary at any moment. On seeing him, all the male chauvinists dropped everything and sprinted to his aid, leaving me wondering what Daz has got and I haven't! After another round of drinks and a photo-call, we settled down to await events, lulled to sleep by loud snores from Rip Van Writtle's bivvy. Getting to sleep was not helped by a firework display coming from the nearest village and by having to watch the club secretary, now stewed as a newt, wandering up and down the dam tripping over guy ropes.

Then a certain Hubby decided that it was time to send a greeting to old Isaac by blowing a paper trumpet for several minutes very loudly – very loudly indeed. Despite Hubby's contention that this procedure always brought results, the only immediate response was a head-on attack from the Holtmeister, whose sleep had been severely disrupted by the row. The offending instrument was confiscated, suffering some damage in the process, and finished up being stuffed down a certain lady's blouse to keep it out of harm's way. Hubby, taken somewhat aback, then proceeded to forecast gloom, doom, death and destruction as a result, and no fish as well.

Just before midnight, there was the sound of a bite alarm and guess who had got a run? It was none other than the club secretary, who had no doubt arranged things beforehand. Now the fun started...

Somehow FH managed to hook the fish, but had great trouble remembering which way to turn the reel handle. After several chaotic attempts, he finally managed to get things right and soon a rather large eel was caught in the torch's beam, ably directed by the Maharishi himself. The Holtmeister and I lowered the landing engine (a sort of landing net on wheels) and FH then treated us to a demonstration of how not to land an eel. Angling and alcohol do not mix! The eel had obviously been caught before as it knew all the tricks, diving under the net when any attempt was made to bring it close in. Eventually, the skill of the landing crew prevailed and what was obviously a big fish was heaved up the wall. By this time, the club secretary was flat on his back, suffering from a combination of exhaustion, alcohol and euphoria. Said gentleman had only pulled off a five (five pounds, two ounces to be precise).

All stood around with looks of admiration at the forty-inch by eight-and-a-half-inch specimen. The Maharishi said proudly, 'It's the same length as mine, but mine is half an inch thicker.'

Of course, I cannot possibly comment!

June

At this juncture, it is worth introducing Big John Holt. John is the archetypal Black Country 'mon' – built like a brick outhouse and covered in tattoos, he has a beer gut that is impressive even by Pensnett standards. John is a major driving force in the Regional Association and organises all sorts of social events, which quite by chance always seem to take place at his local. John is a very competent pike angler and has taken three fish of over twenty-nine pounds, one of them from the Severn, an impressive achievement. It is perhaps a pity that one of them did not go over the magic thirty, but we are not too sorry for him. If there are twenty-pounders in a water, John will find one sooner or later. He has also taken an eel of well over seven pounds. An ex-member of the British Army, despite his formidable appearance, John is terrified of anything with four legs, especially dogs. June once had to lead him by the hand through a field of frisky bullocks while I played matador with my Barbour coat and landing-net handle. John's mode of communication is a Black Country dictionary in its own right; outsiders probably have problems understanding him. This notwithstanding, John has palled up with one Jim Andrew, one time Regional Organiser for the Clydebank branch of the Pike Anglers' Club. Given Jim's thick Glaswegian accent, how this unlikely pair ever manages to communicate is something of a mystery, but Jim is now a regular visitor to our waters and an honorary member of the Dudley region. Jim enjoys catching exotics such as dace and chub, but so far our barbel have been unkind to him. He once drove eighty miles to share a cup of cold coffee with Dick Smith and me when we were fishing Loch Awe.

Big John's sidekick is Terry Watts. If you think John's tattoos are impressive, you should see Terry's! He even claims to have one on a certain very delicate part of his anatomy which cannot be mentioned. Like John, Terry is an organiser and collects the monthly subscription for the region. Woe betide anyone who hesitates in coughing up! One night, while we were eel fishing, Terry gave me a real present. On hooking a fish, he announced that it was an (adjective) bream and that he had no interest in it. He gave me the rod. After a tug of war, the bream surfaced under the dam, glowing deep bronze in the beam of the torch. It weighed fourteen pounds, twelve ounces. He repeated the process with one that went fourteen pounds, two ounces an hour later. Terry has an affinity with eels that almost rivals that of the late John Sidley.

Inevitably, as in any organisation (I use the word loosely) there are fallings-out at times, and members come and go. Things within the Dudley region 'happen'; we do not organise anything, and some people expect a more formal structure. They also on occasions come along for the wrong reasons, wanting information on waters, access to clubs and the like. Such individuals are soon clocked and do not last long. One takes from an organisation in proportion to one's contribution to it; membership is a two-way process (see 'Civilisation Lost (or Gained?)'). Make a contribution and doors will eventually open. We only have two rules. The first is that members will behave in a sporting and gentlemanly manner toward their fellow anglers at all times, and the second is that you will enjoy your fishing. This approach has stood the test of time but owes a lot to the quality and commitment of those involved.

With nearly thirty years behind us, we have only experienced one real tragedy. Some years ago, I had a telephone call from a Stuart Thompson who was new to pike fishing and wanted some advice (Stuart's wife, strangely, turned out to be Jim Andrew's niece – pike fishing is a small world). Stuart had been fishing Tardibigge Reservoir near Bromsgrove and was frustrated by his inability to take a double, something he desperately wanted to achieve. Having fished the water myself, I was not surprised. I invited him to our meetings and put him in touch with Richard Seal, who lived close by. This pairing of novices with experienced pikers always works well, and Richard and Stuart became firm friends. Now, there is no greater kick in piking than putting someone into their first double-figure fish, something we achieved with Stuart fairly rapidly – he was doing nothing wrong, except fishing the wrong water. I well remember a day in my boat when Stuart took a fish of sixteen pounds or so – he was over the moon. It may be my imagination, but there seemed something of an urgency in helping Stuart. In the March of the season when he joined us, he made the long trek up to the Lake of Mentieth in Scotland for an event organised by the Pike Anglers' Club. A fish of over twenty-six pounds took his mackerel tail. We arranged a trophy to be presented at the April AGM. On the afternoon of the meeting, I took a call from Richard Seal, in a state of total shock. Stuart was dead. He had been taken to hospital with appendicitis and had gone into allergic shock caused by the anaesthetic. He was twenty-eight years old and as fit as fiddle. The news was difficult to take in – we had lost the youngest and fittest of our members who had left a wife and child, with Andrea expecting their second. During the two minutes silence at the AGM, the trophy fell off the table for no apparent reason, which unnerved us even more. We now fish annually for the Stuart Thompson Memorial Trophy, awarded for the biggest fish taken on an annual weekend's fishing on Llangorse Lake.

It is difficult to do justice to this band of brothers in one short chapter. Others have made great contributions over many years; Graham Wright, for instance, somehow manages to act as chairman and has represented us, together with Tony Mobley, on the Severn Consultative (before its untimely demise). Both of these stalwarts are also secretaries of other clubs, yet still find time to do a job (delegation is my way of surviving). Where would angling be without such people? Fishing is, of course, meant to be fun and we have fun, though some of it is at one other's expense. Simon Darby has managed to win the Ryobi-Masterline River Trophy for a number of years now, usually with a twenty-two-pounder from the same stretch of the Wye. Many are convinced that it is the same fish with which he has done some sort of deal! Frank Nock is always avoided when sorting the sleeping arrangements at Llangorse due to his incredible snore; someone once suggested that we ring the British Geological Survey to see what it registers on the Richter scale. On returning to his house from Llangorse one day, Dick Smith was heard to mutter 'Where the hell is my tackle?' He had only left the lot on the slipway by the lake. It was a long and tense journey through the night back into the hills, but his tackle was still where he had left it – a close call. He still gets ragged about it. Steve Sault once took to having a plug rod set up in his electrician's van in order to have a chuck or two on the Severn during his lunch break. One day he caught his hand on one of the largish (barbed) trebles. No one at Kidderminster hospital had any cutters strong enough to shear through the shank and eventually Steve had to give a nurse the keys to his van, where he kept a powerful set of bolt croppers. He is now more careful! Pride of place must however go to our Gromit. Staying overnight at Dick Smith's, he announced early in the morning that he had forgotten his toothpaste. 'No problem,' says Dick, 'there is a tube of mine on the window ledge.' Several minutes later, our hero appears at the kitchen door, looking pale and complaining that the toothpaste tasted awful and that his mouth had gone numb. It turned out that he had cleaned his teeth with Dick's hydrocortisone ointment.

Mates – what fishing should really be about. John Holt and Terry Watts, complete with a certain amount of permanent decoration. (Author)

Phoenix Rising: The Legacy of Dr Kuznets

Simon Kuznets' legacy: David Durkin with his three-pound, six-ounce canal perch, taken from the Staffs–Worcester Canal in Wolverhampton. (Keith Higginbottom, Regional Angling Magazines)

Not many anglers will have heard of Simon Kuznets; he did not fish, as far as I am aware, and he popped his clogs some years ago. Kuznets was a fellow economist who made his name with work on the relationship between income distribution and economic growth. He came up with an inverted U-shaped curve – as a country's economy began to grow, income distribution got worse (more unequal), peaked at some point and then improved. More recent research has suggested that a similar relationship may occur in relation to the environment. The work has focused on 'end of pipe' emissions, including the lethal cocktail of nasties that finishes up in our rivers, lakes and canals. It appears to be good news for us anglers – the British economy is well past the peak of the curve and discharges are falling, at least on a per capita basis, and, given relatively low population growth, in total as well. Now, this is not an economics book and the Environmental Kuznets Curve is a controversial proposition in academic circles. It also infuriates the Greens since it suggests that economic growth, long their demon, could actually be part of the solution to problems such as water pollution, rather than being just the cause ('rich is clean' is a violation of their religious principles – they would prefer us all to go back to the caves).

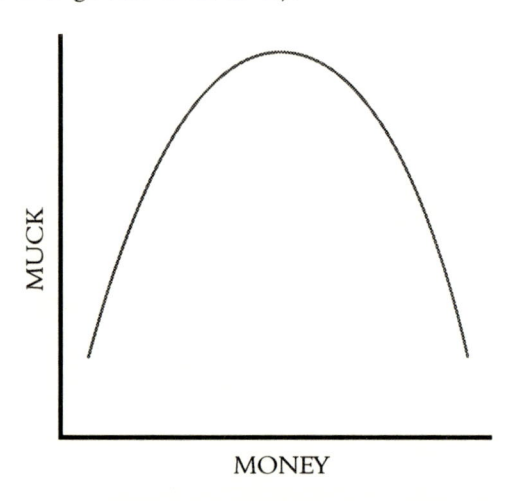

The layman's Environmental Kuznets Curve:
Muck versus Money ('Rich is clean')

For Britain at least, as a rich country, there is thus some hard evidence that we are witnessing the practical manifestations of these ideas. Some of our waterways have, over the past few years, made a remarkable recovery from the filthy condition that they were in when I was a child. I am by no means implying that all is well – far from it – but in certain locations there is a transformation that would have been unthinkable fifty years ago. This is particularly the case in our old industrial areas, such as my native Black Country and many other parts of the West Midlands conurbation. The rivers Tame and Stour, once literally open sewers, are now fisheries for the first time in two centuries, and our canal system, environmentally sterile in many places for so long, is now not just the domain of the match angler, but the specimen hunter as well. To anglers, the Environmental Kuznets Curve describes a real, and very welcome, reality – despite the academic rhetoric and the ranting of the Greens. This chapter tells some of the story of the Stour (I am not qualified to speak about the Tame) and the Black Country canals; for once, we anglers have something to celebrate.

The Worcestershire Stour, unlike its namesakes in Dorset, Suffolk, Kent and Warwickshire, has featured little in angling literature. (The name incidentally derives from the Norse *staurr* – 'a strong, powerful river'). Yet, even when one could smell it from two hundred yards, it always struck me as potentially a lovely little stream. In medieval times, its mills ground the corn produced by local agriculture, and the manufacture of scythes along one of its tributaries at Belbroughton was a nationally important activity. During the Industrial Revolution, its water helped power the newly emerging industry (one iron forge, established in 1660, is still going strong – making lorry wheels) and provided water for many of the processes that were being pioneered along its banks. It was also a means of disposing of many of the toxic fluids being generated, together with sewage from the growing urban population. Attempts to turn it into a navigation between 1662 and 1667 by one Andrew Yarrington failed, partly due to local opposition – shades of the Severn Navigation Restoration Trust! (unlike the latter, Yarrington did succeed in building twelve locks, only to have them destroyed by floods – does no one ever learn?). In the years that followed, a river that had once been run by salmon – and which had its own indigenous trout population – rapidly degenerated into an open, poisonous, waste-disposal system, far removed from its previous self. How lovely it was three or four centuries ago, one can but speculate.

In *Nash's History of Worcestershire*, published as a two volume tome in 1781 (and weighing a ton), there is reference to a long-dead debate as to exactly where the Stour rises. There were (and are) two candidates – Uffmore Wood, south of Hales Owen (possibly incorrectly written as one word these days) and Frankley Beeches, a tree-topped hill and well-known landmark on the Worcestershire/Birmingham border. To quote Nash, the Stour, 'commonly faid to take its life in Uffmore Wood' really 'fprings in a copfe called Twylands, in the adjoining manor of Frankley whence it paffes through Ylley'. In other words, Frankley Beeches (more precisely, Twiland Wood, close by) wins – if one looks on the Ordnance Survey, one can actually see that this arm of the feeder streams is the longer of the two. Nash knew what he was talking about, even before the availability of accurate mapping techniques. Once through the village of Illey, this tributary then flows into Hales Owen town, beyond which it meets the brook descending from Uffmore Wood, this latter running in a deep gorge as it passes through Rumbow and under the A458. Boosted by the Lutley Gutter, it flows through an ever-deepening ravine into Cradley Heath and on to Stourbridge, where it is a fair-sized stream. Leaving the urban area, it is joined by the Smethstow Brook (another candidate as the true source) and into Kinver, now a real river. Here, it used to scream 'fish' despite its condition and, followed by the Staffs–Worcester Canal, passes through Wolverley and into Kidderminster, where, until recent times, its pollution load was augmented by the carpet factories. At Stourport, it joins the mighty Severn – prior to the economy reaching the turndown of Dr Kuznets' curve, its filth did the main river no good at all.

I first knew the Stour as a schoolboy; the Earl's Brook, as the Uffmore Arm is known, passed in its ravine right next to my school. The standard punishment for bullies and other miscreants back in the 1950s was to be thrown 'down Earl's'. It never happened to me, but I did help with one or two of the ceremonies! As a penalty, it was grim – falling down a steep tree- and scrub-lined bank with an open sewer at the bottom was no joke. Explaining the mess you were in to the teachers afterwards was even worse – the cane (or a plank of wood – I've seen that used) was always there in the background. Today, the Earl's is fenced off – health and safety and all that, and of course bullies thrive – we had our own ways of dealing with such problems years ago; teachers and parents did not come into it and school

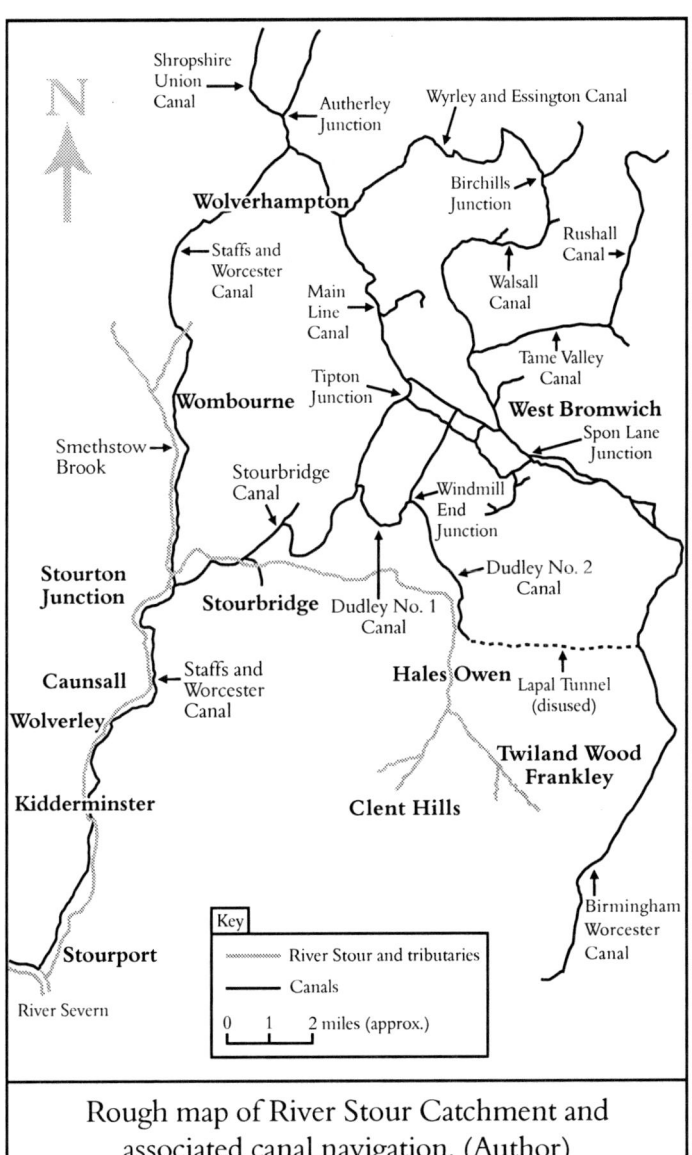

Rough map of River Stour Catchment and associated canal navigation. (Author)

was a safer and happier place. The river's other function was to provide a chunk of the designated boys' cross country running route. Dai Davies, the games' master, was a real sadist – we not only ran along the river but, on occasions, in it – the water was the colour of dishwater and the smell unbelievable. Foul-looking weed, the sort only seen in open sewers, made the experience somewhat slippery in our plimsolls. Add to this barbed wire – one nasty accident here – and an unfenced open mine shaft, plus a vicious hill in mid course, and we were well prepared for direct entry into the Parachute Regiment. One of us actually did just that!

Above the town, even in the 1960s, the Uffmore Arm contained fish, brown trout to boot, especially above Illey. Robin Dunn, living nearby, even tried fishing for them. They were small and not easily deceived. I myself saw trout in other streams running from the Clents into the Belbroughton Brook. These fish survived, seemingly miraculously, above the pollution which began in Hales Owen – it was even rumoured that the town's swimming pool water was discharged into the Stour, chlorine and all! An economy is a dynamic thing, however, and change was thankfully taking place. The old metal-bashing industries were in terminal decline, being replaced by cleaner forms of employment such as financial and other services. There was more concern for the environment as the basic needs of the community were met, bringing pressure for rising standards in water quality. The Earl's Brook was a blight on the town and the council began to take notice. The first indication that something was shifting was when, back in the mid 1980s, a kingfisher was hit and killed by a car on the A458 close to the town centre. Now, kingfishers do not live on sewers and this bird, flying deep in the ravine, had obviously climbed high up to fly over the road, rather than risk the tunnel. It was a fatal mistake. Downstream, above the Severn confluence, fish were beginning to move into the cleaner water and this fishing even received a mention in 1986 by Des Taylor and Dave Phillips in their guide *Where to Fish: The Midlands*. There appear to have been a number of false starts, with fish stocks being cut back by doses of pollution, especially around Kidderminster, but eventually the fish population gained a firm hold.

Notices began to appear along the banks – 'Day tickets £3 a day' was one near Caunsall. Farmers who had previously had to prevent their animals from even getting near to the water now found themselves reaping the rewards of riparian ownership – a liability had become an asset. Matches were held on the lower reaches and even barbel were caught. The angling correspondent in the *Halesowen Chronicle* reported a thirteen-ounce dace, and carp into double figures. Dudley PAC member Steve Sault, who lived close to the river, lost a huge perch. Recently, otter spraints have been found along the banks within Dudley Borough and it is clear that, barring accidents, we have a new (and fascinating) little fishery on our doorstep. Even trout have somehow appeared, an indication of just how clean the water has become. These are not restricted to the upper reaches, far from it. Colin Booth, looking out of his office window in Kidderminster, observed a number of brownies happily feeding in the middle of the town. I have already mentioned the trout in the Illey Brook back in the early 1960s, and it is not beyond the realms of possibility that a repopulation has occurred from here and other tributaries such as the Hoo Brook, which joins the Stour at Kidderminster. It would indeed be remarkable if the current trout population were the descendents of the original fish that have somehow miraculously survived the ravages of decades of pollution by hiding in the feeder streams. Maybe one day we shall see the appearance of fly rods on the river – while the farmers and other owners would benefit, it would be a shame if the current wide access was restricted. As I write, the Birmingham Anglers' Association has leased a stretch of the river below Stourton – an indication of how far things have moved, and I am sure that other clubs will follow suit. A study by the Environment Agency has also identified the urban section of the river (together with the adjacent canals) as one of the last strongholds of the water vole – a remarkable transformation for what was, in living memory, the very antithesis of an environmental asset.

What really attracted attention, however, were reports of pike. A ten-pounder was mentioned in the local press as having come from a weir pool at Kinver. These fish were either migrants from the Severn or had found their new home by more devious means

– the Staffs–Worcester Canal has been known to overflow (this could also account for the carp), or their presence could be the consequences of illicit stocking. Darren Griffiths, one the Dudley PAC's stalwarts, went to investigate. Fishing a weir in the middle reaches with small live baits, he took six pike, the best over seven pounds in weight. Now most modern pike anglers would undoubtedly turn their noses up at such fish – yet weight is not everything, despite what the angling press would have us believe. These pike are important, to us old ones at least. If someone had told us back in the early 1960s that pike fishing would be available on the river less than ten miles from home and within the next forty years, we would have thought them slightly potty – yet it has happened. And it is wonderful.

With all this happening, and with memories of my schooldays fresh in mind, I just had to fish the Stour. I took Dave Hendry, a superb float angler, with me. We began operations upstream of Wolverley. Who owned the fishing, heaven only knows – there were no forbidding notices and we were quite prepared to fork out a quid or two should any owner put in appearance. Despite chatting to the farmer on the bank opposite, we were not bothered. Dave set up above a bend with a tree overhanging a depth of around four feet of water. After an abortive start, I fished downstream in a similar peg – the depth here was nearer five feet. It was not long before Dave put in an appearance. 'Come and see this,' he said. In his keep net were three roach and a lovely dace. They probably weighed between six ounces and half a pound, and beautiful fish they were. They could easily have come from the Upper Wye, such was their condition. My first Stour fish was soon to follow, appropriately a gudgeon, to be followed by a dozen more. Then came a chub and I hooked something that ran downstream, pulling hard, until the hook hold gave. Towards dusk, there was a shout from Dave – a pike had just swum past his feet, tight under the bank. We caught steadily until the December dusk closed in. Make no mistake, Dave and I plan to be back – and we shall have our pike rods with us!

It is not just the Stour that has been transformed; the same is true of the canals. Here I am referring not just to the semi-rural waterways that so characterise our region, but to those that penetrate deep into the urban area – places which, until recently, were characterised by sunken supermarket trolleys, litter, graffiti and all sorts of indescribable filth. Unlike the Stour, which has literally returned from the grave, the canals of the Black Country and Birmingham (the latter is really just part of the greater Black Country!) never really completely died during the industrial era, though it is clear that the effects described by Dr Kuznets' curve have been experienced with some force nevertheless. For this reason, it is difficult to assess the degree of change, though it has been substantial. Grandfather fished for pike around Bilston and Coseley before the First World War, and it is clear that the species never completely lost its hold, even in places where industrialisation ruled supreme. Searching the local papers of 1903 for my great-grandfather's obituary, I once came across a front-page advertisement for pike fishing in Titford Pools, a canal feeder not too far from home. The price was one shilling a day, quite a hefty sum of money in those days. I presume people fished for the pot, and they must have been prepared to pay this sum for the fishing available. Where there are pike, there have to be prey fish – Grandfather always spoke affectionately of the ubiquitous gudgeon. The Soho Loop in the centre of Birmingham always seems to have produced good roach fishing and the Norton Canes Extension, not far from Walsall, never lost its reputation for a whole range of species. I would guess that fish populations were patchy, with pollutions having severe local effects, repopulation taking place once water quality had improved. Nonetheless, the environment was pretty evil and not the sort of place where any reasonably genteel disciple of Isaac would have wished to venture. Outside of the main urbanisation, there was always fishing; clubs such as the Birmingham Anglers' Association having large holdings on waters such as the Birmingham–Worcester since the Association's inception in the late nineteenth century. The fare, even in my childhood, was gudgeon, small roach and perch, together with the occasional 'skimmer'. Specimen waters they were not, though the Birmingham Anglers' Association's annual specimen fish competition usually managed to record a double-figure pike or two from the canals, even back in the 1950s.

Yet the potential was there; the massive roach in the Lapal Arm of the Dudley Number 2 proved this during the late 1950s. Left alone, nature would repair herself and once a consistent improvement in water quality occurred, weed would grow, light would penetrate and a virtuous circle would develop. The main problem with places such as the Lapal Arm was that they were in many senses artificial. Canals are man-made and need constant maintenance. Once they are abandoned, nature will take over, but without some degree of upkeep they gradually decay through silting and leakage. This is where the boats come in. We anglers have to recognise that the canals were built as navigations; boat traffic provides the bulk of the funds for maintenance and therefore should have some degree of priority. This of course does mean that some element of disturbance is inevitable, and that the water will usually have a degree of turbidity which will impact on light penetration and therefore the food chain. On top of reductions in discharges, planners have at last recognised the contribution that an upgraded canal-side environment can make to the regeneration of our towns and cities. Birmingham City Council, to its credit, has been a leader in this renaissance and the Waterfront development at Merry Hill, not far from home, is a catalyst for not just a range of modern office developments but also, emulating Birmingham, for a thriving nightlife as well. A recent edition of the (reincarnated) *Midland Angler* had a photograph of a chap displaying a net of good-sized bream at the Waterfront, surrounded by a rather befuddled group of nightclubbers. Describing it as a 'surreal clash of cultures', the journal commented that 'night-time revellers drinking out on the waterside terraces at sunset socialise as local anglers play, land and drop tench, bream and carp into bulging keep nets not five metres from where the social 'elite' listen to the latest tracks of dance and R&B music'. Such events would have been unthinkable even twenty years ago, when the location constituted the shattered remains of the closed Round Oak steel works. This stretch has, not surprisingly, also been producing impressive match weights.

Paralleling this, and on my doorstep, is the end section of the Dudley Number 2 which, again until twenty or so years ago, ran through the remains of the Stewarts and Lloyds tube works. Dad was a design engineer there during the Second World War and he and his colleagues tested a miniature version of PLUTO (Pipeline Under The Ocean) in its waters. The full-sized version of PLUTO was used to supply the Normandy beaches with petroleum after D-Day. I remember this stretch of canal as a child; it was a grim and forbidding place with K Works towering above it. It had that distinctive factory smell familiar to anyone reared in an industrial area. Massive tubes were moved by barge between the various works – Dad never reported seeing any fish. How different it is today! The old works have gone, the canal has been cleaned up, beds of rushes have appeared, grass has been planted and a lovely, newly painted cast-iron bridge erected by the local canal trust. While the far side of the canal still displays evidence of the industrial past in the form of dock areas and the line of an old railway, the stretch is now Bull Fisheries where, for a couple of pounds, one can fish for a variety of species in a rapidly improving environment. Maurice Eley and I had a go recently and, having got started, were approached by a rather attractive blond (female!) who proceeded to give us advice on how to fish. She was back within the hour, complete with pole, box and all the other paraphernalia and proceeded to demonstrate how canal fishing should be done. Mixing her ground bait as if she was preparing a gourmet meal, she gave us a right thrashing. Talk about precision fishing. I take my hat off to you, lady; you sure are a great advertisement for your gender! Mid afternoon, she pushed off to collect the kids from school.

The renaissance of these urban canals, helped by British Waterways, the Environment Agency and the local authorities, is a remarkable phenomenon. The jargon in professional circles is that it is a 'win-win' situation. Environment, economy and the wider society that they serve all gain from what is essentially very modest investment superimposed over the wider forces of economic change. Boating, angling, bird-watching and other recreational activities such as cycling all now co-exist and fuel a greatly improved quality of life. New, clean employment flourishes in modern offices constructed on canal-side locations, and residential developments on this brownfield land are increasingly upmarket. Occasionally planners get things right!

The fishing seems to get better and better, including that for pike. Dudley PAC members are taking double-figure pike among the new offices and warehouses – Gromit, a pioneer of this fishing, keeps saying 'I told you so!' A pike match held in Wolverhampton was won with half a dozen fish totalling over fifty pounds in weight, second place was a lot lower – twenty-two pounds – but it was one fish! The *Halesowen News* recently carried a photograph of a couple of schoolboys with a catch of quite reasonable pike, I suspect from the Dudley Number 2, and double-figure carp abound. There are reports of chub of over an incredible six pounds – so large that specialist tactics are now evolving to deal with them (lamprey seems to be the bait). Pike angler David Durkin has reported a three-pound, six-ounce perch, from the Autherley Junction on the Staffs–Worcester; again near Wolverhampton, and close by, on Sankey's Pool, a small canal feeder, Mark Taggart has taken a huge nine-pound, one-ounce eel. David Durkin's best canal pike weighed a creditable twenty-two pounds, eight ounces. To top things, a young lad recently appeared at a Dudley PAC meeting with a photograph of his first-ever pike – taken from a canal deep in the Smoke, it weighed exactly twenty pounds.

When he penned *Still Water Angling* back in the 1950s, Richard Walker gloomily foretold the demise of our rivers. He saw still waters, especially the newly-dug gravel pits, as the way forward. In retrospect, he was only partly right. The effects described in the Environmental Kuznets Curve could not have been foreseen back in the early 1950s, and the possible resurrection of rivers such as the Worcestershire Stour (and similar streams like it) would not have entered his head. Yet it has happened. Things do not necessarily always get worse, despite what the Greens tell us. Similarly, I do not recall canals ever featuring much in the early 'specimen hunting' literature. Times have changed. I occasionally walk by the Bratch Lock at Wombourne where Grandfather used to catch his live baits. These were mainly gudgeon; he considered himself lucky to even get a small roach or perch. He would have been astounded at the thought of decent-sized chub or double-figure carp from the canal, let alone twenty-pound pike. The Stour as a fishery would have been a complete pipe dream. Yet the

Stour's twin, the little River Anker at Tamworth, on the other side of the conurbation, having undergone a similar transformation, is now producing double-figure barbel. I will stick my neck out and confidently predict that such fish will soon be taken from the Stour, even if it has not happened already. Simon Kuznets' legacy is a rich one indeed.

Dr Kuznets' legacy – Lee Hoyland with his first ever pike. Weighing exactly twenty pounds, it came from a canal deep in the Black Country. (Darren Griffiths)

Pestered by Riff-Raff

Frank Hodgkiss with a two-pound, eight-ounce roach. (Author)

Following my small success with the roach from Breeches Pool and the Warwickshire Avon, I developed a love of the species that continues apace even today, nearly half a century on. Gromit, dyed-in-the-wool pike angler that he is, professes not to understand this peculiarity of my psychology. For him, roach are a lesser species that can possibly have only one function – bait. Others are not just tolerant but positively enthusiastic and, as a small team, we have recently had some success, even though most of us are now in our dotage. My quest for a big roach has been a long journey indeed.

Over the years, I had managed to learn at least a little about roach and some of this has already been outlined in the context of river fishing. Needless to say, the goal has always been the mystical two-pounder. I well remember 'Skipper' Parker describing in the *Midland Angler* how he managed to take no less than seven two-pounders in one sitting on the Hampshire Avon, and Dick Walker telling of even more impressive catches from an undisclosed southern chalk stream. If they could succeed, why couldn't I? The old adage 'you can't catch 'em if they are not there' of course applied – such fish were not exactly common on my local waters and, since the demise of the canal, I knew that my chances were slim. Pike, tench and barbel took over but the desire for a big roach always simmered in the back of my mind. I missed out on the middle Severn bonanza of the 1980s largely through ignorance, though it is now clear that these fish were probably fairly localised. Talking recently to ex England international Ken Giles, he informed me that in all his years of match fishing on the Severn, he had only taken two roach over the magical figure, a fact that rather put my lack of success in context. Ian Jarvis took to travelling to the Hampshire Avon in his personal quest, to be rewarded with a three-pounder, a fantastic achievement by any standards. I laid plans, which remained just that – plans.

Nonetheless, I did discover something about the behaviour of decent-sized roach, especially in still waters. The first factor seemed to be the role of wind. Patshull Great Pool in the late 1960s/early 1970s was still a lovely, remote spot, untouched by the hand of commercialism. One day, in the teeth of a howling gale, two friends and I fished the Glory Hole next to the old temple with our usual sliding float rig. Fishing maggots with heavyish cloud bait, we caught roach after roach above the pound mark. Fishing in nearly twenty feet of water, the undertow was so great that the situation was akin to fishing a river, our floats 'trotting' upwind as the lake water moved against the force of the wind. When it reached the taking spot, the large float would dive with mechanical regularity; it was fantastic fishing. Subsequent visits confirmed the formula – look for a big blow if you wanted to bag up with the roach, otherwise you were condemned to catch skimmer bream, a horrible fate if there ever was one! In order to fish the place more effectively, I even invested in a sixteen-foot monstrosity of a rod. Made of hollow glass, it was made by Modern Arms and called the Zepherine. It weighed a ton, gave me arm ache, but did the job. Despite all this, there were no two-pounders. I still have the rod, though it hasn't been out of its bag for nigh on three decades. I shall return to the relationship between wind and the feeding of big still-water roach later, but at this juncture it is worth pointing out that Chris 'The Teeth' Phillips, the Dudley PAC's resident dentist, confirms my view. Fishing the clay pit (see 'Middle Earth'), big roach always appeared when he was forced to 'trot' in a big blow – no wind, no fish.

Somewhat more recently, I again had the opportunity to have a crack at some decent still-water roach. Bream anglers on one of my pike waters started reporting two-pounders. Ian Jarvis and I set about a campaign. One thing became abundantly clear – these particular roach reacted to light levels. I remember Dick Walker once writing that roach anglers could learn a lot from taking a light meter with them. How right he was! Since we were fishing from a smallish boat, fishing in high winds was not an option but light levels turned out to be critical. Small roach would feed in bright sunshine, but if you were looking for pound-plus fish, the darker it was, the better. The bream anglers were taking their fish at night and our ploy was to fish through the evening into the darkness, packing up before things became too difficult. On overcast days, fish over a pound would come immediately; on sunny evenings, it was small fish only until the sun went over the yardarm and then, as if a switch was thrown, the larger fish would show. The process was almost predictable – as soon as the light diminished, down would go the float and with luck the fish would be over a pound and a half. My jinx, however, continued – over two or three summers' fishing, we had many fish over one-eight, but the best was one-fourteen. Maybe we should have fished more into the night, for the bream anglers continued to report twos. Or maybe we were just unlucky? Even the one fourteen was something of a let down – Ian hooked it and a rather big pike promptly nailed it, eventually letting go. Needless to say, when returned, the roach was not exactly in pristine condition.

At this juncture, I pretty well gave up; barbel and tench took over as my summer fish and the prospect of a really big roach was dimmer than ever. Fifteen years or so passed. Then recently rumours began to circulate about veritable monsters being taken by carp anglers from an estate lake, which, as far as we were aware, had no pedigree as a roach water whatsoever. These fish included a number of three-pounders. They were not 'scraper threes' either. Interesting? Definitely!

Ian Jarvis was one of the first on the scene, but I was soon let into the loop on penalty of keeping my mouth shut! Keeping things quiet was, however, virtually impossible. The lake was in a semi-public place and was a favourite place for dog walkers, some of whom were anglers. A two-pound roach in the landing net is difficult to conceal! That said, it was the carp anglers who ruled the roost and the roach, to date, have seen very little pressure. A big question has always been how the fish had become so large in the first place. Certainly, the lake has always had a good food supply and maybe the fish have been around for years, but most consider that the volume of carp bait going in has been a significant factor. Bait boats, spods and PVA bags full of boilies and particles all feature prominently as carp anglers vie with one another as to who is going to get the next thirty. Long may it continue, as the roach wax fat! When Frank Hodgkiss invited me for a day, at long last the prospect of a two-pounder seemed realistic. Indeed, I was assured that it would be cakewalk!

It was the last week of the season when I had my first visit, taking a protesting Gromit along to be an extra witness to my first two. The outcome was totally predictable. I caught a number of good roach, including a personal best, but it weighed one pound, fifteen ounces! Gromit, bemoaning the loss of a good day's piking, even managed a five-pound plus tench on his roach gear. Frank Hodgkiss, just to show who was boss, took two roach over two pounds, the better of them going a thumping two pounds, eight ounces. He threw in a two-pound-plus perch for good measure. I was going to have to wait until the next winter, but in the event it would be well worth it.

From what I could gather, these roach were regarded as winter fish. What was more, they lived a long way from the bank. Summer fishing on the lake was mainly for the ubiquitous carp, with a sprinkling of 'pleasure' anglers thrown in (a strange term this – do we not all fish for pleasure? Observing the activities of the carp anglers, I am not so sure). Occasionally a good roach would turn up during the summer months, usually to a carp angler, in which case it was regarded simply as a nuisance. The roach probably are catchable during the summer, but given the pressure placed on the water by others, plus the lure of other species, at the end of the day we have chosen to leave them alone. Given the delicacy of the ecological balance that maintains them, this is probably no bad thing.

A central problem has always been the fact that the roach shoals are a long way out. I have never taken the trouble to pace out my maximum casting distance, but these fish require specialist tackle and rigs if any success is to be achieved at all. Put a bait closer in than around sixty yards and you will go biteless, from the big roach at least. Why this is so is difficult to say, though again it may be related to the activities of the carp anglers. These latter seem to operate on the assumption that carp are only located at great distances from the bank and bait accordingly. Given the use of bait boats and the like, this process becomes a self-fulfilling prophecy, reinforced by the amount of disturbance created close in. With the carp bait all going in at range, is it any wonder that the roach shoals follow suit? Some of this baiting activity is quite ludicrous – having pitched camp on one bank, bait is deposited much closer to the opposite bank. Why not fish from the latter in the first place but keep the disturbance down? Whatever the reason, casting of almost tournament proportions is often needed to reach the roach. (As 'real' anglers, we refuse to even contemplate using bait boats and the like!)

The solution to the distance problem lies initially with the end rig. Whoever invented this will never be known. It has probably been around for donkey's years and re-invented as circumstances demand. When I described it to Dick Smith, he claimed that he had thought it up years ago to catch roach at distance on an entirely different water. Mick Haley and Ian Jarvis can probably lay claim to its development in the present context, though no doubt someone will suggest otherwise. The rig is illustrated in the diagram. I have specified the names of the products we use because they are important, though clearly there are alternatives once the characteristics of each is identified. The rig is a 'feeder-cum-helicopter-cum-bolt rig'. Bolt rigs for roach? Why not? These fish are at extreme range and running tactics have proved a dismal failure. The rig casts like a bullet and is virtually tangle free. We use six-pound Berkley Trilene Sensation as reel line to cope with the force of the cast. This line is quite fine at .23mm diameter but very strong and seems to have the appropriate combination of strength, stretch and diameter. Other makes of line can result in snap-offs on the cast. There is plenty of elasticity at range, though takes from tench and carp can result in breaks. Even at eighty yards plus, takes from roach are powerful – Gromit, half-heartedly joining us one day, almost lost his rod to a fish of less than two pounds when he first tried the rig. Heavy bobbins are the order of the day; mine can have an extra weight screwed in if wind and undertow are a problem. Optonics are optional, but do allow lapses of concentration! The top hook is also optional – strangely, fish caught on this are usually tench and perch, the roach inevitably coming on the bottom hook. Bait is usually a couple of white maggots. This is the sort of set up that would probably have sent Bernard Venables into an apoplectic fit, yet it represents a logical solution to the problems of catching roach at range. While I accept that electronic alarms are a lazy way of fishing, bolt rigs are another matter. Even rigs not designed explicitly to make fish bolt will, if they generate resistance, make fish behave in this way; barbel leger rigs are a classic example. I may be digressing here, but one thing that Dick Walker got totally wrong in my view is the issue of resistance. Fish expect to feel resistance and are certainly not put off by it. In my early days, under Walker's influence, we always tried to minimise resistance and the results were not impressive. With a bolt-type rig, the fish of course hook themselves, and this may be deemed by some to be unsporting. Consider, however, the other factors involved. Accurate casting at extreme distance is a must; ideally, the same spot needs to be hit time and again. This calls for no little skill. When a fish is hooked, it has to be played in on a light bottom (which, incidentally, needs to be changed regularly). When played, the fish 'jag', a phenomenon which can be more than a little disconcerting. The feeder gum at top of the trace absorbs some of this, but nonetheless the short bottom takes a lot of hammer; being so short, it has very little stretch. Big roach also tend to 'kite', and keeping a big fish out of bank-side snags and vegetation without breaking needs what Dick Walker called 'hands'. We do not all have this skill. Bear in mind that the small hook is barbless and I see no reason to apologise for using the rig, Bernard Venables' probable attitude notwithstanding.

Fishing for these roach is now an important part of my fishing year. My first two-pounder did not come easily. The problem, I feel, was that I was trying too hard. This conclusion is explained in 'I Shall Be Glad When I Have Had Enough of This!'. I caught a lot of good roach up to a shade under the magical figure. Frank Hodgkiss and Mick Haley proceeded to wave two-pounders under my nose with monotonous regularity. Friends, mainly fellow members of the Dudley PAC, used to come and watch (and still do). Big John Holt, whose attempts to catch a two were even more jinxed than mine, gave up completely. One day, as a spectator, he turned up with an impressive supply of piping hot bacon and egg triple-decker sandwiches to fortify us against the elements. Where he had acquired them, and how he had kept them hot, remains a mystery. Often, the gallery gets somewhat out of hand and once, when the warden arrived to collect our money, I remember jokingly complaining, 'I don't pay good money to be pestered by riff-raff!' My griping is now something of a ritual when certain spectators are present.

Eventually, the great day came. It was the day before Christmas Eve. On arrival in a murky dawn, Frank Hodgkiss and I had debated where to fish. I finished up in peg 23, which gave access to slightly shallower water, particularly for the right-hand rod. My first roach went one pound, eleven ounces, so did the second. The third went one thirteen. By now Frank had taken two twos. It was the same old story. Around mid morning up rolls the warden, wanting our money and also a chat. Martin is a remarkable character. A retired police inspector, he now reigns supreme over this lovely estate and has introduced a number of sensible measures designed to conserve the fishing (one of which is the restoration of the close season). In his professional life, Martin was once personal bodyguard to the Rt Hon Enoch Powell MP, and we are often regaled with stories about his time in the police and how the whole judicial system has gone to the

Long range still water roach rig

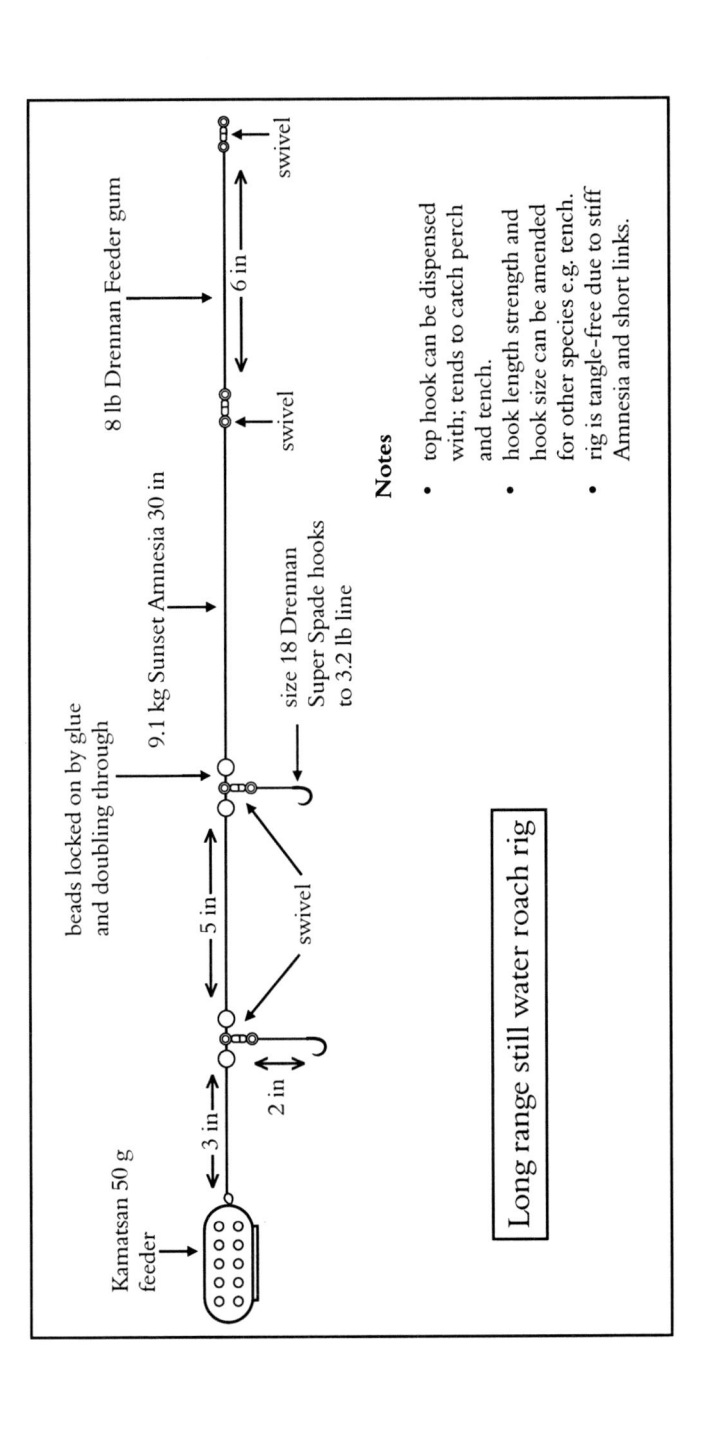

- Kamatsan 50 g feeder
- 3 in
- 2 in
- 5 in
- beads locked on by glue and doubling through
- 9.1 kg Sunset Amnesia 30 in
- size 18 Drennan Super Spade hooks to 3.2 lb line
- swivel
- 8 lb Drennan Feeder gum
- 6 in
- swivel

Notes

- top hook can be dispensed with; tends to catch perch and tench.
- hook length strength and hook size can be amended for other species e.g. tench.
- rig is tangle-free due to stiff Amnesia and short links.

dogs since he has retired! He also has some fairly firm views on how to deal with terrorists. After putting the world to rights, he left me with the following comment and, from the look on his face, he was deadly serious: 'Anyone who fishes peg 23 on the twenty-third of the month always catches a big fish'. I said something like 'Pull the other one'. He placed his hand on my shoulder, said 'Mark my words', and moved off to relieve Frank of his ticket money in peg 22.

At around 1.30 p.m., I had a take, the bobbin pulling violently up to the rod. At seventy yards, it is always difficult to assess the size of the fish, but it was immediately apparent that this one intended to stay well out. At first I thought it was a tench and played it gently – the technique is to wind steadily rather than pump – but slowly I managed to work the fish towards the bank. Gradually, however, it began to kite to the right, a rather disconcerting tactic on a longish line. Pressure brought the fish closer in, the line getting nearer and nearer to a decaying bed of rushes. Deep down, there was a flash of silver and I knew then that my quest was over, provided I could land the thing! The next few minutes were somewhat hairy, to say the least. In front of me, jagging violently, was the biggest roach that I had ever seen. It was within three feet of the net, but would it give in? If I used the words 'It's going to come off' once, I used them a dozen times. Frank oozed words of calm reassurance and eventually, after what seemed at eternity, the fish came over the net. The handle bent over as Frank lifted it. We looked at it. It seemed enormous. Usually, you can hold a roach in one hand; even my two hands did not meet around its girth. I measured it – fourteen and a half inches long and a massive twelve in girth. It went two pounds, nine ounces. My first two was over two and a half! I felt sick; a strange reaction maybe, but that was how it was. The necessary photographs were taken and I sat down, cradling the fish in the pan net. The quest which had taken nearly half a century was now over. The warden's prophecy had amazingly proved correct. (I have since discovered that the number twenty-three has some significance in occult circles, particularly in the Kabbalah – perhaps if I had fished on until 23:00 hours I would have caught a three-pounder?) There was a mixture of both euphoria and numbness; together with feeling sick, it was not particularly pleasant. The fish got lively in the net and I released it, thinking that I would never see a roach of that size again. I was wrong.

The Christmas holidays, pike fishing and indifferent health kept me away from the lake for nearly a month. Given the distance and the weather, driving was something of a problem but by late January I was back, ready for another two-pounder. The problem was that the old pattern re-emerged: Frank Hodgkiss catching the twos and yours truly having to be content with fish up to one-fourteen. No one should complain about catching roach of even that size, and I certainly wasn't, but somehow Frank had the knack. As explained in 'I Shall Be Glad When I Have Had Enough of This!', I feel that I was trying too hard. Frank now had an impressive tally of two-pounders, and, while not complacent, had relaxed into his fishing, knowing that success would follow. In the next couple of trips I began to do the same, and then in mid February, it happened.

The banks were covered in snowdrops as we walked to our pitches, a delightful sight; I always think that the arrival of these beautiful little flowers heralds the arrival of better weather, and indeed, better fishing! The day started with a fight with a four-pound male tench, which at least tested the tackle. Winter tench are not uncommon; Mick Haley managed to land one of seven pounds, five ounces on the rig, something of an achievement on an ultra-short three-pound bottom. In the days of my youth, tench were supposed to bury themselves in the mud in October and not emerge until spring. Whether winter feeding is due to global warming, or whether the old conventional wisdom was wrong, is difficult to say – I suspect that the truth is a combination of the two. After the usual crop of fish around one and a half pounds, I got into what I thought was another tench. There was, however, a certain feel about how the fish was behaving and, when it began to kite, I knew what it was. It almost succeeded in getting into the weeds to my left and even felt snagged for one horrible moment, but eventually it came over the net. It was another massive roach. The top hook was missing; this must have been the snag (maybe in future we resort to using just the one hook?). The fish went two ten, was fifteen inches long and, like the two nine, was twelve inches in girth. The gallery behind was mightily impressed, handshakes all round, and I obtained something I have always wanted, a photograph of a big roach among the snowdrops. This now graces my gallery in the downstairs toilet – the boss will not allow photographs of fish anywhere else in the house! A young lad fishing close by, rather bemused by the whole affair, took a photograph on his mobile phone and in seconds it was being shown around Natalie's office in Birmingham. Such is modern technology – Natalie initially rang the lad back, wanting to know why a total stranger had sent her a photograph of a b—y fish!

Later in the afternoon, I got another big one, at two pounds, three ounces. Two twos in a day – I still had some way to go to beat Frank Hodgkiss' record of five, but there was a great feeling of satisfaction nonetheless. The next session I got a fourth. My jinx was well and truly broken, and I have not looked back since. By way of conclusion, it may be worth reflecting on the influence of weather on these roach. Frank Hodgkiss and some of the others have now accumulated significant experience in this area and it is worth outlining their conclusions. First (and rather obviously), warm weather is better than cold, but the influence of this variable can be overridden by other factors. Temperature only seems to play a powerful role if it is dropping toward freezing – frosts are certainly bad news. Second, low light levels are also an advantage, though the impact is not as marked as it was on my other water. It should, however, be remembered that this is winter fishing, when light levels are low anyway; my previous experience was in high summer. Third, the effect of the wind was confirmed – big still-water roach love a big blow. Our most spectacular catch so far was four two-pounders on the bank at the same time – two in my landing net and two in Frank's, the best going two pounds, five ounces – to me for once. There are no prizes for guessing that it was blowing a 'hooligan'. I took three two-pounders that day and a dozen over a pound and a half. As I write, it is the last day of the season and I should be out fishing. A bitter easterly gale is lashing my study window. Earlier, I telephoned Frank to chicken out; the weather was just too evil and I seem to have some sort of a bug anyway; it is best to take no chances after my recent brush with the other side. The telephone has just rung. It was Frank. His tally of fish is thirteen, with three fish over two pounds. Despite the raw cold, the low light levels combined with the gale have brought the fish on with a vengeance and I am kicking myself for not fishing. Soon it will be time to get out the trout rod, the daffodils will be in bloom and I will be 'fluff chucking' somewhere in Middle Earth. I cannot help but feel, however, that my heart will be somewhere else, riff-raff or no riff-raff.

A brace of two-pound-plus roach, taken within minutes of one another. A similar brace was to arrive on Frank Hodgkiss' rods (background) seconds later. (Author)

Unpestered by riff-raff – two-pound, ten-ounce roach among the snowdrops. (Author)

The Black Beast and Other Frighteners

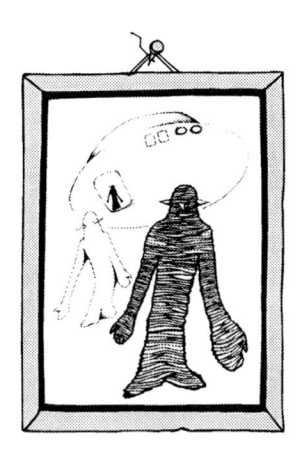

How would you like to share your bivvy with one of these chaps? Artist's impression of the entities that abducted anglers Charles Hickson and Calvin Parker from the pier at Pascagoula, Florida.*

Do you believe in the paranormal – in ghosts, UFOs or strange coincidences? When asked this question, I reply that I 'believe' in nothing. As one trained in economic science – where facts are often elusive (there are lies, damn lies and statistics – trout returns often fall into the same category!) and hypotheses tentative (we economists have our own version of Murphy's law, Goodhart's law, which I will not bore you with) – all one can do is observe, record events or data as accurately as possible and put together some tentative conceptual propositions that just might explain what is going on. I always feel that it is odd

---

* 'Fifty years of UFOs: from distant sightings to close encounters' by John and Anne Spencer, Boxtree, 1997. With kind permission from the authors.

that people who claim to be scientists reject, a priori, evidence provided to them by credible witnesses. Because such observations do not fit into their predetermined scheme of things ('ontology' is the word), such witnesses must, by definition, be either liars or (at best) mistaken in what they observed. 'It can't be, therefore it isn't,' seems almost a mantra in some (but not all) scientific circles. It always seems remarkable that witness evidence, not so long ago sufficient to send a person to the gallows, is perfectly acceptable to the judiciary (and therefore to the wider society that the latter serves) yet is not accepted in the corridors of academe. This seems true even if there is independent corroboration of what is reported.

June once encountered the apparently firm outline of a woman in her room at an old house in Herefordshire and later found details of the apparition (the Grey Lady of the Cedars) in a book on Herefordshire ghosts. My cousin Judy suffered a bad car accident avoiding a woman who appeared through a hedge and walked straight in front of her car – the police later told Judy that it was 'only Bella' and that such incidents along that stretch of road were relatively common. I have had one or two strange encounters myself, and have on four occasions seen objects in the sky that defy 'logical' analysis. Neither June, Judy or I are liars or are deluded (in my case, there were other witnesses to two of the objects observed), yet what we experienced 'cannot' exist – or can it? We anglers are somewhat vulnerable in this respect. We spend time alone (or with one or two fellows) in remote places, often at uncivilised times. On enquiring among angling friends, I have a few stories to relate; if you have any similar experiences, then please let me know. Fishermen are all liars anyway, say the sceptics. Such people are entitled to their opinions; we are at liberty to disagree! (I once did have an idea to write *The Angler's Ghost Book*, but never got around to it – a future project maybe?)

One of the most haunted places for anglers is probably Redmire Pool. Events here have been documented elsewhere and need not be repeated. There is also the card that Chris Yates sent to Rod Hutchison predicting that he was going to break the carp record – precognition, or just a lucky guess? Fred J Taylor has written about the haunted boathouse at Wootton Underwood and also of observing a huge, lit-up, cigar-like object pass silently overhead. In *Fishing for Big Pike*, Barrie Rickards tells (briefly) of his and Hugh Reynolds' encounter with the Lough Ree Monster – one day maybe we shall hear the whole story? In one of my early copies of the *Midland Angler* it is reported that the Severn above Arley has a reputation for being haunted. One angler, standing well out in the river trotting a float, heard the splashing of footsteps behind him. He presumed that it was another angler wading out for a chat. When he turned around, there was no one there!

My first story was initially told by my good friend Vic Bellars at the Pike Anglers' Club Conference (sorry, 'Convention' – why do we always have to emulate the Yanks?). Sitting in the lounge of his and Lindy's delightful cottage deep in rural Norfolk, complete with Sticky Feet the parrot, Vic enlarged on what had happened. It was back in the 1960s, and Vic had discovered a carp lake somewhere well off the beaten track. Obtaining permission from the owner, Vic began a campaign to catch some Norfolk carp. He fished during the day (night fishing was not, I think, allowed). One day, early in the campaign, Vic became aware of a gentleman whose approach through the bushes had been totally silent. The chap stood and watched Vic for some time, refusing to engage in any conversation – Vic thought him more than a little rude. Rather as in my encounter with the White Lady of Lindridge (described later), Vic began to feel uneasy – there was something distinctly odd about his uninvited companion. It was not just the fact that the latter was silent; it was the strange lack of expression on his face and, most of all, his clothes, which seemed the product of a bygone age. Vic poured a drink from his flask and, thinking it would break the ice, offered the chap a cup of coffee. There was no response. Something was not right – Vic was, after all, alone on a remote lake (alone, that is, apart from the person, whose blank stare was becoming unnerving). Vic decided to take the plunge and went to place his hand on the man's shoulder. Imagine his horror when his hand went straight through the apparently solid body! As Vic said to me, 'I have been torpedoed, mined, shelled by German warships and shore batteries, and even had my Number One blown to pieces next to me on the bridge of my frigate, but never in my life have I been so terrified.' This veteran of a dozen sea battles, who was mentioned in despatches for his part in the assault on D-Day, fled the scene in a state of total panic. It was the most unreasoned fear he had ever experienced. Getting into his car, he hit the throttle and hightailed it to the nearest village, bursting into the local and demanding a triple whisky from the startled landlord. Recounting what had happened to the man behind the bar, the latter seemed unmoved. 'No one in their right mind fishes up there alone,' Vic was informed. After another whisky, the landlord accompanied Vic back to the lake to collect his tackle. Of the gentleman in the strange clothes there was no sign. The carp campaign was quietly abandoned.

Now, while the pub landlord was at least in part a witness to Vic's ordeal, he did not actually witness the spectre. My next story is a little more significant in that witnesses to a previous, apparently identical, phenomenon came forward. The victim was Dave Hendry. Now, Dave is an engineer whose thought forms appear as equations – a more down-to-earth witness would be difficult to find. He is also a man, like Vic, not given to fear – a martial arts expert who until recently taught the subject. It was early one January morning at the time when Dave was taking his great catches of roach from the Severn, and occurred just before dawn. Now, positions of transition in space/time were felt by the ancients as being windows through which contact could be established with other levels of existence. Anthropologists call such positions liminal zones – dawn and dusk are classic examples. The following is the unabridged version of what was published in Dave's fishing column in the *Dudley News*:

Cold Morning Brings a Chill to the Spine

For me, roach fishing in the middle of winter holds a special fascination; be it the cold frosty mornings, the numb fingers grasping a hot mug of tea, the cheeky robin helping himself to the free feast of maggots, or the sheer excitement of not knowing how big the next roach will be when the float sinks out of site. Anticipation of what the day will bring is one thing that keeps me heading for the River Severn on days when most sane anglers could be tempted to stay in bed. I was never so tempted. However, one journey was to make me seriously reconsider.

It began as many other days had with the silence of my room being shattered by the 5 a.m. alarm call indicating it was time to get up. Getting dressed was done on auto pilot, as co-ordination between brain and hands was at this time not yet in sync. With some effort and a mug of strong coffee, heavy eyelids were persuaded to stay open and by now the thought of what the day would bring urged me on. With my tackle having been sorted the night before and a couple of flasks prepared, it only remained for me to load the car. Opening the front door of the house completed the awakening process, as a freezing blast of frosty air chilled my face. Ten minutes later saw the tackle loaded in the car and the windscreen cleared of its early morning blanket of frost. I locked the house, made a quick check that I had not forgotten anything, and was on my way.

After three or four miles, I felt the warmth of hot air filtering in from the car's heater, a welcome respite for my cold feet. It was about this time that I began to think of the big roach I was hoping to catch. Would the River Severn be in a responsive mood to allow me to gain victory over my intended quarry? Was I too early, as there was still nearly an hour to daylight and only about ten miles to go? Little did I know what lay ahead! My thoughts changed as I turned off the A449 and headed along the winding country lanes in the direction of Arley, one of my favourite stretches on the River Severn. As the road dipped, I was welcomed by large pools of mist held in the hollows as I drove towards the Fox Inn at Stourton. Rounding the left-hand bend prior to the pub, the road dropped away downhill – what happened next was to take my mind off fishing, and stays firmly in my memory to this very day.

Into the brightness of my headlights appeared the figure of a cavalier! He was standing in the middle of my lane, his feet slightly apart, with one hand on his hip and the other on the handle of his sword. His hat was tilted to one side and he stood there motionless as my headlights reflected back from the buckles on his clothing. Headlights were quickly changed from dipped to main beam, illuminating further the booted figure, but still he did not move. What followed lasted only seconds but seemed like hours – time had slowed down to a veritable crawl. He appeared to be looking straight at me, with yours truly looking back in total amazement. My mind became awash with questions: was this person real? Is he (it?) flesh and blood? If I do not change course will I go straight through him or will there be a nasty accident, with me held responsible? If I was to stop short, what then? Would I be abducted into another dimension? All these thoughts and more flashed through my mind as I hit the brakes, closing rapidly on the still immobile figure.

Headlights were repeatedly flashed as impact seemed imminent, but I managed to swerve around the obstruction. Time slowed even further as I crept past the motionless, but apparently solid, cavalier. The air in the car became cold, so cold I could see my breath, the hairs on the back of my neck standing up in a way I had never experienced before. A freezing chill passed through my spine, causing me to shiver. I turned to look back. The spectre, if that is what is was, had turned his head and was looking straight at me! I quickly turned to look away in the direction I was going. But should I look back again? Was he still there? What if he was? So I looked, and yes, he was still there, slowly turning his head away as I drove on. The figure remained in my rear view mirror until I had rounded the next bend. That was the last I saw of this amazing 'man'. Who he was, what he was, I don't know. Was he real? I do not know that either. Is this story true? Yes – the date was Saturday, 25 February 1984, and no, it is not a fisherman's tale.

As for the roach fishing, that was a bit of an anti-climax after such an eventful journey – a good day all the same with some fish approaching two pounds, but a day I will remember for reasons far removed from the river bank.

Dave adds:

A footnote to the encounter came following the printing of this article in an angling column I was writing at the time in a local newspaper. I received telephone calls from two gentlemen who had experienced similar events some eight years and twelve years before respectively. Both events took place within two hundred yards of the Fox pub. Food for thought, but the most interesting and informative response came from an elderly woman who was able to inform me of her almost identical experience over twenty-five years previously, as well as providing an historical explanation.

Following the battle of Worcester on 3 September 1651, between the forces of Oliver Cromwell (supporters of the Rump Parliament) and the cavaliers (supporters of King Charles II), many cavaliers fled to take refuge in parts of the countryside north of Worcester, including some of the houses in the Stourton area. It is reported that, during skirmishes between the two forces, some cavaliers were killed in these houses – it is thought that the sightings of cavaliers in this area are the ghosts of those men.

Now who says fishing is not educational?

Dave Hendry is not the only person to have experienced something strange. Adrian Writtle had an experience at Eastnor Castle, south of Malvern. Adrian is another angler not easily frightened by a bump or two in the night, though he and Nigel Povey sure had a bad time one night carp fishing at Eastnor. Now, Eastnor Lake is reported to not only be haunted by a previous keeper – Jack – and his dog, but ghostly figures have also been reported by carp anglers walking along the battlements at dawn and dusk. The lads had set up in a dense, wooded area adorned with thick undergrowth. As the night sounds took over, Adrian was dozing when something bumped into his leg. He ignored it. It happened again. Shining his torch on to the ground, he was astounded to see dozens of rats running through his peg! Moving peg didn't seem an option, so he made a footrest with the net handle and sat back in his seat – at least the creatures would no longer run over his feet. The pressure on the canvas of his seat was suddenly too much and, with a loud ripping sound, his rear was deposited straight down into the rat run. Horror! Struggling to get up, standing seemed the only option and eventually the rats reduced somewhat in numbers. It was about this time that Adrian began to have the 'I'm being stared at' feeling. It seemed to be coming from the undergrowth behind. Was his mind playing tricks? He turned and could not see anything. Carp splashed out in the lake. No, he thought, someone is watching me! As with Dave Hendry, the hairs on the back of his neck were standing up as he turned again to peer into the darkness. There, only feet away, in front of the undergrowth, was the form of a human face. The problem was – it had no body! There was just this face, staring at him out of the blackness, seemingly floating unsupported above the ground. Forgetting the rats, he turned and found his torch. The face vanished. I've had enough of this, thinks our Ade, and ponders what to do. He decides to visit a totally silent Nigel. At this very moment, there was an almighty crash, followed by a pregnant silence. Then, out of Nigel's peg, comes an hysterical shout, the contents of which are unprintable. Rushing around, Adrian encounters Nigel, crawling out of his bivvy, next to which, unaccountably, has fallen a huge elm, the main branches having missed Nigel by inches. It was two very shocked carp anglers who packed up rather early that morning. Why all the rats charging along one bank? Why an ancient elm crashing down when there was hardly any wind? Were these events anything to do with that horrible, hideous face?

Let me now relate one of my own experiences. There is probably a rational explanation for it, but it was faintly unnerving nonetheless. I was barbel fishing by myself on the River Teme, sitting quietly at the bottom of a steep bank (a typical Teme swim), rod butt tucked under arm with the middle supported by a long rest. Now, biologist Rupert Sheldrake has published a book entitled *The Sense of Being Stared At* and, like Adrian, this is just what happened to me. The peg was remote and both banks, especially the far one, were lined with trees. Suddenly, I felt uncomfortable. Turning, I saw standing at the top of the bank a woman in a white cardigan and yes, she was staring at me. Like Vic's phantom, she was silent. She looked to be in her mid thirties. I smiled, said 'Hi' and switched my attention back to the rod top. The uneasy feeling continued. I turned again and she was still there – her expression was one, I felt, of sadness. I carried on fishing; to look back again might be embarrassing. Eventually, of course, I did so and there, still, was the woman, apparently rooted to the spot. There was nothing to be afraid of, I rationalised; it was only a flesh and blood female after all (wasn't it?). She posed no threat – I was fit and had an array of improvised weaponry if needed (angler's catapult, bait knife, spiked rod rest). I turned away, feeling strangely vulnerable and distinctly uneasy. No, I'll confront her – politely, of course, thinks I, and I stood up making to climb the bank. She had gone. It had only been seconds since I had been looking at her. Mystified, I climbed to the top, expecting to see her on the path. Nothing – she appeared to have vanished into thin air. I checked the pegs either side of me, looked across the open hop field; nowhere was there a woman in a white cardigan, or anyone else for that matter. What had happened to her? I just do not know! I christened her The White Lady of Lindridge and got well and truly ragged by the Dudley PAC lot when I recounted the story. These days I am not too happy fishing alone in remote places. Maybe I had fallen asleep and was dreaming, maybe I was hallucinating, maybe…

Another weird experience involving someone dressed in white occurred while fishing in mid Wales. Strangely, I cannot recall who my companion was that day. At the other side of the river was a field, sloping up to scree and a near-vertical rock face, above which was a mountain. About mid morning, we noticed a white figure moving around the edge of the field. Curious, we took out the binoculars and had a closer look. The form was human, apparently dressed from head to toe in a monk's habit, complete with cowl pulled over the head. It was slowly traversing the circumference of the field, probably twenty feet or so from the surrounding hedge. This continued for about an hour with little or no deviation of path, then the figure was gone – where to, heaven knows. There was no one else around, no car in the lane and frankly no obvious explanation either (other than the local nutcase). We christened the person the Phantom White Monk of Llanbister – a white witch conducting some pagan ritual maybe, or the farmer playing a practical joke? June even suggested that it was a scientist in protective suit doing tests for radiation following the Chernobyl accident. I shall never know.

To me, when fishing, different waters appear to have particular atmospheres. Is this just imagination or is there something more to it? Psychics like Derek Acorah claim to be able to plug in to such background manifestations. Is there really such a thing as 'spirit of place'? Is this related to Carl Jung's collective unconscious (see 'Quantum Field')? I do know that I am less happy fishing some waters alone than others. One water comes to mind where wild horses would not have got me there alone, particularly at night. I understand that the place has now been turned into some sort of country park, but years ago Kyre Pool on the Worcestershire/Herefordshire border had a reputation for being a real frightener. Paul Williams and friend once tried to carp fish it at night, setting up under the pines which covered the steep eastern bank. By the middle of the night, the atmosphere was, in Paul's words, so oppressive that eventually panic set in. The two decided that discretion was the better part of valour and, hurriedly packing their tackle, literally fled the scene. Some time after this, June and I went to explore the place; Natalie, then a toddler, was in her buggy and we proceeded to walk around the pool. We had barely begun when Youngster started to scream. She screamed and screamed and screamed. Nothing would placate her. In the end, we retraced our steps and returned to the car. Daughter promptly quietened down and, once the car doors were shut, returned to her usual, bubbly self. Could she, at less than two years old, sense something that was not apparent to her parents? Anyway, I removed Kyre Pool from my list of potential carp waters.

It is not just ghosts or even oppressive atmospheres that can interrupt our contemplations. Over the years, the media have carried stories concerning large (usually black) cat-like creatures roaming the countryside. Photographs and even video recordings have been taken and published or shown on television. Last summer, Frank Hodgkiss and I encountered such a creature while barbel fishing on the River Teme. Being eyeballed by the black beast was a remarkable experience, to say the least. We were packing up one evening, having fished side by side opposite a sunken tree. At the top of our bank was a narrow stretch of field, followed by a sleep slope up on to an open ridge. Frank climbed up our bank with some of his tackle. On reaching the top, he stopped, rooted to the spot. 'Come up here quick,' he hissed.

'What's the problem?' I retorted.

'Make it snappy,' was the response. On the ridgeline stood a creature, motionless and silhouetted against the blue sky. It was jet black and the shape of a cat. But what a cat! What was more, it had its gaze firmly fixed on us, as if trying to stare us out. The distance I would guess was around a hundred yards. If it was a cat, then it was huge, but it was the d—m thing's demeanour that was so off-putting. It was as if it owned the place and was telling us in no uncertain terms that our presence on its patch was very much resented. The situation was what the Americans call a stand off.

Neither side budged. We did not have any binoculars and after a time I thought of the camera in my bag, back in the pitch, but before I could move, the creature moved slowly to its right, as if reading my thoughts. Like a skilled infantryman, in doing so it reduced its silhouette but was still able to keep its gaze firmly upon us. We brought up the rest of the tackle and it was still there. A decisive move towards it would have probably spooked it, or resulted in one of us being savaged, so we left it where it was. Back at the farm, Frank flagged down the farmer in his tractor and told him of our experience. Of yes, he had encountered the beast himself – 'It's an (adjective) great (unprintable)' was the response, 'I don't know where it has come from and I wish it would (expletive) go away. It is an (adjective) good job I don't keep sheep.' As a countryman, he appeared not too phased by the creature and seemed to see it purely in terms of his financial balance sheet. When you are high off the ground, driving a rather large Massey Ferguson and protected by sheet metal, I suppose that you can take such a line. When on foot and encumbered by tackle, it seemed appropriate to take a rather different view of the farmer's unwelcome and uninvited guest.

At least the black beast was a denizen of this earth (or was it?). I have been fascinated by UFOs since my undergraduate days, have read widely on the subject and am firmly convinced that, in legal jargon, there is a case to be answered. What they are and where they come from is another matter. Well-known sea trout angler, the late F W Holliday, had a similar interest – rumours persist that his tragic and premature demise was not as natural as it was made out to be. As stated earlier, I have had four sightings myself, though not when fishing. Fred J Taylor had his experience while returning home from fishing. The same happened to Dick and Pam Smith while returning to Leominster from a carp trip at the well-known lake at Llandrindod Wells. They were driving, at night, through the lonely Radnor Forest, when they spotted a bright light in the sky to the right of the car; it appeared to be keeping pace with them. This went on for miles and was more than a little disturbing, especially given their situation. Even though the object was at times screened by trees, it stuck with them and only disappeared when they reached the built-up area.

Ian Jarvis and Rob Andrews had a similar experience. They were once eel fishing in the canal close to Powis Castle not far from Welshpool. Sometime around midnight, a light appeared in the sky above the castle and began silently to dance. They were on their own and more than faintly unnerved. It shot off, only to be replaced by a second such object, which repeated the performance. Neither witness had a clue what they were. This experience was rather similar to one of mine when, early one morning, I observed a single, silent light cavorting in the sky, apparently at low altitude, through our bedroom window – it was well below the cloud base. June actually hid under the bedclothes and refused to look at it! It eventually disappeared behind our neighbour's house.

These UFO experiences pale into insignificance, however, when compared with what happened to seventy-eight-year-old angler Alfred Burtoo. This is a well-known case in the UFO community but is worth airing here. Alf was a local historian and had been a regular soldier, serving throughout the Second World War. On 12 August 1983, our Alf was fishing by himself at night on the Aldershot–Basingstoke Canal, close to Buller Barracks near Aldershot. Suddenly, a brilliant white light appeared close above the building behind him, moving in his direction. It seemed to land somewhere further down the canal. Minutes later, he was confronted by two small beings (he described them as 'forms') about four feet high, who indicated to him that he was to follow them. Most people would have turned and run, but for some reason Alf did as he was asked. Parked on the towpath was a circular, luminous craft, about forty to forty-five feet across. He was escorted on board to be greeted by two other, similar, beings. All four were dressed in pale green one-piece suits that seemed to cling to their bodies. Their faces were covered by visors. The inside of the craft was black and appeared seamless, with a central shaft from floor to ceiling. Alf was instructed, presumably in English, by his new friends to 'come and stand under the amber light,' and was then asked his age. He was then informed that 'you are too old and infirm for our purpose' and was ushered back on to the towpath. The craft left and Alf, being a true disciple of Isaac, went back to his fishing! Alf apparently never claimed that he had been involved with aliens; he maintained that the craft was terrestrial and probably came from Asia. Anyway, he went on to take five rudd, three roach and a tench, and was rather miffed at losing a big carp in the weeds. He reported the incident to a patrol of Royal Military Police which had conveniently appeared, and who seemed to have been already aware that something odd had happened. His main fear was telling his wife – he was afraid that she would ban him from going fishing! Alf stuck to his account until his dying day. You can make what you will of this story.

It gets worse! Back in 1973 (11 October, to be precise), keen angler Charles Hickson took a colleague for a night's fishing off a pier at the abandoned Schaupeter Shipyard in Pascagoula, Florida. Like Alf (and me), Charles preferred to fish in seclusion, but this was to be his downfall. A revolving, egg-shaped object appeared and hovered over the pier, cutting off any retreat. They estimated it to be thirty feet maximum in diameter and ten feet high. Terror struck, both men observed an opening in the 'thing', out of which 'floated' three weird entities. 'My flesh crawls even now when I think of them,' Hickson stated years later to British investigators. The visitors had long arms with mitten-like hands, and feet that resembled those of elephants. Pointed projections on their heads replaced noses and ears. The two anglers were seized and taken aboard the craft. The second angler, Calvin Parker, at this point seems to have lost consciousness, whereas Hickson, following a searing pain in his arm, appears to have been placed on some sort of scanner. The next thing both men knew was that they were back on the pier, amongst their scattered tackle and deep in shock. Confused, and with Hickson's arm bleeding, they finally made it to the sheriff's office. They were separated and asked to write down details of their ordeal – the sheriff even bugged a room in which they had been left to rest. Following medical examination by a doctor, Bernard Best, the authorities concluded that both men were telling the truth; joint hallucination or fabrication was completely ruled out. Their conversation while alone showed fear and great agitation, as well as concern for their own credibility. Parker, terribly traumatised, subsequently suffered a severe nervous breakdown.

In a parallel incident in August 1976, identical twins Jim and Jack Weiner, together with friends Charlie Foltz and Chuck Rak, were fishing at night on Eagle Lake in the Allagash National Wilderness in Maine. Abducted by buglike creatures, they seem to have been taken into a ball of what appeared to be plasmic energy and subjected to procedures that are best not described. After being returned to the beach from which they had been fishing, all four subsequently passed polygraph tests and, feeling that they have been 'tagged', go in terror of a repeat abduction.

We seem then to have another set of reasons for not fishing alone (or even with friends, as in the above instance) in remote places. When you think of the literally thousands of people who disappear each year in Britain alone, maybe these anglers had lucky escapes. Alf Burtoo seems to have inadvertently stumbled on one of the more bizarre benefits of old age – being rejected as an abductee! At least therefore I do not have to worry; neither do a significant number of the members of the Dudley region of the PAC. This happy band have such idiosyncratic ways of dressing when out plying their rods that the sight of them would be enough to cause even the most determined of aliens to think twice! I wonder what the good inhabitants of Stephen Hawking's Dimension 11 would think of a man who goes pike fishing wearing a top hat, bow tie and tails?

Have you ever come across weird coincidences? Dick Smith has a good one. He had been pike fishing on Loch Awe, in Argyll. On his way home, he stopped at the delightful little town of Inveraray, on the shore of Loch Fyne, which is a sea loch. Standing looking over the water next to a lamp post, Dick noticed a flight of mackerel feathers festooned around the lamp. Some poor devil has made an impressive mis-cast, thinks Dick, and forgot about the incident. Two weeks later, back home in Herefordshire, Dick goes into the local tackle shop for some bits and pieces. Inside, a young angler is speaking of his fishing holiday in Scotland – 'We did some mackerel fishing at Inveraray.'

'Did you lose a rig up a lamp post?' says Dick.

'How the hell did you know that!' exclaimed the young man. Now, as one versed in statistics, I would find it difficult to calculate the odds of such an event happening – two weeks later and over four hundred miles away, Dick not only encounters the guy who lost the rig, but is able to identify him through a conversation the latter was having with a third party. Can such an event be pure chance? Just how far do the tails of the statistician's normal curve stretch? Is something else going on here? Eminent thinkers and scientists such as Arthur Koestler, Carl Jung, Camille Flammarion and Wolfgang Pauli thought that this might be so. It certainly seems to be true in the case of the Library Angel, beloved of academics.

I was aided twice by the Angel while writing this book. On holiday in the Algarve, we were watching a show in the hotel and I was mulling over what to include in this chapter. Alfred Burtoo came to mind but I needed to check the details and could not remember the reference. Behind me, twenty feet away, was a bookcase containing novels which could be borrowed by the guests. Next morning June, a whodunnit addict, went to the case to change her book. Casting my eye across the shelves, I noticed a small, black tome that seemed familiar. It was Timothy Good's *Alien Base*. Intrigued, I took it from the shelf and opened it – facing me on the page was the story of Alf Burtoo! There were over a hundred books in the case, and it was the only non-fiction work – when thinking of Alf the night before, I had been within twenty feet of the reference, and we were hundreds of miles from home in Portugal! The next day, the book had disappeared. Earlier, when writing the first chapter, I wanted to check on Albert Oldfield's roach catches. Thinking that the *Midland Angler* might be a place to start, I took one from the many on the file – it fell open and there was a piece on roach by Albert Oldfield. This sort of meaningful (and helpful) coincidence is referred to as a 'synchronicity' and can produce some weird results. Sometimes, similar paranormal phenomena can save you from injury or even death – I will conclude with such an account.

On 7 July 2005, June and I were in the USA. Back home, Natalie took a telephone call from June's brother, Stephen (an angler, my only formal justification for including the story here). Uncle Stephen was obviously very shaken indeed. He had travelled to London to attend a conference and, in order to complete his journey, had boarded a tube train. Stepping on to the train, he had an overwhelming feeling that all was not right. The feeling was so powerful that, before the doors could close, he jumped off, deciding to wait for the next train. The doors closed and the train disappeared into the tunnel. Seconds later, the suicide bomber on board triggered his detonator.

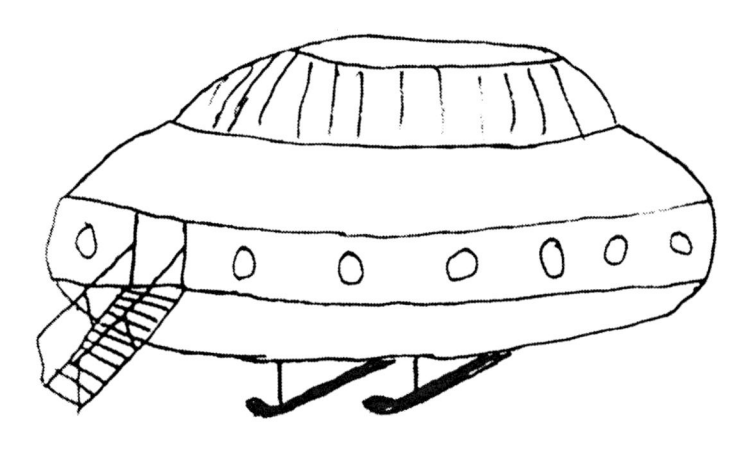

A tracing of Alfred Burtoo's UFO.
('Beyond Top Secret' by Timothy Good, Sidgewick and Jackson, 1996,
with kind permission from the author and publisher)

David Hendry with a brace of big Severn roach and not a cavalier in sight!
(David Hendry)

I Shall Be Glad When I Have Had Enough of This!

Get Hooked on Fishing. (Anne Moyle, GHOF)

Just why do we do it? I have just returned from a tench fishing trip. It all looked good – in the planning. Up at 3 a.m., I collected Frank Hodgkiss an hour or so later and we motored through the half light, way into deepest Shropshire. The weather forecast had been reasonable and we had high hopes, even to the extent of personal bests. It was drizzling when we arrived – I never like tackling up in the rain, but warm, light rain in my experience borders on ideal tench-fishing weather. The problem was that this rain was anything but warm. We were sure that it would clear, anyway. I got into a reasonable tench first chuck which, after a bit of a scrap, came adrift. The rig was a stepped-up version of our roach rig (see 'Pestered by Riff-Raff') – such events happen with small hooks. The wind increased and so did the rain.

Despite waders and 'waterproof' coat (waterproof when bought twenty years ago!), the wet soaked onto my back and down my arms. I needed a warm jumper and my poncho – the cold penetrated deep. I started to catch a fish or two, including one just under five pounds, but it was more than uncomfortable. Frank huddled under his brolly; mine kept blowing over. I took another couple of fish. It warmed slightly as the morning wore on. Tiredness set in – getting up so early, age and medication were taking their toll. I dozed off. The alarm clock sounds strange, I thought, waking to just about rescue one of my rods from disappearing into the depths. The three-pound male tench was a poor reward. Soaked, frozen and shattered, we drove the sixty miles home. The rush hour traffic in Wolverhampton was a nightmare. A hot shower, a (too) large glass of whisky and I just about collapsed. The title of this chapter, a saying publicised by Fred J Taylor, had been foremost in my mind all day.

The sacrifices we make for our sport ('opportunity costs' to the economist) are huge. Add the cost of petrol, bait, time taken to set up rigs at home and pack the whole lot up, and the above trip (in retrospect) could be construed as irrational behaviour writ large. Examine the big picture. Angling is a way of life, it can take you over; other (important) things get pushed aside. I have lost track of the number of marriages that have failed because of it. Once the demon gets hold, it can control almost your every thought. I remember an anti, in a debate, claiming that angling is an addiction, presumably trying to make a link to drug-taking (BB did, after all, write *Confessions of a Carp Fisher*). An addiction can simply be defined as 'something that you can't stop doing'. On this definition, angling is an addiction. But then again, so are many other things. Addictions, defined thus, are not necessarily bad, but they do need to be managed and set within the wider context of life. It is when imbalance cuts in and things get out of proportion that the problems occur. I have always tried (not totally successfully) to balance my fishing with other interests and with those of my family and career. I changed my academic contract at my university to give me more fishing time – it cost a lot of money, though I never counted that cost; my fishing was beyond monetary value.

And that is the point. There is a massive upside to all this. We have dealt with the costs, let's now do our economics and look at the benefits. We live in a mad world, increasingly soaked in inconsequentiality and suffering from information overload.

Despite all the hype about education, one gets the distinct impression that there are many members of modern society who cannot think at all. British educational standards have declined massively over my lifetime – I know, I was in the thick of it. Most individuals these days seem to swim in a sea of trivia eagerly devoured from tabloid newspapers, trashy magazines, the internet and computer games, plus implausible and often downright nasty soap operas. Their conscious minds must be getting so constrained that there is a distinct danger that the media are becoming the collective unconscious, with the human brain being eventually supplanted by the microchip. A society made up of mindless, amoral non-entities who have lost the ability to reason or think critically borders on an Orwellian nightmare, especially when one considers the impact of literalist religion, the human race's penchant for killing and torturing in the name of 'god', and the ever-growing threat of environmental catastrophe. If there are aliens out there, is there any wonder they keep their distance? We, as individuals, can do little to alter things. But we can attempt to stay sane. 'Follow your rod' and you will find a way out – fishing is the escape tunnel, and for an increasing number of people. The places one visits, the incredible interface with nature that is the reward, the intellectual stimulus, all set the thinking angler above the man in the street. I never cease to be amazed at how far removed from reality many people are. Not long ago, the environment correspondent of the BBC's *Midlands Today*, a science PhD no less, was revelling in the fact that he had seen his first kingfisher! I have seen half a dozen in the last three days – where had the man been for the last forty years? And he is employed to be an expert on the environment! Is there any wonder that Bambi reigns supreme (see 'Civilisation Lost (or Gained?')? When I was a child, we were taken pond-dipping in nature study lessons by a teacher who herself had grown up close to nature – the waterside is a fantastic, therapeutic place. Today, kids cannot be taken near to water they might fall in and catch a cold. As Robin Page has pointed out, it is this being close to nature that so defines the field sports enthusiast – we are not the products of a bygone age, but ought to be pointing the way to a saner, more civilised, world. Dick Orton used to liken anglers to the Native Americans, always being driven back, forced to give ground, in the face of an urban, materialistic colossus that will eventually overwhelm us. Let us hope that Dick was wrong – the power of our genes may drive us forward, but we should not forget angling's powerful self-destruct mechanisms, which are explored in 'Civilisation Lost (or Gained?)'.

There has recently been a study of children's attitudes to life conducted by the British Market Research Bureau, as well as the results of a survey of similar research by the Children's Play Council. It is encouraging stuff which destroys many of the myths concerning kids today. They do not prefer television and computer games – far from it. Eighty-six percent in the survey preferred outdoor activities, including building dens and getting muddy. The Children's Play Council stresses that children have a deep-rooted sensitivity to the natural world – play is actually the process by which kids fulfil their drive to affiliate with nature. The corollary of this is that lack of outdoor activities impact on environmental awareness – computers, overprotective (and litigious) parents, and sheer lack of space, all result in a breach in that all-important connection with the natural environment. Salmon grow in tins, milk comes from the supermarket, legs are replaced by the four-by-four. Is there any wonder that anti-field sport attitudes abound, that we have an epidemic of child obesity and drug-taking, and that feral youth roam the streets causing mayhem in their communities? It is not the children's fault – they are no different from Phil Burford and me half a century ago. It is up to us adults to put things right. I am reminded of Gromit's granddaughter Alex, who can out-fish her grandfather, cast a fly, and insists on killing her own trout. She quite happily hooks and lands decent pike, treating any offer of assistance by her elders with disdain – a model for the future if ever there was one.

To be anything like a competent angler, one needs a blend of many skills, both intellectual and physical. Meteorology, geomorphology, biology, chemistry (especially if modern baits are factored in), ecology, mechanics, field-craft, physical stamina, powers of observation, the ability to handle a boat and to manage risk (controlled exposure is far preferable to avoidance) – the list is long. Angling's contribution to healthy living, and not just in the young, is a powerful one. The Countryside Alliance's 'Get Hooked on Fishing' is a pioneer effort here, and has demonstrated the positive impact of angling, particularly on young people from inner urban locations. The initial pilot was in Durham, run by PC Mick Watson. Since 2000, some five hundred and forty-three youngsters attended, of whom two hundred and twelve were on final warnings or had received reprimands. The results were astounding – there were no reports of reoffending and the truancy rate fell by seventy-five percent. The participants submitted some three hundred and fifty pieces of written work, and over two thousand mentoring contracts were made. Local to where I live, the Bournville Village Trust, aided by Charles Jardine and Andy Walker, has refurbished a local pool and instigated courses in fishing for local youngsters – reoffending rates among those attending are less than two percent. These initiatives are being replicated elsewhere – the results are not totally surprising to those of us reared the 'old way' and are a powerful step forward. Soon, hopefully, fishing will be on the school curriculum, providing, of course, that politicians change their attitude – a major obstacle that I explore (pessimistically) in 'Civilisation Lost (or Gained?)'. The benefits, of course, accrue to all participants. For adults, fly fishing is being pioneered as therapy for breast cancer patients both in the USA and in the UK – the latter initiative being driven by the Countryside Alliance. Similar work is being done in relation to patients with epilepsy.

So why is fishing so therapeutic? I am going to stick my neck out here and develop my own perspective. I have studied yoga for some years now and have come to the conclusion that there are links between both activities that should at least be considered. Such a perspective might even improve your catches, as we shall see. Modern life can push the human system beyond its design parameters; stress is now a significant problem for many. PEST (Protestant Ethic Syndrome Trauma) is endemic in modern society. Some anglers, of course, carry modern attitudes into their fishing – competitiveness, pressure, selfishness, one-upmanship, 'got to catch 'x' number of doubles this season/get my photograph in the press/get another personal best' etc. This, to me, is the very antithesis of what angling is all about, just as it was to Bernard Venables and BB. Was it not Isaac himself who called our sport 'the contemplative man's recreation'? Yoga and contemplation go hand in hand – to me, angling is applied yoga. Yoga is not a religion but a profound and powerful path to self-realisation. It is about being balanced, centred, and co-ordinated – a path into inner stillness where one's higher self can take over from the churning madness of everyday existence and synchronise one's mental processes with the quantum energy field of which we are all a manifestation. As one who has led a fairly pressurised existence, it was only when I began to study yoga that I realised why I had such a desire to fish. Central to the process is the ability to focus, to shut off from the maelstrom of chaotic thought that characterises our everyday existence. The resulting mental (and physical) relaxation ultimately moves one onto a higher mental plane – things fall into perspective, one sees the world in the light of a greater purpose and, ultimately, one's higher self takes over. This, of course, is meditation – self-realisation follows – the essence of being, engaging with the very energy that we are made of. Just what do we do when we go fishing? We focus. Even major problems get pushed into the background and can be observed from a different perspective. When the rod top slams over and a barbel charges for the nearest sunken tree, one does not have time to worry about the mortgage payments! Simply sitting on a river bank, in tune with nature and interfacing with other creatures and flora, is, to me, the very essence of meditative practice, the gateway to engaging with one's higher self. Candle-staring is one way that yoga teachers train students to focus – does not watching a float do exactly the same thing? A pike float, bobbing on a gentle swell, or being pulled gently around by a live bait, is a mesmerising experience – the coloured top (often, if not usually, red – the colour of the base chakra) surely performs the same function as the candle flame. Trotting a float on a gentle stream is little different, and even a rod top or pike 'drop-off' can fulfil the same function. Forget electronic bite alarms! Seen thus, angling is a process of renewal – at the end of a day's fishing, good or bad, one sees the world in a different light, things have fallen into place a little and sanity has, albeit temporarily, returned.

Water is immensely powerful stuff. I am drawn to it like iron filings to a magnet. I can sit by a river for hours, just watching the stream. Its very presence is calming. When frozen, ice crystals can be demonstrated to react to their environment, even (as Masaru Emoto has spectacularly demonstrated) to human emotion. It comprises the major component in our bodies. Its more subtle properties still generate controversy among scientists, as the debate over homeopathy demonstrates. Anglers interface with it in a gentle way, unlike power-boaters, water-skiers and the like. We treat it with respect and at least a minority of us actively fight those who wish to abuse it. It rewards us with its bounty and soothes our shattered nerves. Interacting with it can be a vehicle in achieving a higher state of consciousness, students of yoga would be clear about that. Peace, the attainment of higher values, self-realisation and a more profound understanding of human purpose can be the end result – we anglers (at least those of the old school) may be on to something pretty profound here. It is a pity that many of our fellows increasingly attempt (sadly often successfully) to turn our sport into an extension of the very thing from which we are in reality attempting to escape – pressure, competition, stress, infighting and downright nastiness can all feature, sadly, in the modern 'scene' and are abominations to the soul. Such anglers have really lost the plot – possibly they have come to things too early in their spiritual evolution or maybe, just maybe, after a time, the values of the true disciple will become apparent and they take on board the real message. Angling then becomes a vehicle for the development of their very souls, and a profound one at that.

To anyone infected with the competitive spirit, this is probably ballyhoo, rubbish of the highest order (if rubbish can have a highest order!). To such anglers, I would add a caveat – such New Age perspectives might just improve your catches, so read on, I dare you! One major implication of accepting the existence of the quantum field is that mind and matter become unified – an 'unbroken wholeness' in physicist David Bohm's words. We, and fish, are no longer individuals, but all are components of a greater whole. All life, including plants (vegetarians please note), is constantly exchanging information with the zero point field. Our individuality becomes a myth – where do we end and a shoal of roach begin? Part 2 of Lynne McTaggart's book *The Field* is entitled 'The Extended Mind', and begins with a quote from Krishnamurti – 'You are the world'. This says it all. Maverick biologist Rupert Sheldrake draws out implications that could impact profoundly on us anglers. Among his many works, three stand out: *The Presence of the Past: Morphic Resonance and the Habits of Nature*; *Dogs That Know When Their Owners Are Coming Home, And Other Unexplained Powers Of Animals* and *The Sense of Being Stared At And Other Aspects Of The Extended Mind*. Take a look!

Let me give you an example of what is being proposed. In 'God's River', I introduced Bob Allen, with whom I fished the Teme nearly forty years ago. During the Second World War, Bob had a pet dog which lived with his parents in Stourbridge. Despite the acute danger of his flying raid after raid over Germany, the dog remained unfazed. As far as the timing can be ascertained, however, the moment that his aircraft was hit by the German night fighter, the dog, hundreds of miles away, went berserk. Sheldrake gives many similar examples to demonstrate just how far we are all interconnected. He gives evidence, for example, that, statistically speaking, we have an idea who is telephoning before we pick up the receiver. More recently, in the 2004 tsunami, the animals plus the primitive tribes all made good their escape, leaving the more left-brained and 'sophisticated' humans to do the dying. If dogs know when their owners are returning and when the latter are in mortal danger, if animals know that a big wave is on the way, it follows that fish may also know when they are being angled for! Have you ever thought of that? There were hints of a parallel idea back in 1980 in an article by Duncan Kay in *The Third British Carp Study Group Book*, but, by and large, the idea does not seem to feature in angling literature. We accept that physical concealment is all-important for successful specimen hunting (I am reminded of my Teme chub), but what about psychic concealment? It is all very well staying out of a fish's sight and avoiding vibrations, but if your churning mind is sending out a quantum signal which effectively says, 'I'm here – trying to stick a hook in your mouth' then you will probably not catch anyway! Think about it – how often have you tried so hard to succeed that you seem to simply reinforce your failure? In the end, you give up trying to get a pike run and go gudgeon fishing instead! In the winter of 2004/2005, Gromit got himself into this sort of pickle – blank after blank, twenty-three of them on the trot (twenty-three – that number again). He tore his hair out (he still had some), kicked the dog, swore at Sylvia his long-suffering 'missus', got ratty with me (my waving a twenty-pound pike in front of him did not help), stormed out of meetings, and generally got himself into a right old flap. In the end, he gave up trying to catch a pike and went carp fishing instead – success immediately followed. If you doubt all this, read what Sheldrake (and McTaggart) have to say – if still in doubt, log on to Princeton University's Global Consciousness Project on http://noosphere.princeton.edu, and view some empirical results for yourself. Sheldrake specifically deals with angling in *The Sense of Being Stared At*, p.153. Get too excited and tense, let your heart race, and the fish will know. This may explain an often-observed phenomenon in pike fishing – huge fish caught by total novices. The latter succeed because of their mental attitude.

So what can you do about it? The answer is simple – relax, don't try so hard! We students of yoga know a bit about keeping our psychic heads down. You must do the same, though I would not advise the use of whisky as recommended by Sheldrake's angler correspondent! However, does correct mental attitude explain why some anglers do better than others, despite fishing the same waters with similar methods and at similar times? My arch example is Robert Pashley (see 'God's River'). He shared his beats with others and even fished with inferior tackle, yet no one came anywhere near to approaching his catches. A lot of his salmon were taken on a battered old trout rod that, after each fish, had to be placed on the ground and walked along to get it reasonably straight again! His Devon minnows were so heavy they cast like bricks and moved through the water like bricks. Was his mental attitude a factor? Just as modern military aircraft can no longer rely on physical camouflage for concealment, was Pashley able to conceal himself within the electro-magnetic spectrum in the same way as a stealth aircraft or via the equivalent of a Tornado's jamming pod? The former, I feel, is a better analogy. Or, like the Vulcan XM607 that attacked the airfield at Port Stanley, was he able to 'fly' under the fishes' 'radar'?

Let me introduce what I shall term the Pashley–Stevens Conjecture (Stevens is Gromit's surname). A conjecture is just that – it is not as specific as an hypothesis and is something that may never be supported by mathematical proof or even unequivocal empirical evidence. My copy of the *Concise Oxford English Dictionary* defines the term as the 'formation of opinion without sufficient grounds,' so it may be total b—s (and probably is!). But the PSC is worth an airing. In the diagram, there are three curves. The background curve represents the characteristics of the underlying field (or fields – who knows?) in terms of frequency, amplitude, wavelength and so on. Lynne McTaggart describes this as a 'system of exchanged and patterned energy'. The Pashley curve represents the characteristics of the signals relating to the interaction between the mind of someone (like Pashley?) who, through some mental process, is able to screen his or her presence from other biological units to which he/she is linked via the quantum field (the term 'coherence' come to mind). The Gromit curve, by contrast, represents the signals from some poor so-and-so who is struggling to catch, getting het up, and who is generally frustrated and out of sorts (the term 'incoherence' comes similarly to mind). Such a person may be literally sticking out like a pair of bull's b—s, even if they are physically concealed and doing everything else right. Angling success thus may not be just about technical competence.

The PSC can be summed up as follows: an angler's ability to capture his or her intended quarry does not just depend on technical skills such as fish location, tackle, bait, and physical concealment – mental attitude, which determines the degree of psychic coherence with the quantum field, is possibly a significant variable in accounting for individual success or failure.

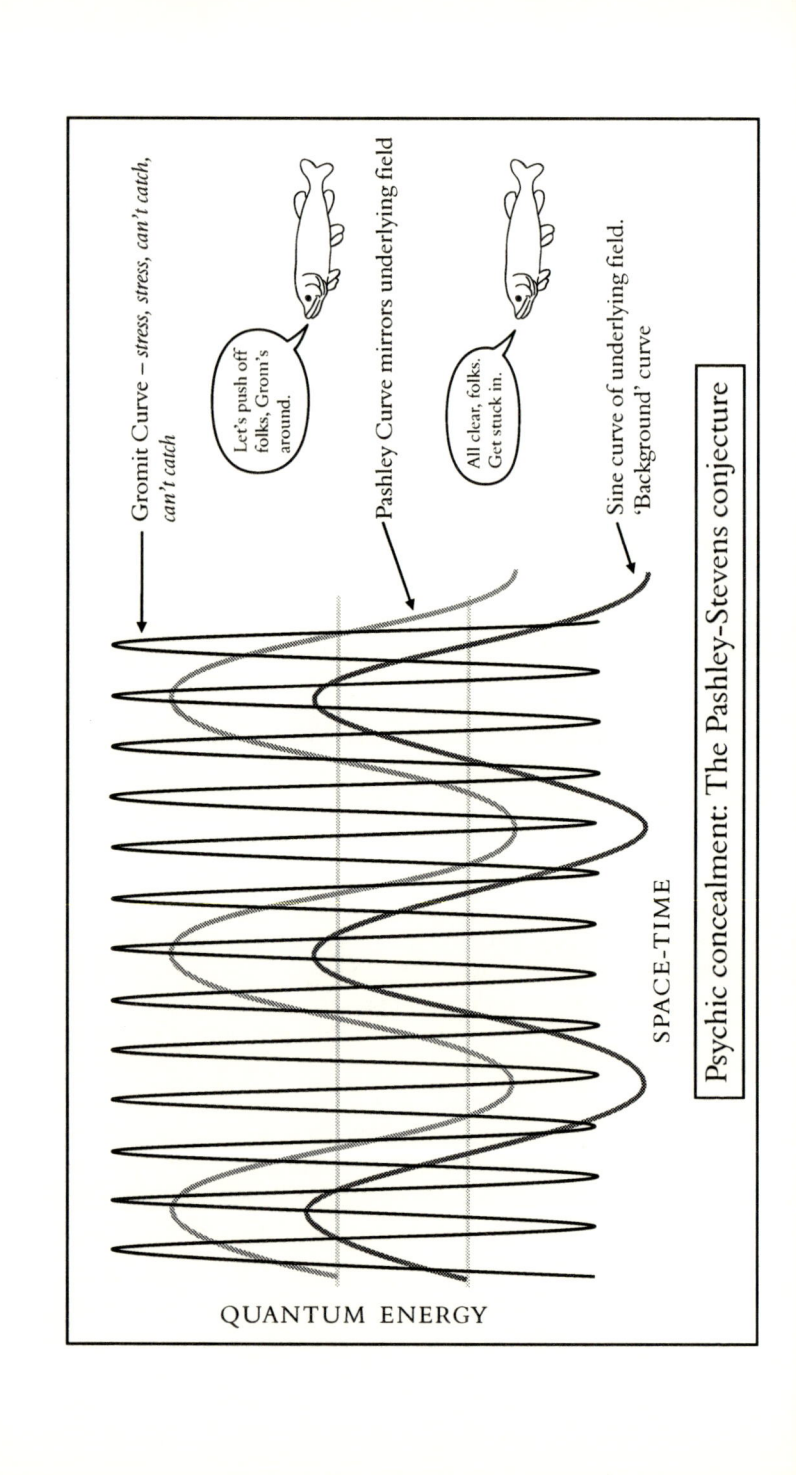

Psychic concealment: The Pashley-Stevens conjecture

So, how do you go about keeping your psychic head down? It is easy to say 'stop trying'. Yes, you must do things correctly – location, tackle, bait and so on. But you must also shut off mentally. How do you do this? Back to yoga! Yoga is the Sanskrit word for 'union'; the Pashley curve is in union with the background field, the Gromit curve is not. As old Isaac stressed, contemplation is the answer – to succeed it may help to be in a meditative state. My dictionary even defines contemplation as 'meditate on', and meditation as 'serious contemplation'. There is nothing new here – Isaac got there first! Maybe it is time that this ancient perspective on angling success was resurrected? It is not the purpose of this chapter to teach you meditative practice, let alone put you through an introductory course on yoga, but if you can shut off and let your higher self take over, you may be able to reduce your psychic signature and get through or below the fishes' radar. Is this what Richard Walker meant by his famous remark, 'You have got to be deadly'; words that upset Bernard Venables? Perhaps the latter misinterpreted their underlying meaning – no one was more for back to basics than Mr Crabtree! Or was Walker simply the supreme technician? Was catching fish just an extension of the principles of engineering that he studied at university? Or was he another Pashley, his penchant for better tackle and physical concealment being a veneer to cover something more profound? I do not know. My own experiences possibly back up the PSC. I struggled to catch my first tench from the Breeches Pool and failed dismally – my first such fish was taken bream fishing on a river when tench were far from my thoughts. It was the same for my first double-figure pike – after catching nines almost by the dozen, my first fully confirmed double came while roach fishing. The harder I tried to get a two-pound roach, the more one twelves, one thirteens and one fourteens I caught. Is the PSC species-specific? Is it size-specific? Or is it cobblers? Put it to the test and form your own opinion. I tentatively suggest that individual angling success will never be fully explained without taking the psi variable into account.

One final implication of all this is that there may be a link, however tenuous, between our sport and the practices of Eastern mysticism. Given what is happening in modern society, this may be no bad thing and may underpin angling's popularity, something that seems to have a momentum all of its own despite the forces that wish to restrain it. Given the individual benefits I have outlined, plus the undoubted environmental spin-offs from our sport, you would think that angling would have broad societal support, with government resources to match. The reality is dealt with in the following chapter. What is more, on the *Richard and Judy* programme last night, there was a piece on a trout fishery in the north of England which had been 'sabbed' by a bunch of animal rights activists who, unable to vent their wrath on a local shoot, had attacked a small group of anglers instead. The latter, including two women, were heavily outnumbered. One angler finished up in hospital, having been repeated stabbed with a hypodermic syringe (the consequences are unthinkable); one woman was set upon by a group of thugs of both sexes – her fishing rod, a gift from her father, was smashed. It was a cowardly display by sub-humans who, of course, concealed their identity with balaclavas. Typically, despite police being called out, no arrests were made.

Such an incident is far from unique. So what has gone wrong? Why attack an activity that appears to be so beneficial, that unites professors and plumbers, and has such a rich literature? Why is so little government money put into our sport? Why does it receive so little attention from the media, and why is that attention usually so negative? Was Dick Orton right and are we condemned to be swept aside by the current tide of madness? You will not find the following chapter comfortable reading, particularly in view of my contention that we anglers are, at least in part, responsible for our own predicament. It is time for all anglers to wake up before it is too late. Our very existence is at stake. If the truth hurts, then be prepared not only to feel pain but, for society's sake as well as your own, do something about it.

Civilisation Lost (or Gained?)

Bambi has a lot of answer for.

I have a confession. I am an anti-angler. No, I have not become a member of Pisces, a childish organisation if there ever was one. Being an insider, my objections to anglers are much more fundamental. Note that I say anglers and not angling. The latter has been a lifelong passion and will continue to be so; my concerns relate not to cruelty to fish but to the attitudes and activities of my fellow brothers of the angle, which in my estimation comprise far more of a threat to the sport than all the animal libbers put together. There, I have said it – angling's great enemy is the anglers themselves. There is nothing new to this phenomenon, but, of late, I do feel that we fisherman are in danger not just of losing out, but of losing the plot completely. I make no apologies for making such statements. It is about time that someone stuck their head above the parapet and said it out loud. I speak as a coarse angler who does a fair bit of trout fishing as well, though I do not include sea anglers in my comments. Recent experience suggests that some trout anglers are the worst of the lot!

Of course, you, good reader, are at liberty to disagree and you probably will. That said, I have spent the last thirty years or so sitting on a variety of committees and have made many attempts to get anglers to engage in some serious thinking about their position. Of course, I have failed dismally. In the round, I have been subjected to some pretty severe abuse, either from people who have never bothered to lift a finger to help in running our sport or from those whose egos, once they gain some sort of position, completely take over, and who object in principle to having their errors pointed out. As I write, the angling press has been full of reports of well-known 'pike anglers' (I use the term loosely) who have allegedly been caught by Customs and Excise, attempting to take live fish across the Irish Sea for use as bait in a country where live bait is illegal. Some of these fish were reported to be carp, a non-indigenous species in Ireland and a notorious carrier of disease. The case is sub-judice and the 'facts' are allegations only, but the incident, if it happened, is typical of what is occurring in our sport today. Apathy, long recognised as a core problem, is being supplanted by ego. Adding another thirty-pound pike (albeit possibly full of spawn – the month is May) to the list and getting the photograph in the press is apparently far more important than preserving the ecology of the entire island of Ireland. Laws, what laws? They do not apply to us! Having spent years and much effort trying to preserve our right to use live fish as bait, I am perhaps entitled to wonder why I bothered in the first place.

So, let us examine how our sport may become history – together with the self-destruct mechanisms that are dragging us into the mire. We will put the psychology of the individual angler, vital as it is, on one side for a moment and examine angling's – largely implicit – 'strategy' (if one can dignify it with such a grand title) both to deal with those who would restrict or even abolish our activities and to preserve the waterside environment for our future enjoyment. This strategy has two underpinning components – isolationism and appeasement. I will take each of these in turn.

There is no doubt that there is a real political threat to angling's very existence. When one mentions this to fellow anglers, they appear to go into denial. There are between three and four million of us, they say, no politician would dare touch us! Yet many non-anglers regard angling as another blood sport (even the BBC, of which more anon), and hunting, shooting and fishing are inextricably linked in the public's collective psyche. Now the term 'blood sport' is, to me, a derogatory one; yet its use persists, despite all sorts of legislation and rules/regulations designed to prevent language that causes offence. Doesn't this tell us anglers something? In my (admittedly pessimistic) view, the threat is there, even if it not in our face. I have no strong political affiliations, being the archetypal floating voter, but it is worth pointing out that the threat does not just come from the Labour Party alone. That said, it is a fact that a ban on all blood sports was seriously proposed in Labour's Draft Manifesto of 1979. This was withdrawn when it was realised just how many anglers there were – in other words, angling was deleted from the hit list for reasons of pure expediency. Recently (March 2006, to be precise), Labour's earlier view surfaced in the House of Commons in a statement by the (then) Secretary of State for the Environment, Food and Rural Affairs, Margaret Beckett. She said, 'I've always said that when we got rid of all the other blood sports there will still be the House of Commons'. Other blood sports – with hunting illegal, such a statement could only be referring to shooting and fishing! Furthermore, when the hunting community appealed in the High Court, the judges made it clear that the legislation was 'overlaid by a moral viewpoint that causing suffering to animals for sport is unethical and should... be stopped'. If it really is Labour's moral view that basic human rights can be infringed in the case of field sports (let's get the terminology correct), then angling is in real trouble in relation to the Labour Party, no doubt about it.

It does not stop there. I have had some dealing with the Liberal Democrats and yet when it comes to this issue, the party appears neither liberal nor democratic. Many members of the party seem to take a similar view to Labour, though this is never made explicit. I always thought that being liberal was to be tolerant and to be a supporter of minority interests – when this is pointed out, there is just a choking sound on the other end of the telephone. I'm not sure that these people have even thought the thing through in relation to their core values, and have little confidence that, push come to shove, they would not jump into bed with Labour's old guard if it was felt to be of advantage. And what of the Greens, those hearty defenders of environmental values? Surely, they are angling's natural allies, you would think? After all, the Environment Agency itself has described anglers as 'the guardians of the water environment'. When the Greens first appeared on the scene, the late Ken Sutton wrote a piece in the *ACA Review*, entitled 'Greens Are Good For You'. I felt at the time that there was a need for some sort of rejoinder – too many Greens can give you serious digestive discomfort! I believe that I have subsequently been proved correct. In 'Quantum Field', I detail the behaviour of some of these people elsewhere in the quantum field and have no reason to believe that their behaviour in this dimension is any different. Trespass, vandalism, illegal notices and the construction of a huge bird hide on someone else's land without permission were all justified on the grounds that, as a wildlife trust, they had some God-given right to elbow the anglers out – the means were justified by the ends.

In his book *The Hunting Gene*, Robin Page reproduces a paragraph from the Green Party's Animal Rights Working Party. This document stresses that the Greens are in total opposition to all blood sports, including angling. The latter is alleged to cause 'unnecessary suffering', and it is made clear that the party is ready to support a ban on angling when the political climate is right. Furthermore, the reader is invited to examine the party's formal statement of policy on the subject. Animal rights and opposition to field sports are central to the party's stance – policy AR411 makes this quite clear ('AR', incidentally, stands for animal rights). This is not a green agenda at all! Such people have no right to call themselves green. Field sports have an environmental record second to none; levels of biodiversity on land that is hunted, for example, have been demonstrated in study after study to be significantly higher than elsewhere. Anglers could even lay claim to having coined the term 'conservation'. One is left to wonder how much these latter-day champions of the environment really understand about the very thing that supposedly drives their agenda. Any organisation interested in environmental enhancement should be actively supporting field sports, rather than using the law to abolish them. Both David Bellamy and HRH The Duke of Edinburgh have made this powerful point on a number of occasions, and have been castigated by the egotistical rent-a-mob groups who wish to hijack environmental concerns for their own ends. Such people are melons – green on the outside, but red in the middle. Science, facts, ethics, even their fellow human beings, are trampled underfoot in the sheer passion of the moment. In truth, environmental degradation is actually a means of bashing the nasty capitalist West rather than reflecting any real concern on issues such as biodiversity, pollution, climate change and the like. 'Environmentalism' is sadly a Western, urban, left-wing, middle-class activity more linked with vegetarianism and animal rights than with what actually constitutes good land management. One only has to look at what has happened in Germany to see the above philosophy put into practice. Following pressure from the Greens, the German government made it illegal to return any fish to the water after being caught, on the grounds that the experience caused the creature so much stress that being put down was the best option. What absolute hogwash! We pike (and, of course, carp) anglers know that fish can be caught time and time again without any harm whatsoever – pike happily take another bait after having been hooked and landed only minutes before; I once took the same fish three times in a morning, same location, same bait – so much for capture causing stress. It is no coincidence that in late 2006, it was Eleanor Scott MSP, a Green representative in the Scottish Parliament, who was a major mover in a vote proposing a ban on live baiting in that country. Make no mistake, these people are dangerous! My impression of many of the Greens is they would not know the difference between a chub and a chimpanzee; world revolution is their game, Joe Stalin their great icon.

This leaves angling relying on the support of only one major party. I do not find this position a comfortable one, especially when no attempt is made to forge any sort of strategic alliances with other field sports and organisations sharing similar interests. Can angling stand alone, as many seem to think? If there are really between three and four million of us, would many of these vote accordingly? Would anglers really put their sport in front of entrenched political allegiances? Are there even three million of us? What is an angler? Someone who owns a fishing rod and has the occasional chuck off the cliffs when on annual holiday? Would such a person be prepared to stand up and be counted if push came to shove? Or would they just take up bird-watching instead? Less than two million rod licences are sold in England and Wales each year (the latest figure I have is 1.26 million); take into account the rest of the UK, together with the sea anglers, and three million might be plausible – just. Incredibly (to me, anyway), the Environment Agency claims to have survey results for 2005 that suggest that eight million people in England and Wales alone have an interest in freshwater fishing, over half of whom have fished in the last two years. This may be good news for the isolationists, particularly if such support could be translated into votes and money. Whether this could be done, I just do not know – anglers' psychology is discussed later. What I do know is that angling has only stood alone once; on the issue of lead shot and alleged swan deaths. We were slaughtered, yes, slaughtered. Powerful and well-funded bodies such as the RSPCA and RSPB walked all over us, aided by the media (especially the BBC). No votes were involved, no political party took up our cause. To those reared on Bambi, a swan allegedly dying of lead poisoning was an awful sight and we stood no chance. Without lead shot, float fishing on our rivers died a quiet death – witness the undergrowth covering the banks of previously popular stretches of the Severn and Warwickshire Avon.

There are many ways of killing a cat, as the saying goes. Slow death by a thousand cuts can be far more effective than one massive blow. As I write, the latter approach with regard to hunting has generated exactly the opposite of what was intended; a revival in hunting's fortunes seems on the cards – the Labour Party is actually being hailed as hunting's saviour, Bruce Anderson in *The Times* waxing lyrical on a remarkable paradox. It would indeed be ironic if hunting was again made legal but the use of live fish as bait was banned – it could happen. By contrast, shooting is being treated to the 'thousand cuts' approach. The strategy is to chip away at the foundations without making too much noise ('onion peeling' – it may be no surprise that lead shot features yet again). Our enemies, stinging from the backlash following the hunting fiasco, now know this and will apply it – slowly. Would angling on its own be able to deal with such as approach? Personally, I doubt it, and so do others who have experience of dealing with fellow anglers. Tony Mobley, a man now in his fourth decade of angling administration, and who has virtually stopped fishing because of disillusion with anglers and taken up shooting instead, commented recently that 'if shooting went, angling would collapse like a pack of cards'. Such a view should be taken seriously. Do we anglers really want to be isolated? We face a multi-faceted enemy which operates on a divide and rule basis. In order to get rid of hunting, you reassure shooters and anglers that they have nothing to worry about – this false sense of security hopefully helps isolate hunting. Pour in the propaganda and down go the hunters (OK – the frontal attack may eventually prove counterproductive, but the principle survives intact). Then apply the same approach to shooting (this is exactly what has happened following the passing of the Hunting Act). Reassure the anglers that they are the good guys – just as Mr Blair did in early 2006. Quietly strangle shooting. Anglers then are on their own, lack any sort of allies, and can be quietly picked off over a number of years, bit by bit. First, establish that sticking a hook in fish is wrong by making live baits illegal, and then go for keep nets and other live baits (worms, maggots). Then state your high moral position that abusing animals for sport is ethically unacceptable, and hit the media with some carefully crafted propaganda about barbed hooks, 'scientific' evidence that fish feel pain, and birds getting tangled in fishing line. Back up your stance with statements about not encouraging youngsters to take up the activity, encourage or force local authorities and other public bodies to ban angling on waters they own and you are virtually there. A few good adverts by PETA, the RSPCA and the RSPB showing wild birds tangled in fishing line (money with these people would be no object; the propaganda value and extra recruitment would soon compensate for the loss anyway) and it's game, set and match, with no major piece of legislation involved. Alternative perspectives (see 'The Rocks Remain') and liberal values, based on human rights and the hard logic of the philosopher, would not get a look in.

I sincerely believe that angling needs as many allies as it can lay its hands on. We have a great supporter in the Environment Agency, which knows about the contribution of angling in protecting the water environment – after all, we contribute significantly to the salaries and running costs of its Fisheries Department and the Agency is involved on a day-to-day basis with angling bodies working on angling/environmental projects. The Agency is uniquely positioned to provide government and responsible non-government bodies such as the RSPB (I do not include the RSPCA here) with the facts about the benefits of the sport both to the individual and the environment. Anglers need to keep the Environment Agency on side – licence-dodging and the breaching of bylaws does us no favours at all. But that is not enough. I come back to the 'hunting, shooting, fishing/blood sports' perspective. Hunters and shooters are our natural allies and it is about time anglers recognised this. United we stand, divided we fall, literally. Many anglers shoot and even hunt, so what is the problem?

The problem, when I put this point of view to our fishing club's (ex) chairman, is that hunting and shooting are doomed anyway and to be seen to be allying with them would drag angling down as well. All we need to do is clean up our act (that is, get rid of live baits, keep nets and the like – where do you stop?), and all will be well. The otherwise excellent journal *Waterlog* seems also to take this view – my (ex) chairman is in distinguished company. I am afraid, given what I have already said, that we are back to the hogwash factor. I would humbly submit that this view, for reasons already given, is literally fatally flawed. My (ex) chairman was a shooting man as well, a lawyer who had even handled cases on behalf of shooters against the League Against Cruel Sports. To sit back and cynically let other field sports go the wall is not just bad strategy, it is plain lunacy. In the process it makes enemies of our natural allies and sends exactly the wrong signals to our real enemies. This is serious stuff! There appears to be no debate and no attempt to understand the enemy's strategy. I have recently been re-reading Robin Page's book *The Hunting Gene*. It is a stout defence of hunting on environmental, social, economic and ethical grounds. Every angler should read it. If they did, they should be worried, very worried, about the author's attitude to angling. Here is an influential countryman who should be angling's friend. He demonises angling. Match anglers and those who fish all year round in over-stocked 'holes in the ground' come in for particular stick. A potential friend is virtually siding with the anti-anglers in a book defending hunting! In 2006, the Environment Agency announced a programme to popularise angling among women and other less well-represented groups. Who hit the press with a scathing attack on the scheme? None other than Robin Page. Sorry, fellow anglers, but you have brought this upon your own heads – (ex) chairman, please note. Some of you need to sort out in your own minds who are your friends and who are your enemies – you do not have to agree with everything that shooters or hunters do, and they, no doubt, do not agree with all that anglers do – witness Robin Page. Strategically, we are all allies and have a great commonality of interest – that which unites us is of far more import than that which comes between us. War (and it is a war, despite what is said by those in denial) does make for strange bedfellows at times – witness the allies in the Second World War – but unity against a common enemy is the glue that keeps everyone together. The ACA has publicised its membership of the Fisheries and Angling Conservation Trust in 'A plea for unity in angling', published in its annual report for 2005, but where are the links to shooting and hunting? United we need to be, isolated we may become nevertheless.

So much for isolationism – what about appeasement? The latter seems to be the preferred policy of many commentators. It can be defined as 'feeding your friends to the crocodile in the hope that it will eat you last'. Buy the enemy off by giving ground, just like the Danegeld of old. Apart from encouraging the enemy to go on increasing the pressure, this strategy actually weakens angling by causing disunity. It also uses up valuable resources which could otherwise be deployed against our enemies. If the Dudley region of the PAC had spent the time and resources wasted in fighting live bait bans supporting, say, the ACA, angling would be a trifle more robust; instead, weeks of time and many hundreds of pounds were spent fighting our fellow anglers. Banning live baits could easily cause predator anglers to disengage from the fight, and yet the strength and professionalism of organisations such as the Pike Anglers' Club is the very thing that angling needs if it is to defend itself. It seems that those in power within angling will do anything but actually stand up and fight. When they do fight, they fight the wrong people! Appeasement, involving ritual sacrifices, may be great for the ego merchants, but is, at the end of the day, totally counterproductive. After all, where do you stop? Live baits (maggots and worms as well?), match fishing, keep nets, non-biodegradable line, hooks even? Hooks are literally the bottom line – or are they? Perhaps the appeasers would like us to give up using these as well? This ludicrous idea is even mentioned by John Bailey in the above ACA annual report. He, it would appear, would be quite happy fishing with the point removed from his hooks! Now I am all for respecting our quarry, but I cannot help feeling that Bambi (in Robin Page's eyes, our main problem) has taken over somewhat here. Bailey's perspective is illustrative of how far the appeasers will go to avoid facing the real issue – with such 'thinkers' in our midst, who also needs enemies? Theirs is a philosophy of despair; to them, the war is already lost – in any case, our enemies were right all along. Bailey and those like him are doing the antis' job for them. Just keep pushing, RSPCA and PETA – anglers will voluntarily abolish themselves! Appeasers will apparently do anything other than construct an intellectually robust defence in the way that the hunters have done; yet the material is there, waiting to be used.

Professor Roger Scruton is an eminent philosopher and a huntsman. A few years ago, he published a work entitled *Animal Rights and Wrongs*. I wonder how many of angling's leaders have read it? If they had, they would realise that there is no reason to be on the defensive at all – quite the opposite; it is field sports which actually occupy the high moral ground. The 'other lot', by misrepresenting our fellow denizens of the planet, not only do them a great disservice but their position, if translated into action, actually results in very real cruelty. Bambi, a cuddly quasi-person, who thinks and feels as we do, is a creation of a human mind, that of Felix Salten – foxes, peregrines and pike are the product of thousands of years of evolution. The appeasers have, I feel, been taken in by the very effective propaganda machine run by the other side. John Bailey calls for us to 'polish up our sport' – he intends a lot of good things, but, at the end of the day, we do not have to buy into the enemy's philosophy at the same time. What is more, we anglers have our own Roger Scruton; his name is Alexander Schwab and, in 2003, he published a mould-breaking book entitled *Hook, Line and Thinker: Angling and Ethics*. Schwab's is a tour de force. Patiently, systematically, he takes the whole animal rights philosophy apart. It is compelling stuff; with the sort of propaganda machine available to our opponents, the contents of Schwab's book alone would turn the tide in anglers' favour. I will not spoil your enjoyment of the work here (though if you are a cat owner or a vegetarian, watch out!). Andrew Herd, in a piece entitled 'A Short Treatise on Killing', published in *Waterlog*, has also demonstrated how a robust defence of field sports can be assembled and how out of touch a lot of people are in relation to the environment that sustains them. My point is that angling not only has a robust defence, it has a powerful means of attack. Why do we not use it? I am sure that most anglers can read, write and (hopefully) even think. Our enemies have only appeared as a force over the last few decades; we could, given the resources and the effort, have a good go at putting them out of business altogether and move society into a saner world, for the benefit of all. So why are we in such a parlous state?

The Liberty and Livelihood march through central London in September 2002 was a classic example of isolationism in practice, and did angling no good at all. Between four and five hundred thousand people from all walks of life took part, and there were substantial contributions from abroad as well. Anglers were conspicuous by their absence; little wonder that shooters, hunters and other field sports enthusiasts regard us with open contempt. From the Dudley region of the PAC, Richard Seal, Natalie and I went along, in a coach organised by a shooting syndicate. Down there, out of tens of thousands of people, we saw one (identifiable) angler – a chap holding an Irish tricolour attached to an old cane fly rod. We met Tony and Irene Mobley, representing their shooting club, and, returning on the Tube, bumped into ex Dudley PAC member Simon Stokes, now living deep in the rural West. Barrie Rickards tells me that he and Des Taylor were there also. That makes nine! Farlows of Pall Mall gave us all a welcome, but where were the missing three million from the angling fraternity who ought to have been there? Many and varied were the excuses from the others in the PAC – 'Nothing to do with me'; 'Want to start pike fishing that weekend'; 'We are simply being used'; 'Hunting is cruel, fishing isn't', and so on. My (ex) chairman, despite being a shooting man, was not there – it had nothing to do with him! The march was an amazing success – how much more of a success would it have been if the many hundreds of angling clubs had got off their behinds and produced something of a reasonable turnout? The number taking part could have easily exceeded half a million and maybe even approached the magic seven figures that would have had immense psychological significance. What a powerful message would have been sent – not just to government, but to all of those who oppose us!

It all comes back to psychology, and this is the root of the whole problem. It is why I am an anti-angler. Anglers are just great at being beastly to one another – this seems to give the egotists in particular great kicks. This whole psychology thing is impenetrable; it almost amounts to a death wish. Apathy, obviously; ego, certainly; an inability to think straight, in my estimation, yes; and there is the penny-pinching factor as well. It is a complex, lethal cocktail. I have given up trying to understand it, let alone change it. A growing problem is not the numbers of young people joining the sport, but their complete lack of willingness to put anything back into it. One committee I sit on once calculated its average age, which was over seventy. I am a young whippersnapper! Getting replacements for people who burn themselves out is increasingly difficult. Tony Mobley has run his club, almost single-handed, for well over thirty years; Frank Hodgkiss has been secretary of his club for only marginally less time. Dick Smith is in a similar position. I have done nearly thirty years as a Regional Organiser for the PAC. Where are the youngsters in their thirties who ought to be taking over? What happens when we literally peg it? On top of this, those who do give of their time are often subjected to what can only be described as abuse from the very people they strive to serve. In the club of which I am currently secretary, we are facing major issues of water quality, one planning inquiry with another potential one looming, cormorant damage, issues of trespass and security, the need to de-silt two of our pools, plus constant negotiations with sailors, bird-watchers, DEFRA, the Environment Agency, Natural England, the Rural Payments Agency, the National Trust and a number of local authorities. It is a massive, thankless job. Over the past year or so, a tiny group of trout anglers have seen fit to barrage us with letters, telephone calls and e-mails concerning such 'major' issues as a poorly fitting spout on the fishing hut, a loose gatepost and a dodgy rowlock on a boat. Since the club, by definition, belongs to all of us, these insignificant items could have been fixed by the persons concerned during the time it took to write the letter, but we are the committee and it is our task to sort all the problems. Maybe they would like us to ghillie for them as well? In a separate incident, I was asked to produce a report on pike conservation. This was done and accepted in its entirety by the committee. Once the coarse anglers heard about it, all hell broke loose. I was vilified by the very people whose fishing I was attempting to preserve. Had I possessed a tape recorder, I could have sued for slander. One of the ringleaders was an ex shop steward from a well-known (ex) Birmingham motor manufacturer (and, of course, proud of it). The pike fishing is now going the same way as the car firm – both demises were totally predictable, and both were caused by the same bloody-minded destructiveness. Just what drives these people?

The great economist Arthur Pigou made the proposition that human beings have what he called a 'defective telescopic faculty'. The key word is 'defective'. By this he meant that we are so short-sighted that we damage our own interests in the process. This proposition certainly applies to anglers. A more colloquial word might be 'stupid'. Any new gadget or bait flavouring is worth every (extortionate) penny. Hundreds of pounds (and more) are spent on tackle, baits and permits, and on travel, chasing some elusive thirty and the like. Try getting someone to join the ACA! For a member of an affiliated club, currently membership is a little over ten pounds per year and around twenty for full membership. Very few of our three million could not afford this sum. Yet membership of the ACA struggles to top ten thousand. Despite this (almost complete) lack of support, the organisation continues to achieve remarkable things. Not long ago, it received high praise from the Institute of Economic Affairs, which cited it as one of the most successful environmental protection agencies in Western Europe. It has recently led a successful campaign to persuade the Veterinary Medicines Directorate to suspend the use of pyrethroid sheep dips, which over the years have done terrible damage to the waterside environment. In economics, we have a proposition that 'willingness to pay' is a measure of how much one values some unit of good or service (including the services provided by the environment). Judging by the amount anglers seem to spend on tackle and the like, they value their sport very highly indeed. Yet there is a strange duality here. The latest rods, reels, baits and the like are seen as essential for their sport, but not clean water! Think what the ACA (and other national angling bodies) could achieve if they had the support they deserve. I could preach about this for days, but it would be a waste of time. One once well-respected (ex) member of the Dudley region of the PAC left us because we put the monthly subscription up by one pound in order to pay for our room, trophies and other running costs. He valued us at less than twenty-five pence a week, despite us having essentially reared him as a pike angler and recommended him for membership of clubs that, without our support, he would never have got within a hundred miles of. Economists call such people 'free riders' – they are happy to reap the benefits of others' efforts and expenditure, but are not prepared to contribute themselves. The work of organisations like the ACA, PAC and Countryside Alliance is in the nature of what is referred to as a 'public good'. Everyone benefits from their activities but it is impossible to compel payment from those who benefit. The vast majority of anglers free-ride on the back of the

ACA – they benefit, a tiny minority pays the bill. Great, isn't it? What a comment on the wider angling community! The word 'disgraceful' is not strong enough.

All this, of course, means that anglers tend to get pushed around. The late Dick Walker was mightily critical of the BBC thirty years ago and, if anything, things have become worse. When did you last see angling featured on the BBC? The series *A Passion of Angling* was fantastic all those years ago. You would have thought that Aunty would have learned something. If there really are eight million people in England and Wales interested in angling, this amounts to well over fifteen percent of the entire population. The BBC is a public corporation – should we not be asking how our money is being spent? It sure isn't on angling! It is worse than this – I suspect that Aunty is actually well into the anti camp, though it would not admit such. Not so long ago, there was publicity concerning some research done on rainbow trout involving injecting their mouths with snake venom. The fish showed some nervous reaction, which was hardly surprising. It was latched onto by the antis as an argument that fish feel pain. Now, I have not come across us anglers tipping our hooks with snake venom, but the BBC had a field day – the *Today* programme, the national news, the lot! Quite what the research had to do with angling (or anything else for that matter) is a mystery. A swan gets caught up in line and again the propaganda machine swings into action. The ACA wins a major case on sheep dip and not a mention; the perch record tumbles and Britain's first twenty-pound barbel is caught, again not a mention; re-offending rates among young criminals introduced to fishing were reported to be near to zero, a quite remarkable phenomenon – what does the BBC make of it? Not a lot. It continues to refer to angling as a blood sport – why has someone not taken this up with the Broadcasting Complaints Commission? Even the Liberty and Livelihood march was played down. Maybe if the marchers had stormed Broadcasting House and staged a sit-in until an apology was forthcoming, Aunty might have listened. Here is a real enemy, yet it is allowed to walk all over us – pathetic.

Other bodies are not much better. The National Trust took over Bosherston Lake in Pembrokeshire many years ago when the

Cawdor Estate was sold. It was a wonderful fishery, especially for pike, perch, eels and tench. The Trust still allows fishing – on paper. Anglers have to purchase their ticket prior to fishing and the latter is restricted to marked swims. On arrival, any angler will find that most marked pegs are totally unfishable – overhanging trees all year round and solid weed during the summer months. No attempt is made to cater for anglers; the Trust's sole contribution is a notice by the Eight Arch Bridge, informing everyone that live baiting is banned, and this is predator water. Now, there is a piece of legislation called the Trade Descriptions Act – why some enterprising person (or local club) has not taken the National Trust to court over the mis-selling of fishing permits is beyond me. It is not as if the Trust lacks money – thousands have been spent on footpaths, car parks and premises in order to 'open the place up' for the public (and wreck it in the process). To advertise angling is disingenuous to say the least; it would be more honest to state that angling is banned, which effectively it is, certainly during the warmer months. But that would land the Trust in hot water – so do it by the back door instead. As I have said, there are many ways of killing a cat. As far as the consumers are concerned, our fellow anglers, apathy reigns yet again. Now, June and I might retire to Pembrokeshire – anyone know a good solicitor?

I will conclude this chapter with the Countryside Alliance, our one hope for a unified stand. Its 'Campaign for Angling', run by Charles Jardine, grandson of the great pike angler Alfred, is a great effort not just to promote the sport but to integrate it with its sister activities. I wonder how many anglers are members. Not many, I would guess; yet, as Barrie Rickards has pointed out, we anglers rely heavily on farmers and country landowners for our sport. It is surely in anglers' interests to support our sponsors in their time of need, even if one does not shoot or hunt. I am reminded of a comment made by a senior member of the British Field Sports Society (forerunner of the Countryside Alliance) at a regional meeting in Birmingham some years ago. When the question of gaining support from anglers was raised, he remarked, 'Anglers are a waste of space'. In the light of what I have said, it would be a bold person who disagreed.

Isolationism is one of UK angling's great weaknesses. Adrian Writtle and Natalie at the Warwickshire Hunt. (Author)

One for the Mortuary

The brown rat (Rattus norvegicus).

Some years ago, in the twilight of my career, I voluntarily signed up at my university for a professional course on teaching and learning in higher education. Having already been teaching for thirty-odd years, you may rightly say that this was somewhat late in the day. Together with a couple of colleagues, I enjoyed the course immensely. The final module was on learning technology, a little daunting given my limited IT skills. I need not have worried. The module was led by a guy called Alan Staley who was extremely user-friendly and supportive. At the start of the module, we had to introduce ourselves on a web board from our own personal computer. Alan started things off with a brief résumé – one of his selling points was that he was an angler and had caught a big carp. I responded in mine, politely pointing out that I had caught one even bigger. Oops! Anyway, Alan and I became firm friends and have a day or two fishing together each season. Alan's great ambition is to catch a thirty-pound pike, a thirty-pound carp and a thirty-pound catfish, preferably all from home waters. His initial target was the catfish. Some local lakes held a head of good ones and he had already had some success, but no thirty. One day he popped the question, 'Ever caught a catfish, John?' Now, I had never really been into exotics, but the chance of seeing such a creature, let alone catching one, was attractive to say the least. Broadening one's angling horizons in old age is not a bad thing. It was early September and the barbel could take a back seat for once.

I was advised to bring strong tackle – I elected for my old glass T72 pike rods, big Shimano reels and fifteen-pound line. A running two-ounce lead with a size one barbless catfish hook to twenty-five-pound Mantis Braid completed the rig. Bait was to be halibut pellets on one rod and trout live bait (bought on site) on the second. On arrival, we drove down the hill to the lake, parked the car, unloaded, and trekked down some steep steps to the water. It was a mild evening and we were going to fish throughout the night. I hadn't bothered with the bivvy and was not exactly overdressed, having forgotten how cold a late summer night could be. We set up each on either side of a bay, opposite to an adjacent island.

I positioned the live bait to my right, in the channel between me and the island, and cast the left-hand rod with the pellets out to the left, close to the island. Alan had made himself comfortable on a rather high-tech bed chair, and we sat back to await events. Deer wandered the banks, quite tame, and soon darkness closed in. We did not have to wait long. Around midnight, Alan's live bait was away and, pulling my baits in, I walked around to watch the fun. The fish fought hard, not giving much ground, but Alan is a skilful angler and soon I had the net in hand, headlamp switched on. At the end of the line was the most hideous creature imaginable, and it was big. Alan brought it, protesting, towards the drawstring. Then, horror of horrors, his lead, on a short link, snagged in the top of the net. The fish could neither come forward nor go back. There was only one thing I could do. Reaching down and taking hold of the trace above the link, I pulled – hard. The link broke and, hauling on the line, I drew the fish over the net. It was a close run thing; had the link been stronger or the trace weaker, the fish could have been lost, but there it was, in the net and on the unhooking mat. It went thirty-one and a half pounds. Phew! Alan had achieved his first objective. I cannot say that the fish was attractive, but it was impressive, that I cannot deny. After the photographs, the brute was returned and I walked back to my rods. When I arrived, to my consternation one of the damn deer had its head in my rucksack! Shooing it off, my sandwiches seemed intact, though the wrapping was torn. Whether this had any bearing on future events, I cannot say, but a certain bacterium thrives in the kidneys of herbivores. I recast and settled down. It got cold and sitting on my seat became increasingly uncomfortable. In the end, I finished up lying on my Barbour coat next to my brolly, propped up by the wall. I was not to stay cold for long.

An hour or so later, my left-hand rod was off, the light on the Optonic stabbing red in the darkness. This was it. I connected with something fearfully strong. I was reminded of that massive pike I had lost all those years ago. Attempts to put on too much pressure simply resulted in an enormous wrench on the rod top; surely something must give? Alan Staley came around and shone his torch on the rod top so that I could gain some idea of the direction the fish was taking, together with the strength of pull on the tackle. It was an impressive fight; at one point, the reel handle spun backwards and took a small piece out of my left index finger. Alan's comment later on was that I was excessively hard on the fish, but I am used to Teme barbel and that is the way I do things. After an eternity the fish was in the net, another ugly brute. Alan said thirty; the fish was significantly shorter than his, but thicker across the back. The hook was lodged in the top of the mouth and removed with my short trout forceps. In doing this, I received a small abrasion on my right hand. Like the previous cut, it did not bleed and was insignificant compared with pike wounds. Little did I realise it, but these minor pieces of damage were to change my life for ever.

In the event, the fish went twenty-nine pounds exactly. In a sense I was glad it didn't make thirty; it was appropriate that this should be a goal which required some extra effort on my part.

Photographs taken, the catfish was slipped back into the lake. I cracked open a small bottle of whisky I keep for such occasions, sharing a tot with Alan Staley and a lad fishing to my left who had walked over to witness the weighing. Two big catfish in a couple of hours! Across the lake, another light came on as another angler prepared to land a fish. Recasting the pellets, I soon had another run; a good fish was hooked, but it lacked the power of its predecessor; a fifteen-pound common carp. A fourteen-pounder soon followed. Dawn broke and we packed, shattered but successful. Little did I realise as I trudged up the steps in the September sun that I was leaving with more than I had brought with me. Through one of the two wounds on my hands, now barely visible, a tiny bacterium had entered my bloodstream. The clock was ticking – within a fortnight it would overwhelm me.

My diary records a day on the Teme with Colin Booth the following week. Apparently, I took two three-pound-plus chub and a beautiful barbel of eight pounds, nine ounces. I remember very little of that day, though I have a great photograph of the barbel taken by Colin. June pushed off to Greece for a couple of weeks and Geoff Round, her boss, invited me for a day's flying from Wellesbourne in his Piper Cherokee. This was on the Sunday. On the way home we stopped for a meal. For me, it was five minutes to midnight. Thirteen days had passed and the incubation period of that bacterium was around two weeks. I felt strange. The lasagne and chips went uneaten. Little did I realise that this was a symptom of the onset of liver failure; my liver was quietly being ripped apart by leptospirosis, an evil infection generated by the mixture of rat or cattle urine with warm water. I drove home feeling groggy and went to bed. Missing time is a strange experience; I remember little of the next five days – broken conversations with June over the telephone and telling Emma, my last PhD student, that I was 'all messed up'. I do not remember the doctor who diagnosed severe 'flu on the Wednesday. My first real memory is of two green-clad paramedics bending over me and the voice of Dr Alan Carr, my GP, speaking forcefully on the telephone downstairs. I do not remember how they got me down the stairs and into the ambulance. It was Friday. I do remember being put on a drip and Natalie, who unbeknown to me had taken leave from work, informing me that our local hospital could not take me and that I was going to Sandwell General Hospital. I had barely heard of the place. The whole thing was totally surreal. I was dying – fast. I was told later that had Natalie not called the doctor I would have pegged it in bed that evening, and no one would have had a clue as to the cause. The GP's last words were, 'It's no bad thing you are going to Sandwell'; prophetic words indeed. When we arrived, Natalie was already there, having burned rubber up the motorway. It seemed like a scene out of *Casualty*. I was wheeled through crowds of people, complete with drip, and into a lift. I was losing it. Someone took my watch, given to me by my parents for my O levels in 1961. This worried me. There was talk of penicillin, dialysis and moving me to intensive care. These were almost my last experiences on this planet. I lapsed into oblivion.

I can only describe the process of dying as 'going within oneself'. The holding place between this world and the next was a benign nothingness. All I remember of the next days (weeks; I am not sure) was a lady with a strange accent telling me that she had to put an incision in the bottom of my throat (a tracheotomy), it wouldn't hurt and that it was necessary to gain better access to my chest. She was Polish and the ITU's consultant anaesthetist. Why she bothered speaking to me, I don't know; she must have brought me partly round to do it. It was then back to oblivion, totally unaware of the drama unfolding around me. Thanks to British Airways, June returned from Greece in double quick time. Sister in the ITU gave her 'the' talk. It was pretty much a message of no hope. Coming from such a professional, it must have been shattering. My liver had packed up, so had my kidneys; yellow bile oozed from my pores. Massive septicaemia had set in. My lungs were full of fluid and the only things between me and the next world were the life-support machine, dialysis and transfusions of blood. When Emma (these days virtually a 'non-biological' daughter) enquired of my chances, the nurse put her thumbs down and walked away. On the following Wednesday, I suffered circulatory collapse. Only swift intervention by Nurse Technicians Kumar and Joseph stabilised me. June paced the streets – practical as ever, she began to organise my funeral. A crucifix and artificial flowers were placed on the chair next to my bed. At the Dudley PAC meeting, no one spoke. Old Dr T was off to the great pike water in the sky.

Kumar told me later that what had separated me from other dying people was the high level of electrical activity in my brain. My body might have had it, but I had a beloved wife and daughter, a wonderful family and a great circle of friends, not to mention a thirty-pound pike to catch. Something held me there, and I am not at all sure that all the strength came from me. Prayers were said, the yoga class held a silent vigil, directing healing energy to my bed. If you think that such an external effect is fanciful, there is now hard medical evidence that it exists. We all are, after all, packets of quantum energy resonating within a background field – such energy transfer is far from impossible. I held on. As I moved away from the brink, weird, terrifying hallucinations cut in. I was in a Canberra bomber piloted by Gromit and Frank Hodgkiss. We crashed in a forest, hardly a surprise! I was piloting a Hawk jet. June was flying a second aircraft. There was a vicar driving a kid's pedal car. Natalie was standing next to my bed, and my blood was spraying over her. There was something about John Sidley and a canal. The latter was a terrifying, surreal place. Great Aunt Tilly, highly decorated as a nurse in the First World War, was in charge of the nurses, rapping out orders just as she must have done all those years ago. The hospital was a ship in a storm. June's face floated in front of me, so did Natalie's. Frank and Penny, Gromit and Sylvia; my sister-in-law, her face etched with horror, fled from the room. These visions, a mixture of fact and fiction, were fleeting; my only real sense was my hearing. Someone said my chances were fifty-fifty. No they're not, I thought, I'll get through this. The words 'one, two, three' and strong arms would turn me over. At this juncture I apparently developed violent hiccups, which became something of a concern to the staff, not that I remember anything. I became more aware of my surroundings; a nurse went into raptures over a catheter bag with half a cup of my urine in it. Joseph explained what had happened; they were worried about something called creatinine. For the technically-minded, this is a protein produced by the muscles and removed by the kidneys. Its level in the blood is a key measure of kidney function. In a fantastic gesture, Natalie had apparently been to the consultant and offered me one of her kidneys. The staff felt, however, that things were potentially reversible. They had already christened me the Miracle Man. Communication was impossible for me; every time I tried to speak, air rushed through the hole in my throat and no sound was forthcoming. The staff tried to get me to point to letters on a card but I could not manage it. Eventually, I found myself being lifted, precariously, with some sort of crane and placed in a chair. Speech was eventually partially re-established with a nurse pressing a gloved finger on my tracheotomy. Cousin Judy arrived, and I was mortally offended when she refused to take me down to the pub for a pint of bitter shandy.

Later, the A&E consultant came to see me and told me that I had had a 'near death experience'. I would not have survived had I not been so fit (!), or had I been a diabetic or a smoker. When he initially examined me, I was 'one for the mortuary'. At my age, getting a 'stiffy' is one thing; being one is an entirely different matter! Amazingly, I had apparently self-diagnosed. I do not remember doing this – how I had concluded that I had Weil's disease (the most deadly form of leptospirosis) I have no idea, but Natalie is adamant that I was most forceful about it. As the consultant said, 'self-diagnosis is not uncommon, getting it absolutely right is rare; getting it right and thereby saving one's own life is unprecedented'. He had me down for Legionnaire's disease until I had spoken, then 'it all clicked into place'; he had thrown the book away and gone with my diagnosis. As he said, 'in emergency medicine, sometimes you have to run with your instinct'. His instinct was that I was correct. The statistics he gave me were frightening – in the West Midlands over the last fifteen years, there had been twelve cases. Ten had died. I was one of two survivors. Talk about a close shave. Just to round off the fun, as a marker for staff wishing to see this medical curiosity, above my bed was pinned a large photograph of the twenty-nine-pound catfish.

Eventually, after thirty days in the ITU, I was moved to the High Dependency Unit. Some of the tubing was removed and my neck stitched. However, my battle had only just started. Being conscious, I gradually became aware of my predicament. My feet were the size of footballs and felt red hot; I looked at my hands, which were withered and unrecognisable; I had lost six stones (eighty-four pounds) in weight. For the first time, I encountered other patients. It was a harrowing experience. I was told to rest, but to start with it was futile. I somehow managed to pull my feeding tube out, thinking that I was taking off my glasses. Eventually, I did manage to reach that calm, safe place that my yoga teacher had always spoken of. I was tried with semi-solid food and immediately had my first encounter with a bed pan, another bundle of laughs. The physiotherapists arrived and I discovered that my legs would not support me. In many respects, this was one of the worst moments of all; I had an awful vision of spending the rest of my life in a wheelchair. Do we not all take standing up for granted? Praveen and Padma were just brilliant. After a few attempts, I managed to stand, supported, for a count of ten before collapsing, shattered, into the chair. Getting tangled in the catheter line didn't help! One of the nurses, Dexter, who hailed from the Philippines, decided to give me a bed bath. With me lying stark b—k naked on my high-tech bed, he and Staff Nurse Sharon got to work with sponge and towels. Suddenly, and shockingly, Dexter exclaimed, 'John, you are the first Englishman I have ever seen who has been circumcised'. This was news to me!

Outraged, I retorted, 'I b—y well haven't!'

Dexter responded, 'You have, John, you have'. A fierce argument ensued, during which the entire HDU was treated to a lesson by Dexter on the subject of circumcision. Sharon was doubled up laughing, Sarah the Sister looked dumbstruck and the consultant's secretary quietly left the unit. There are apparently various approaches to this delicate operation and in the end I was forced to concede. I wish my parents had had the decency to tell me though! Discovering this sort of thing after half a century is more than precious.

I will not dwell on my remaining weeks in hospital. My first 'walk' using the Zimmer frame produced a shock – on looking out of the window, all the leaves were brown and littered the hospital lawn. What had happened to the summer? 'You have been in here for two months, John,' I was informed. Another shock; I had thought it was about two weeks. I was put on a high-protein diet; great fry-ups for breakfast, bacon, egg, beans, fried bread, the lot. Who says NHS food is poor? Loads of hilarity followed. I developed an addiction for a proprietary brand of soft drink. Cans littered the ward. McDonald's cola ran it a close second! A nurse called Sara was given the delicate job of removing my catheter after I had gone on strike, wanting it left in (convenient things, catheters). She was probably younger than Natalie but did a great, painless job. I christened her Sara the Catheter – she was one of many angels I encountered. I fell out of bed in the middle of the night, nearly got mowed down by a runaway coffin while trying to get to the loo, and was treated to Praveen and Padma's stairs routine. This followed the 'throwing away the Zimmer frame' ceremony. I had no chance of escape from the hospital until I could do three flights of the back stairs, albeit aided by a stick. The stairs were not for public use and were steep, concrete blocks. I puffed and sweated, tripping over the damn stick more than once, but eventually my tormentors were satisfied. On my release, my consultant, Dr McCloud, himself an angler, advised me to 'stay away from stagnant ponds in the future'. You can say that again.

Clearly, on returning home, a big question was whether to keep on fishing. Does one stop driving after a bad accident? I could not conceive of a life without my rods. I had fished for over fifty-five years without mishap and none of my angling friends, many of whom fished more frequently than I, had had any problems. Even if lightning does occasionally strike in the same place twice, I was not exactly in the full flush of youth and felt it important to get as much out of such time as remained as I could. I would keep fishing, taking rather more precautions along the way. Stagnant ponds I would probably avoid.

In late January, I accompanied Gromit on a pike trip, not to fish but just to get the feel of things. I did not freak out, and felt quite relaxed about the whole thing. The next week, I took my rods. Old *Esox* settled the question once and for all with a truly great 'welcome back' ceremony. Everything was quiet until mid morning, when a big fish rolled between my baits. Seconds later, the sardine was away and I was into something heavy. After a sullen fight, a big fish hit the net. Gromit had a job lifting. It went twenty-one pounds, twelve ounces. What a comeback! With the words 'you jammy g—t' ringing in my ears, I returned the lady to her watery home, my protective rubber gloves glistening in the winter sun. I found out later that she was the biggest fish from the water so far that season. Was the capture just a freak event or was there more to it? I like to think the latter. Poor Gromit blanked.

Rotten weather, roach fishing and a chest infection cut in and my return to piking was complete, or so I thought. The season closed. Out came the fly rod. In late April, on a rather windy day, I was fishing with an intermediate line a hundred yards or so off the dam and had taken a number of rainbows, the best going four twelve, all on an orange Montana. Then came a savage take. The six-weight rod arched over and the fly line whipped through my fingers, disappearing into the water at a rather disconcerting rate. Within seconds, the backing was following. Having the entire fly line way out over the water gives a feeling of not really being in control. I looked at my watch – this was one hell of a trout; how long would it take to land? The backing continued to disappear. If it runs much further, I thought, it will be down the sluice! The fish stopped, feeling solid, even if it was a hundred yards away. The backing bowed in the wind. There was something odd about this fish. I pulled, the fish pulled back. Several minutes' tug of war followed. I regained some line. Then, eighty or so yards from the boat, a familiar tail came out of the water, with my fly clearly visible, impaled in its leading edge. A big pike, foul hooked! With a five-pound point, I did not fancy my chances and rather hoped that it would come off. Somehow I worked it towards the boat. Still weak from my illness, I was feeling groggy – I do not suppose that the pike was too happy either! Netting it with my (admittedly large) net was a nightmare. I could get the tail and midsection of the fish over the net and then it would simply swim away, forwards, and we were back to square one. Exhaustion was setting in for both parties and, with the boat both rocking in the wind and tipping, I threw caution away and resorted to brute force. How the tackle stood this, I do not know. The fish was in the net. I guessed it at mid doubles. I tried to lift it, but it would not budge. I wondered if the net was snagged on the bottom of the boat. I tried again. Up it came, a magnificent, fat pike. I looked at my watch – half an hour exactly. The fly fell out in the net. Luckily I had my Avon scales with me and, unscrewing the net, hooked them up. With the boat rocking and me feeling faint, I took a reading. Twenty-three pounds! The net went one and three quarters, making the fish twenty-one pounds, four ounces. A quick photograph and back she went, waving her tail to me as she sank into the depths.

Returning the fish had been instinctive, but I realised that I had a problem. The trout anglers that populate this particular water are mainly of the old school. The only good pike is a dead one. Killing the fish would have been immoral and, given that it was the coarse-fishing close season (the place is a Site of Special Scientific Interest) would also have been illegal. So would moving the fish. The event had lasted over half an hour, and I was secretary of the club. What was more, I had a meeting with the chairman within the hour. Supposing someone had seen me – the keeper, even? I decided to come clean and report what I had done. After the usual pleasantries, I began, 'Mr Chairman, I have a confession to make' and explained what had happened. He didn't say a lot but it was clear that he was not particularly happy. We let the subject drop. I have already said something in 'Middle Earth' about this sort of attitude and it requires no further elaboration. My first two pike on my return from the pearly gates turned out both to be twenties, though in most respects the latter did not count. A couple of weeks later, I had a thirteen-pounder off the same water; it even had the decency to take the mayfly nymph properly. My comeback was well and truly complete.

In concluding this chapter, it may well be worth reflecting on the dangers to which anglers are exposed. Big John Holt once fell out of a boat while obeying a call of nature; his boat partner shifted position, tipping the boat and causing him to lose his balance. Gromit broke a bone in his knee falling off a wooden platform made slippery by rain, and made a mess of his shin at the same time. Worse, he once fell in the Wye when the bank collapsed – had I not been on hand he would have been in serious trouble. David Hendry has had so many accidents they could not be realistically catalogued. Dick Smith once tried eating some fresh maize found near his peg on the Teme; the pesticide on it almost resulted in us calling the air ambulance. Some years ago, Colin Booth found a big shoal of good barbel feeding well on the Severn. He spent all day hooking, playing and landing them. The case of tennis elbow that resulted was so serious that the medics banned him from fishing for twelve months! Also, it should be remembered that the banks of rivers like the Teme and Severn, particularly in winter, can literally be deadly. Wading on the Wye tributaries is treacherous at the best of times; so is the use of small boats on big waters – I once made a bad mistake myself. The gentle art does have another side. The events described in this chapter have left me with impaired kidney function, numb and at the same time painful feet, and damaged lungs. Medical advice is to properly cover with waterproof dressing any wound suffered at the waterside and to keep it clear of contact with the water. Have your medical records marked with the fact that you are an angler – most people die from Weil's disease due to it manifesting as 'influenza'. Delayed diagnosis is the main cause of death. I do not remember even putting my hands in the water that fateful night, yet the public health people were convinced I contracted my illness through fishing. Presumably, even handling fish can lead to infection, so be warned.

It was not all bad. In many senses, the experience was a spiritual one. Death is not something that is miles away down the road; it walks alongside each of us at all times. I no longer fear it. My yoga teacher often reminds us of the transience of our physical existence, together with the need to focus on the present while at the same time being aware of our eternal nature. As BB was wont to point out, our fishy friends know this, as do all animals. Perhaps it is time we humans took note. Pick up your rods and the rest of your gear, make your way to the waterside and enjoy yourself – it may well be later than you think.

Alan Staley with his thirty-one-pound, eight-ounce catfish (Danubian Wells). (Alan Staley)

Author with what was very nearly his last fish – an eight-pound, nine-ounce River Teme barbel. (Colin Booth)

Author with 'November Foxtrot' minutes before the onset of symptoms.
(Author)

The Rocks Remain

Walking off into the sunset.

'Steer 180 degrees,' the controller's final instruction came loud and clear over the radio. 'November Foxtrot,' we acknowledged as we left the Halfpenny Green circuit and set course due south. Below us, following the same valley, the Worcestershire Stour and its companion, the Staffs–Worcester Canal, gleamed in the summer sun. Was that Graham Wright cycle–trolling along the towpath, I wondered? Here was part of my angling future, should I be spared – fishing the canal for its pike, perch and chub, and trotting the Stour for its roach and dace. The latter's pike are an unknown quantity but will undoubtedly get some attention as well, providing I can drag myself away from those huge estate-lake roach and the grayling of the upper Wye and its tributaries.

We climbed steadily to two and a half thousand feet and soon, to our starboard, the mighty Severn hove into view. Ahead was

Worcester, the cathedral an easy marker for the disorientated flyer. Its weirs, the scene of Colin Booth's great triumph and Gromit's and my encounter with the Great Sea Monster, were clearly visible – as was the confluence of Teme and Severn, the former's winding path marked by a line of willows tracking across the battlefield of long ago. Beyond the Malverns, dimly visible in the mist, lay Hay Bluff, the sentinel that heralds entry into my mystical land of pike, shad and grayling. We changed course to ninety degrees, heading east. Bredon Hill loomed out of the haze and there, underneath its dark silhouette, was the Avon, the Swan's Neck a giant curving snake cutting through the water meadows. I thought of Phil Burford and the roach and bream of all those years ago. Strangely, Phil had telephoned the week before, our first contact for some time. Like me, he too had just survived a close call entailing a long stay in intensive care – our lives were still running in parallel, it would seem. Phil and I agreed to have a pike trip (or two) in the autumn, before it was too late! We made a turn above Stratford – perhaps somewhere below Alan Staley was trying for the barbel, or was it zander?

That final turn led into the Wellesbourne circuit and we completed our cockpit check – make sure that fuel pump is on! With the flaps down, the forty-year-old Piper Cherokee seemed to stand still in the warm summer air. Flying is an exhilarating (and mentally exhausting) experience – while not quite matching the thrill of a sinking pike float or the tension of keeping a big Teme barbel away from a sunken branch, it sure runs them a close second. Thinking back, it is odd how angling and aviation were two paths laid before me in my youth. Dirac's Sea contains a myriad of possibilities, but by some mysterious means these were the two recreational opportunities that seemed to fit the Tate psyche. Since that first pike, angling always had priority, yet the reverse could have been the case – I wonder what adventures that route would have held in store? After taxiing past XM655, Wellesbourne's famous Avro Vulcan, we secured 'November Foxtrot' and headed home, passing over the delightful River Alne en route. I wondered who owned the fishing at Wootton Wawen these days. Was it worth a look on the internet or in *Where to Fish*? Perhaps Phil and I could take up from where we were forced to leave off by the pollution of nearly half a century ago? If so, I must remember the stewed wheat!

And what a half century it has been. Angling has changed almost beyond recognition, a mixture of the good and not so good. On the good side, there has been less pollution and greater choice of water, bigger fish, superb tackle and undreamed-of developments in bait and technique. I wonder how 'moderns' would get on pike fishing with my Allcocks Isis, Luron 2 and *Fishing Gazette* float? How many doubles, twenties and thirties would they manage on that sort of gear? To the greats of the past, such issues were unimportant. How many doubles did C W Thurlow Craig catch, I wonder? I doubt whether he would have given the issue even a second thought, yet he has a distinguished place among Barrie Rickards' and Malcolm Bannister's ten greatest pike anglers. Today, as I have indicted, ego is all, particularly if money is at stake. Sponsorship, 'consultancy' and guiding are the things to aspire to, fuelled by a press that creates its heroes in the same way that it hypes up overpaid footballers and soap stars. One member of the Dudley region of the PAC, before he came into the fold, paid a three-figure sum to one of these wonder boys in order to put his grandson into his first pike. The ploy was devastatingly successful – the lad's first pike weighed over twenty-five pounds. It was a miracle that he was not finished as a pike angler before he had even begun. We now live in a world of instant and fast everything – there must be many youngsters with impressive tallies of twenty-pound carp who have never known the real reward of starting with gudgeon on the canal and working their way up, savouring each step on the way.

Here, of course, we have the downside. What we geriatrics decry in angling today is simply a reflection of how society itself has changed. There is a PhD project for some enterprising sociologist or social anthropologist in comparing the angling press of the 1950s and 1960s (and its social context) with that of today. Gone are the intellectual gems produced by Walker each week, gone are the pioneering pieces by the Taylor 'brothers', gone are the stories penned by Peter Stone. Gone also are values and respect. Values that went back to old Isaac and before; respect for the waterside and its flora and fauna, respect for one's quarry and for one's fellow anglers and for rules, even if the latter are laid down by committee men long past their sell-by date in a vain attempt to maintain some semblance of order. Respect has even gone for the law of the land. All has been replaced by sensationalism, pages of lurid advertisements and the promotion of role models who cannot hold so much as a candle to the greats of the past.

Where is it all leading? Just before he died, Richard Walker asked the same question in one of his weekly pieces. He concluded that angling would survive, though not necessarily prosper. Would he take the same view today? As I write, there are some positive signs, though anglers' attitudes remain as intransigent as ever. Thanks to a proactive Environment Agency, interest in angling does seem to be increasing; noises from politicians are marginally more supportive and, following high profile and adverse publicity, the animal rights camp is on the defensive. The Countryside Alliance now has nearly one hundred and ten thousand members, whereas the League Against Cruel Sports seems to have only around five thousand. On top of this, the ban on hunting with dogs seems to be backfiring spectacularly. Yes, there is hope, though I cannot see a return to the kind of angling that inspired me and many others all those years ago. The forces that shaped that world are gone for good. There never will be another BB, or Bernard Venables, and probably not a Richard Walker.

One significant feature of the new order is the growth of commercial fisheries, or 'holes in the ground' if you wish to be derogatory. One not far from home has on its sign 'The Future of Angling'. In my most pessimistic moments, I feel like adorning it with the words 'Over my dead body', but that would be going too far. Such places will undoubtedly play a key role in angling's future, and they are a vital breeding ground for future generations. Here, the young can fish in reasonably safe and supportive surroundings and enjoy success at the same time. After all, every budding angler wants to see a float go under! Whether continuing easy success is appropriate is another matter. Certainly, cramming hundreds of pounds of carp into a keep net in a match is not my idea of sport, and neither is fishing for coarse fish in such places for a full twelve-month period. One enters the close season debate at one's peril – to me, the issue is not so much one of protecting our quarry during breeding, but one of simple respect. Fish, especially those in such pressurised environments, are entitled to some relief. The best time is surely when they are at their most vulnerable. Even on the rivers, I do not relish the idea of barbel, spawning on gravel shallows, having feeders and lumps of lead dropped among them, but I am a traditionalist and many will disagree. Yet other field sports rigorously impose a close season; the much-maligned fox hunters have one of six months. Hammering our quarry day in and day out, which happens particularly in commercial fisheries, falls the wrong side of the line for me – and I am a confirmed and unapologetic live baiter.

This brings me to pike fishing, my great love. Among the old guard, there is currently a lot of disillusion with the modern scene. Big fish at all costs seems to be the order of the day, to be a 'name' one needs a string of big fish to one's rod. How they were caught is immaterial. Enjoyment at outwitting one's quarry and feeling at one with the natural environment and the forces that made it do not feature in the new order of things. What a contrast this is to the attitude of one Gromit, a pike angler who stands head and shoulders above the moderns. When fishing with him, one is treated to a commentary on the local birdlife, drawing from an encyclopaedic knowledge of the subject that can only come from being reared a true Black Countryman. Even today, he will ring me to proudly announce the capture of a three-pound jack from some obscure canal arm deep in the industrial wasteland. For him, using his knowledge and skill to locate and outwit such a fish is the real reward; its size is irrelevant. And make no mistake – Gromit has taken more than his fair share of twenty-pounders as well, his best being twenty-eight pounds, eight ounces.

Barrie Rickards has recently come up with the idea of an Old Farts Club within the PAC for those who, like me, are not only longstanding or even founder members, but are succumbing to the growing feeling of disengagement. One such stalwart is Graham Stead, who has proposed that we dignify the organisation with the title 'society', so OFS it is. Graham's suggested set of rules is given below:

Conditions of Membership

1. Members must have twenty-five years continuous membership of the PAC.

2. The aim of the Society is to straighten out the hearts and minds of those old souls who have become befuddled by the stresses of modern pike angling and who yearn for the peace and quiet of yesteryear.

3. Annual meetings will be held annually except in special circumstances when they will be held each year. Other meetings will also be held whenever necessary. All such meetings will start with a glass of sherry to commemorate the first PAC Regional Organisers' meeting held in Cambridge in 1978.

4. Members entering the Society do so with a clean slate. It is an offence for any member to bring up past arguments no matter how serious these were felt to be at the time, or to refer to a fellow member's past conduct.

5. The Chairman has the right to move progress should a debate be deemed to be becoming overheated and likely to cause stress or other illness to the participants or onlookers.

6. Grumpiness is a prerequisite condition for entry. Any proposed member must be able to explain why he or she is so pissed off at the time of his or her application for membership.

7. Deceased members are eligible to become honorary ghosts of the Society. This includes deceased non-members who would have been members at the time of their demise had the Society been in existence at that time.

8. Throwing teddy out of the cot, taking home of the bat, etc., are qualities which must be endured, and members will be expected to return to the fold once the tantrum is over. No action will be taken against any member who

has thrown a tantrum and he or she shall be allowed to rehabilitate without sarcastic comments by fellow members.

9   Members must be able to get up people's noses, and an annual trophy (known as the Bogey Cup or possibly renamed after a favourite member) is to be awarded to the member who, in the opinion of fellow members, has committed the best bit of s—t-stirring during the course of the year.

10 Members are expected to enjoy what is left of their allotted time and remember those wonderful moments that were surely there before we became bogged down with it all.

The OFS held its inaugural meeting in Norfolk following the service in St Mary's, Old Hunstanton, in memory of Vic Bellars. Sheila Chillingworth's renovated forty-year-old built-cane pike rod, made originally by Chapman's, was the ceremonial mace. A handful of Grumpy Old Gits railed at all (well, most) things modern. Vic was elected President of the Honorary Ghosts Section and asked to save us some decent pegs and a supply of bait in the pike anglers' matrix of the quantum field where he now resides. He already faces some tough decisions – should Alf Jardine be allowed to join up, for example? A great pike angler, but something of a stroke puller as well? Maybe he has reformed? We shall never know the truth about his thirty-seven-pound 'record' fish (number 205 on Fred Buller's list) – was it really thirty-seven, or thirty-five, or? Anyway, Grandfather will undoubtedly be there, gaff and all – I look forward to showing him the sunken float paternoster and to putting him into a double on a sea dead bait; this latter will surely amaze him. He will certainly be pleased at how pike conservation has progressed since his embryonic attempts between the wars.

For me, there is a sense of time closing in. My tiny corner of the quantum field is getting uncomfortably constrained. Yet there are still patches of blue mist to be entered. The local waters newly available through Dr Kuznets' legacy and the streams of the upper Wye are not the only opportunities. As I have stressed, it is up to us to make things happen (this includes anglers collectively – our futures are in our own hands). Another double-figure barbel from the Teme is a great thought; so is the prospect of my first double from the Wye (though I have already come close). Thanks to Alan Staley (now sporting the title of professor), I have taken my first barbel from the Warwickshire Avon, and more time on this lovely river is certainly on the cards, as is a return to pike fishing on the rivers. A thirty-pound pike from the Wye is not beyond reach and neither is a twenty from the Teme. I have already had a stab at sewin, my first attempt for nearly forty years. The location was Ian Heap's delightful stretch of the Eastern Claddau in Pembrokeshire. A decades-old Teal Blue and Silver produced a savage take early on – nothing changes – the fish came adrift! Back in Ian's caravan, June and he (plus two friends) were quietly demolishing a second bottle of Bell's when I groped my way back through the night, torch failing. Ian, despite not being a pike angler, would certainly qualify for membership of the OFS – we seemed to hold similar views, angling-wise. World champions get disillusioned as well!

I would like to fish abroad some more. Cousins Rich and Guy, natives of the state of California, have already introduced me to rainbow trout in the latter's native environment. We took them on plugs using lead core lines on Pine Mountain Lake in the Sierra Nevada Mountains, adjacent to Guy and Mimi's lovely cabin. Trolling over ninety feet of water certainly puts our canal reservoirs into perspective! We also took trout, including American brook trout, from the Middle Fork of the Tuolomne River where the tree trunks were as wide as railway tunnels (well, almost) and the rocks as big as double-decker buses. This was stalking, as one would do for chub on any small river back home. Bait was salmon eggs; fly fishing was impossible in the rugged terrain. Procedures were livened up somewhat when a rather large snake swam past my bare legs, a rather disconcerting experience!

It was in the mountains and forests of the north-west of the USA that the quantum field almost delivered a real blinder. Cuz Rich, June and I were staying with Rich's sister Elizabeth, up in Washington State. The Lewis River runs not far from the end of the garden and upstream is the Merwin Dam, with the vast Lake Merwin beyond. Salmon hatcheries line the valley. At one, after being shown around, Rich and I were talking to the lady scientist in charge. I mentioned pike. 'You want to see a pike?' she asked. 'Follow me!' She walked quickly to the concrete outflow where water left the hatchery and entered a small river not unlike my native Teme. Keeping low, she pointed into the clear water. There, by golly, was a pike – and what a pike! It was twenty pounds if it was an ounce, and could have been a lot larger – I tend usually to underestimate the weight of fish when they are in the water. It lay there in the current from the outflow, its fins barely moving. But there was something different about it – before I could sort out what it was, our friend muttered the magic words 'tiger musky'. That was it! Unlike *Esox lucius*, this fabulous creature had stripes in its flanks. Incredibly, as we watched, it was joined by a second fish, equally impressive. Out came the camera and I took some shots – it was a once in a lifetime experience.

'You can have a go fishing for them if you wish,' said the scientist. Wish, boy, did we wish! 'No State rod licences,' bemoans Rich.

'No problem,' was the response, 'I am the law around here.' But there was a bigger problem – no tackle! Rich's kit was back in California, and my faithful T72s were five thousand miles or more away. The mind ran wild – a small float, a couple of swan shot and a single treble baited with a couple of parr. Hooking one of those tiger muskies would have been easy – landing it would have been another matter. It would have been the ultimate in small river pike fishing. We were informed that the fish were not regular visitors and that no one on Lake Merwin seriously fished for them, accidental catches being the order of the day. The lake is a massive sheet of water, not unlike a Scottish loch – what monsters lurked in its deeps, we could only guess.

There is always tomorrow, the saying goes. It isn't true. Less than a year previously, I almost ran out of tomorrows. Standing (crouching, actually) watching those fish, still convalescing from my 'little adventure', was a moving experience. Rich and I had been born within days of one another, albeit on different continents. Twenty years ago, we would have both been in the truck, high-tailing it down to the tackle store in Woodland to lay our hands on anything that would handle a tiger musky (and purchasing rod licences!). Maybe *Esox ultimus* would have finished up on the bank, maybe not. Somehow, the capture did not matter anymore. We were both content to watch those two great fish in their natural environment. For me, it was a feeling of having come full circle. For the first time, perhaps, and possibly as a consequence of my illness, I held fishing in its true perspective. I was just content to savour the atmosphere; the cohoe leaping in the holding pools, the sunshine and the forest, the glint of the lake downstream through the trees, and the encounter with my favourite species in what is still essentially frontier country in that far west corner of the USA.

Is being an angler hereditary? It is odd that my two male cousins are both anglers and felt that same sort of pre-destiny and lack of choice in the matter that I did, despite us being brought up thousands of miles apart. All three of us had seemingly been hardwired to a fishing rod from birth. Are we, I wonder, part of the same soul group, destined to travel the anglers' road for karmic reasons beyond our understanding? I estimate that I have spent over three thousand days of my sixty-odd years by the waterside. It has been a hefty commitment, the equivalent of over eight years of my entire life. Was it worth it? What on earth was it all about in the first place? Did I ever have any choice in the matter? I am still at a loss to answer these questions.

What I do know is that, as I write, I am planning a barbel trip on the River Teme, and, by golly, am I looking forward to it. Is that not enough? Beyond the next session, I no longer make grand plans. There is a saying, attributed to Colin Sisson: 'Be true to the moment, for it is the essence of life, and it is all that there is.' This is now my core philosophy. I wish I had adopted it forty years ago! Life is a miracle, however it developed, and an incredible gift not to be squandered sitting in board rooms, offices or traffic jams. To a lesser or a greater extent, we anglers (maybe implicitly) have always recognised this, and some of us – witness the late John Sidley and Ray Webb – took it almost to its ultimate. Fishing is all about the moment – perhaps that is its great power? If so, we anglers may be an evolutionary step ahead (or is it back?)

compared with much of Western society – we should therefore beware of being seduced by its values and attitudes, and of being trodden underfoot by its machinations. My journey through life is now on that last (hopefully long!) roll downhill, and it is time to hand over to a younger generation of anglers. They will, I fear, have a lot on their hands in the years to come. But enough of this pessimism! I have a reel to spool and a rig to make up, and I bid you, good reader, a fond farewell.

Twenty-pound-plus tiger musky, Lake Merwin, Washington State. (Author)

*Philip Burford and the author, forty-five years on.
(David Hendry/Robin Brown)*

Acknowledgements

This book would never have even been begun had I not known that I could rely on the support and encouragement of a wonderful group of people. It is difficult, and potentially embarrassing, to even attempt to prioritise, but I must single out three individuals as the 'first cause'. It was Richard Smith, to whom the book is dedicated, who first suggested that I 'owed the fishing world a book'. Coming from an angler of his calibre, the remark was somewhat precious, but a seed was sown.

The idea was reinforced by comments from my wife, June, who, whenever the subject was mentioned, always said, 'You can do it'; so here is thanks number two. Over the past six months, she has had to put up with me coming into her office (territory she jealously guards), often for two days each week, taking over the auditor's technology, wrecking the printers, denuding the organisation of paper, and generally creating mayhem. The coffee (gallons of it), glasses of wine, cakes, biscuits and sweets were all downed with gusto. (June's concept of a 'wine moment' for stressed staff is her great, politically incorrect, contribution to management practice.) Thanks again, Miss, I will mow the lawns now, promise! (Thanks also, in passing, to all your colleagues at Birmingham Civic Housing Association for their tolerance and good humour.)

Thirdly, there is Professor Barrie Rickards. I find it difficult to put into words my appreciation to Barrie, not just for his encouragement with this work, but for all his help and support over a period of nearly thirty years. A number of chapter titles derive from his suggestions, as does that of the book itself – I had originally planned to call it *Tales from a Worcestershire Weirpool* – the 'Whirlpool' thing is rather more subtle and, given the content (especially the chapters 'Civilisation Lost (or Gained?)' and 'One for the Mortuary'), more appropriate. Incredibly, Barrie read the entire final effort in one night, and got back to me within twenty-four hours of receiving the manuscript. Anytime you want that day's grayling fishing, Barrie, just let me know.

The book contains contributions from a number of my angling friends, all of whom, broadly speaking, come within the ambit of the Dudley Regional Association of the Pike Anglers' Club. David Hendry has provided two pieces (despite suffering at the time from a badly shattered ankle), Colin Booth tells the story of his potential record Severn pike, and Max Taylor gives some of his side-splitting Black Country humour. In addition, there is a piece by June on coping with us all during one hilarious spring night. I regard these contributions as central to the book's theme, and hope that you, the reader, will agree. Others, such as Adrian Writtle, have contributed stories which I have had to précis (Adrian's written piece was almost a chapter in its own right). Thanks to you all. Of course, without all of my fishing companions my angling career would never have been anything like as rich, and you will have met most of them in these pages. I owe them all a great debt, none more than Philip Burford, who, on reading about our schoolboy exploits, complimented me on my memory (memory – what memory?).

During the production process, I have regularly bounced draft chapters off various long-suffering friends. First and foremost, there have been Colin and Jenny Booth who, despite busy professional lives, have fed back comments on a regular basis over a number of months. Jenny is not even an angler, though she is a bibliophile and a fellow student of yoga to boot. The pair of you kept me going! Tony Mobley and Dick Smith have commented on the chapters 'God's River' and 'Quantum Field', and Emma Fieldhouse, who has the dubious distinction of being my last student, on 'One for the Mortuary'. Emma was there in the ITU with June and daughter Natalie and many others, when I was doing a recce of where we all finish up when we leave this mortal coil. Some of the gory stories are hers! Emma's mom, Jean, my yoga teacher and guru, has also checked out 'I Shall Be Glad When I Have Had Enough of This!' – she is the expert!

I would like to thank all those who have given permission for me to reproduce material for which they are copyright holders.

Keith Higginbottom of Regional Angling Magazines Ltd very kindly allowed me to use material from the *Midland Angler*, and Simon Evans from the Wye and Usk Foundation, in addition to helping me trace the holder of the copyright for H A Gilbert's book, gave similar permission in relation to the guide to the Foundation's Passport scheme. The committee of the Pike Anglers' Club of Great Britain, plus Professor Barrie Rickards, have allowed the reproduction of the Pike Anglers' Club badge, albeit doctored, and Anne Moyle of Get Hooked on Fishing enthusiastically embraced my request to use that organisation's logo. I am extremely grateful to Timothy Good for the use of Alfred Burtoo's UFO sketch – Tim is one of the few courageous people to go public with rigorous appraisals of the nature of this worrying and perplexing subject. In addition, John and Anne Spencer kindly gave permission for the use of Bryan Ellis' sketch of the Pascagoula incident. I would like to give special thanks to H A Gilbert's granddaughter, Athene English, for not only giving me permission to quote from *The Tale of a Wye Fisherman* but also making helpful comments in relation to the material on the River Wye. Our sport needs many more lady anglers such as Athene to introduce some sense into what often appears to be an insane (male) world. Similarly, I must thank Mrs Eileen Venables for permission to quote from one of her late husband's classic works. I must also thank my publishers, Athena Press, not just for support over a longish production process, but for being so incredibly efficient. Working with you has been a privilege.

Last of all (they should, in one sense, be first), there is Dr Dwight McLeod and his team at Sandwell General Hospital, especially those who looked after me in the Emergency Assessment Unit and in Critical Care during those dreadful weeks in the late summer and autumn of 2004. I love you all, and will never forget your kindness. It is invidious to mention names, even if I could remember them all, but I owe my very existence to Kumar, Jeffrey and Joseph, as you discovered in 'One for the Mortuary'. How do you say thank you for such a gift? Trying to do this is a humbling experience and one finishes up failing – dismally. Due to the professionalism of these heroes and heroines of the National Health Service, I have been almost literally reborn and, as June and cousin Judy emphasise, am now into my second life! Without them, this book would certainly not have been written – the fact that it has, and that I am catching again, is a tribute to their dedication.

John Tate,
Hales Owen,
September 2007

Useful Websites

Anglers' Conservation Association	www.a-c-a.org
Barbel fishing	www.barbel.co.uk
Countryside Alliance	www.countryside-alliance.org
Environment Agency	www.environment-agency.gov.uk
Get Hooked on Fishing	www.ghof.org.uk
Pike Anglers' Club of Great Britain	www.pacgb.co.uk
Latest pike news	www.pacnews.blogspot.com
Global Consciousness Project	http://noosphere.princeton.edu
Rupert Sheldrake	www.sheldrake.org
Specialist Anglers' Alliance	www.saauk.org
The Great English Outdoors	www.greatenglish.co.uk
The Wye and Usk Foundation	www.wyeuskfoundation.org